THE GODS AT PLAY

THE GODS AT PLAY

Līlā in South Asia

Edited by
WILLIAM S. SAX

New York Oxford
OXFORD UNIVERSITY PRESS
1995

Oxford University Press

Oxford New York
Athens Auckland Bangkok Bombay
Calcutta Capetown Dar es Salaam Delhi
Florence Hong Kong Istanbul Karachi
Kuala Lumpur Madras Madrid Melbourne
Mixico City Nairobi Paris Singapore
Taipei Tokyo Toronto

and associated companies in
Berlin Ibadan

Published by Oxford University Press, Inc.,
200 Madison Avenue, New York, New York 10016

Vasudha Narayanan, chapter 8 in *The Vernacular Veda: Revelation, Recitation and Ritual* (Columbia: University of South Carolina Press, 1994). Used by permission.

Library of Congress Cataloging-in-Publication Data
The Gods at play : Līlā in South Asia / edited by William S. Sax.
p. cm. Includes bibliographical references.
ISBN 0–19–509101–9 (cl). —ISBN 0–19–509102–7 (pbk.)
1. Play—Religious aspects—Hinduism.
2. Gods, Hindu. 3. Play (Philosophy)
4. Hindu drama—History and criticism.
5. Hinduism—Doctrines.
I. Sax, William Sturman, 1957– .
BL1215.P56G63 1995 294.5′2—dc20 94–10215

2 4 6 8 9 7 5 3 1

Printed in the United States of America
on acid-free paper

This book is dedicated to Leela,
of course.

Contents

THE GODS AT PLAY

1

Introduction

WILLIAM S. SAX

God is playful. God creates the world and enters into it in a spirit of play. These are the sorts of ideas that lie behind the important South Asian concept of *līlā*. Because *līlā* is so much a part of ordinary Hindu life, it should come as no surprise that when my wife, Sylvia, and I went to India in 1983 to do doctoral research, accompanied by our infant daughter, Hindus were almost always delighted that my daughter's name was Leela. When she grew older and began to be naughty like children everywhere, people would smile knowingly and say, "Oh, yes, that is the true play, the true *līlā* of God." And, in fact, the image of God as a playful and naughty child has great currency in India: when I asked people what *līlā* meant, they often answered that God created the world in a spirit of *līlā*, like a child who builds a sand castle and then, unattached to his or her creation, knocks it down and builds it up again. The same image is used by Tagore, who adds that "in truth, in self-willed joy, there is something in common between the *līlā* of childhood and the works of God."[1]

Līlā, then, is God's play: it refers not only to the supreme being's playful actions but also to the dramatic "plays" staged by human beings in memory of those actions. Thus *līlā* appears to mark a delightful difference between European and South Asian traditions, embodying a ludic dimension in Indian religious life that is muted or even absent in the dominant religions of the West.[2] Though there may be examples of "playfulness" in Judaism, Christianity, or Islam, still it seems fair to say that Hinduism has developed the doctrine of play more than any of the other so-called world religions, and that this idea has supported, particularly in the more recent religious history of the subcontinent, a pervasive attitude of joy and delight in God's *līlā*.

There are several references to the playful nature of the gods as early as the *Veda*s and the *Upaniṣad*s (see Coomaraswamy 1941), but the first use of *līlā* as a theological term is in the *Vedāntasūtra*s of Bādarāyaṇa at 2.1.33, where the author maintains that the Supreme Lord creates the world "merely in play" (*līlākaivalyam*). The idea is that God's creation of the world is motivated not by any desire or lack, since these would be incompatible with his or her self-fulfilled and complete nature, but rather by a free and spontaneous creativity. Later commentators explain this passage through the metaphor of a great king who plays at sports in order to amuse himself, or a healthy man who, upon awakening from a sound sleep, dances from sheer exuberance. The doctrine of *līlā* thus becomes one way of dealing with the problem of theodicy since, from an ultimate perspective, human suffering is part of the mysterious play of God, and when Hindus are confronted with baffling or tragic events, they are more apt to say "it is God's play" than "it is God's will." *Līlā* also comes to refer, beyond God's world-creating activities, to his or her incarnation in any of several forms in order to sustain and protect the world; thus the *līlā*s of such deities as Rāma and especially Kṛṣṇa are the subject of much devotional art and literature. These and related ideas have been developed and elaborated by various Indian religious traditions: Vaiṣṇava (Haberman 1988; Hein 1987; Hospital 1980; Narayanan, this volume), Śaiva (Bäumer 1969; Bäumer, this volume; Goodwin, this volume), and Śākta (McLean, this volume).

But *līlā* is much more than a theological concept. It is also a kind of religious drama that is found throughout India, especially in the north (see Haberman 1994; Hawley 1981; Hein 1972; Sax 1990; Schechner 1983, 1988; Lutgendorf 1991; Kapur 1990). Such performative *līlā*s usually dramatize the lives and actions of incarnate gods, and thus have much in common with devotional and artistic notions of *līlā* mentioned earlier. They involve the living presence of gods upon the stage, who temporarily inhabit the bodies of the "actors" who "play" their parts, so that going to see a *līlā* often involves a heightened religious experience. It is striking that those who have written about *līlā* as performance usually have not been much concerned with its theological aspects, while those who have written about the theology of *līlā* usually have ignored its performative dimensions. Scholars of *līlā* as drama and scholars of *līlā* as theology often seem to "write past" each other, leading us to ask if the two sorts of *līlā* really are separate things or if the lack of communication has rather to do with the division of academic labor.

The problem is partly one of essentialism: if we fasten on some characteristic or set of characteristics that we deem to be the "essence" of *līlā*, then we will have to define some of our texts and/or performances as *līlā* and exclude others. But who are we, as a group of (predominantly Western) scholars, to tell our Indian colleagues, friends, and informants that some of the things they call *līlā*s aren't really *līlā*s? Would it not be better to adapt the Wittgensteinian notion of family resemblances, the idea that several phenomena (in this case, the various kinds of *līlā*) may be members of a class, not by virtue of some shared essence or common property but because of a "network of partial, but overlapping, similarities"? (Poole 1986:426). The definitional problem is aggravated by disciplinary boundaries. Because *līlā* is generally thought of as a "religious" concept, it has most often been studied by historians of religion, who have traditionally focused on scripture and theology, that is, on texts. While such scholars may have been aware of performative *līlā*s, they did not usually regard these as falling within their disciplinary expertise. On the other hand, when *līlā* is considered as a dramatic performance, it is a "cultural" item and therefore more likely to be studied by anthropologists and folklorists, whose knowledge of classical Indian thought is sometimes rather superficial. This creates problems for textual scholars because they fail to consider those performative contexts in which *līlā*s are dramatized and in which they receive what is arguably their most public and influential expression. It creates problems for anthropologists and folklorists because in slighting or ignoring the ideology of *līlā,* they fail to grapple with the intellectual history that lies behind their informants' understandings. Attending exclusively to performance is ahistorical, while an analysis of *līlā* without attention to its performative aspects easily degenerates into theology. Both approaches risk becoming, as Hindus might put it, "mere *līlā*s."

For these and other reasons, I organized a conference at the Center for the Study of World Religions at Harvard University in April 1989 entitled "The Concept of Līlā in South Asia." One of the main goals of the conference was to unite the theological and anthropological approaches, to see if there was any common ground in their definitions of and approaches to *līlā*. What we came up with was a definition that does not hinge on essences but rather on a number of family resemblances, the most important of which are freedom, spontaneity, and playfulness.

Play is, of course, an important part of the idea of *līlā,* and this is recognized by all of the contributors to this volume. Bäumer, for example, finds that the notion of divine playfulness (*krīḍā*) pervades Śaivism "like salt is mixed with food." Indeed, absolute divine freedom and spontaneity were so important to this school that, as Bäumer tells us, it was sometimes called *svātantriyavāda*. But it is important to remember that precisely what freedom, spontaneity, and playfulness might entail in different contexts and at different times in Indian history is not necessarily self-evident and certainly not always the same. For example, Hospital asks whether play in India is contrasted primarily with work, as it is in many Western cultures, while Wulff reminds us that although spontaneity and playfulness are among "the major characteristics of *līlā*," performances often involve grief and sorrow. In his conference paper (not reprinted in this volume) Neal Delmonico emphasized a dimension of "terror" in *līlā* that is often ignored. *Līlā* may invoke the idea of games, as in Bengal, where, as McLean tells us, the goddess's *līlā* is "like the game of a child." For Hawley the playfulness of *līlā* involves reversal, deception, and thievery; he argues that one of its main functions is to undermine everyday assumptions about life. Or, again, the sort of "play" that is connoted by *līlā* may be of a predominantly erotic kind, as it is for the Śrī Vaiṣṇava community, for whom, according to Narayanan, play is in part "a celebration of the intimate and passionate love that [the Lord] has for Śrī and for his devotees." This erotic dimension of playfulness is especially important in Kashmir Śaivism, and is explored in detail by Goodwin in relation to the famous Sanskrit play *Śakuntalā*.

One of the most salient kinds of "play" included in the idea of *līlā* is that of a theatrical play or drama. India, of course, has a rich tradition of dramatic and aesthetic theory, and Haberman (1988), among others, has written of the influence of this body of theory on Vaiṣṇava religious practice. It has been suggested that the notion of *līlā* actually originated in Vaiṣṇava circles (see, e.g., Hein 1986), but this is disputed by Bäumer, who argues that the hypothesis has not been demonstrated. In their essays Bäumer and Goodwin show how classical dramatic theory was also an indispensable part of Kashmir Śaivism and its theory of *līlā*, in which, as Goodwin puts it, the universe "is a work of art, a play (in both senses), for it is nothing but transcendental consciousness taking form for its own delight." Clearly, the notion of *līlā* has been appropriated by a wide variety of religious traditions in India, and the question of its origin is still open to debate. Moreover, there are many genres of religious drama that owe little to classical dramatic theory. Some of those described and analyzed in this volume are *rās līlā* (Hawley, Wulff), *pāṇḍav līlā* (Hiltebeitel, Sax), *rām līlā* (Kumar, Hiltebeitel), *utsava* (Narayanan), *līlākīrtan* (Wulff), and *terukūttu* (Hiltebeitel).

Līlā involves not just play but also freedom and spontaneity. This point is developed by Bäumer and Goodwin in relation to Kashmir Śaiva philosophy, as well as by Wulff, who writes that *līlā*'s connotations of freedom and spontaneity characterize not only the subject matter of *līlākīrtan* but "also to an important degree its form." McLean writes of the spontaneous or willful (*icchāmoy*) nature of a goddess whose actions "are never entirely predictable." For the Śākta devotee, to live in this world means to participate is such a goddess's *līlā*, and this leads to an attitude of resignation. But for most traditions that have embraced it, the concept of *līlā* has been regarded as emancipatory. In a very illuminating passage Goodwin notes that important precursors of the full-fledged ideal of *līlā* conceived as leading to freedom and spontaneity are to be found in the *Chāndogya Upaniṣad,* in Rāmānuja's writings, and especially in Kashmir Śaivism—but not in the philosophy of Śaṅkara, the great Vedāntin. All of these systems, including Vedānta, can generally be said to agree upon the evanescence of the conditioned world. But whereas the response of Vedānta, the most prestigious tradition of Hindu philosophy, is to renounce that world, *līlā*—and associated ideas like *krīḍā*—are integral parts of philosophical and religious alternatives to renunciation. Such systems are reluctant to turn their backs completely on the world of experience. As Goodwin puts it, they embody "an impulse to recuperate the phenomenal world in the face of a radical ascetic drive to renunciation."

Clearly the notion of *līlā* has important philosophical implications. But does it have concrete social and historical effects as well? In addressing this question, our authors attempt to mediate the disjunction, noted earlier, between textual approaches, on the one hand, and anthropological and historical approaches, on the other. Something of this sort had already been attempted by Hein (1986), who argues that the freedom represented by the irrepressible, reckless Kṛṣṇa was a desired relief from the social bondage of the Gupta age, a bondage that continues into our own day. He related this liberating, social freedom to contemporary and well-known Hindu child-rearing patterns, contrasting the freedom of childhood with the constraints of adulthood. Hein reiterated this hypothesis in his thoughtful and provocative remarks during the conference, and a lively debate ensued in which most of the participants appeared unwilling to grant that the *līlā* concept was so closely associated with a particular ("Krishnaite") religious tradition. Nevertheless, it is indisputable that the antinomianism seems to be an important aspect of *līlā,* and perhaps to be applicable to performative *līlā*s as well as textual ones. In the present volume Hawley focuses on aspects of reversal and trickery in *rās līlā,* while Sax sees *pāṇḍav līlā* as an opportunity for participants to "play with" their own identities. Other social and historical implications of the *līlā* concept are suggested by Wulff, who argues that the notion of *līlā* is related to a "democratizing process taking place within Bengali society" between the fourteenth and seventeenth centuries, and by Kumar, who finds, by contrast, that when *līlā* is analyzed as a gendered concept, it serves to exclude women in both performance and everyday existence. Concluding his comparison of *rām līlā, durgāpūjā,* and *pāṇḍav līlā,* Hiltebeitel boldly suggests that at least the first two "developed against the background of Muslim, and then British, rule as symbolic expressions of the ideal of an alternative mythical and ritual Hindu *rāj.*"

It might be thought that these performative *līlā*s are closely analogous to

Christian "miracle plays"—and perhaps they are—but there is at least one important difference. In most or all of the Indian traditions there is a tendency to assert that the performers are not merely "playing a part" but in some profound sense embody the characters they represent (cf. Vatsyayan 1987:454). Over and over, participants tell us that a player "is" Rāma, and nearly as often we turn around and write that he "symbolizes" Rāma. But rather than worrying about the epistemology of our translations, we should perhaps be examining more closely the ontology underlying them. Indeed, it makes little sense in the Hindu context to say that performers in these ritual dramas merely "symbolize" some character or other when scriptural precedent, ritual action, and native exegesis all insist that the relationship is one of identity and not merely representation. Such ideas were the subject of much lively discussion and virtually unanimous agreement at the conference, and they are illustrated by many of the selections in this volume. For instance, the *pāṇḍav līlā* discussed by Sax clearly involves a kind of behavior sometimes called "possession" by Westerners and academics, even though the English word refers to a great many things that Garhwalis consider quite distinct—for example, auspicious possession versus possession by ghosts and demons, which is a kind of affliction. Narayanan describes the way in which the *araiyar* reciter of the Tiruvaymoli is identified with both the *āḻvār* poet and the Lord. Hawley tells us that the boys who play the parts of Kṛṣṇa and Rādhā are regarded as divinities by the spectators at *rās līlā* (cf. Sax 1990 for a similar description of *rām līlā*). Although various goddesses possess their devotees in a variety of ritual performances, incarnations of Śiva are rare, perhaps even absent. As Hiltebeitel notes, the main *līlā* traditions have to do with *avataraṇa,* more specifically with the human "descents" of Rāma and Kṛṣṇa. Perhaps the salience of these two gods derives from the theological meanings of *līlā*. Hospital reports that he is struck by the fact that in the *Bhāgavata Purāṇa* the notion of *līlā* is more closely associated with divine incarnations (*avatāra* and *līlāvatāra*) than with creation, preservation, and destruction. The idea that gods should temporarily incarnate themselves in the bodies of human devotees is not at all unusual in Hinduism, which, unlike the religions of the West, does not posit a sharp ontological rift between humans and gods. In other words, gods are people, too, and people sometimes become gods.

As John Carman remarked at the conference, there is something almost ludicrous in writing so seriously about a lighthearted topic like *līlā*. What can we do? As scholars and academics it is our *dharma* to write, but perhaps this is one occasion where we ought to take ourselves a bit less seriously. Speaking for myself, I'd like to report that I had lots of fun organizing and participating in the conference, and I'd like to thank those who attended it for that.

NOTES

1. Quoted (in translation) in Dimock 1989:159. Dimock's essay was first presented at the Harvard conference in which this volume originated. (see p. 5).

2. As Hospital puts it, "The theologians of play find contemporary life in North America in general too beset by the ordered, the serious, the Apollonian—to the extent that even the playful is itself imprisoned within the structures and tensions of the Apollonian way" (1977:289). See also the beginning of Hospital's essay in this volume.

REFERENCES

Bäumer, Bettina. 1969. Schöpfung als Spiel: Der Begriff līlā im Hinduismus, seine philosophische und theologische Bedeutung. Ph.D. diss., Ludwig-Maximilians-Universität, Munich.

Coomaraswamy, Ananda K. 1941. Līlā. *Journal of the American Oriental Society* 61: 98–101.

Dimock, Edward C., Jr. 1989. Līlā. *History of Religions* 29(2): 159–73.

Haberman, David L. 1988. *Acting as a Way of Salvation: A Study of Rāgānuga Bhakti Sādhana*. New York: Oxford University Press.

———. 1994. *Journey Through the Twelve Forests: An Encounter With Krishna*. New York: Oxford University Press.

Hawley, John S., in association with Shrivatsa Goswami. 1981. *At Play with Krishna: Pilgrimage Dramas from Brindavan*. Princeton, N.J.: Princeton University Press.

Hein, Norvin. 1972. *The Miracle Plays of Mathura*. New Haven, Conn.: Yale University Press.

———. 1986. A Revolution in Kṛṣṇaism: The Cult of Gopāla. *History of Religions* 25(3): 296–317.

———. 1987. Lila. In *The Encyclopedia of Religion*, ed. Mircea Eliade, et al., vol. 8: 550–54. New York: Macmillan.

Hospital, Clifford G. 1977. Kṛṣṇa and the Theology of Play. *Studies in Religion / Sciences Religieuses* 6(3): 285–91.

———. 1980. Līlā in the Bhāgavata Purāṇa. *Purāṇa* 22(1): 7–8.

Kapur, Anuradha. 1990. *Actors, Pilgrims, Kings and Gods: The Ramlila at Ramnagar*. Calcutta; Seagull Books.

Lutgendorf, Philip. 1991. *The Life of a Text: Performing the Ramcaritmanas of Tulsidas*. Berkeley: University of California Press.

Poole, Fitz John Porter. 1986. Metaphors and Maps: Towards Comparison in the Anthropology of Religion. *Journal of the American Academy of Religion* 54(3): 411–57.

Sax, William S. 1990. The Ramnagar Ramlila: Text, Performance, Pilgrimage. *History of Religions* 30(2): 129–53.

Schechner, Richard. 1983. *Performative Circumstances, from the Avant Garde to Ramlila*. Calcutta: Seagull Books.

———. 1988. *Performance Theory*, rev. ed. New York: Routledge.

Vatsyayan, Kapila. 1987. Drama: Indian Dance and Dance Drama. In *Encyclopedia of Religion*, ed. Mircea Eliade et al., Vol. 4: 452–55. New York: Macmillan.

I

THE THEOLOGY OF PLAY

2

Līlā

NORVIN HEIN

Līlā is a Sanskrit noun meaning "sport" or "play." It has been the central term in the Hindu elaboration of the idea that God in his creating and governing of the world is moved not by need or necessity but by a free and joyous creativity that is integral to his own nature. He acts in a state of rapt absorption comparable to that of an artist possessed by his creative vision or to that of a child caught up in the delight of a game played for its own sake. The latter comparison is the basis for speaking of God's acts as *līlā,* or sport. Although the translation is the best available, the English word *sport* is a rough rendering that suggests a frivolity not necessarily implied by the word *līlā*. In the Hindu thought-world in which this term arose, the description of God's acts as sport was intended to negate any notion that they are motivated, like the acts of human beings, by acquisitive desire (*kāma*) or are necessitated by the retributive impetus of the actor's previous deeds (*karman*) or by the requirements of duty. Since God forever possesses all, he has no wants and no desires. His ever-desireless acts entail no retribution. He is not the instrument of duty but duty's creator. The spontaneity and autonomy of his actions are absolute.

The word *līlā,* used in this theological sense, began to appear in Hindu religious literature in about the third or fourth century C.E. Partial sources of the concept are found in earlier writings that mention, even in the Vedic age, the frolicsome nature of the gods and the ease and freedom of their acts. The attribution of joyous freedom to the one supreme being made its appearance in the Upaniṣads in reports of experiences of unity with the Divine that were expansive states of blissful release from care. It was not in the monistic systems, however, but in the great Hindu monotheisms that the notion of divine sportiveness became a major concept. Even the worshipers of Śiva—a violent and dangerous deity not easily credited with playfulness—explained the universe as formed in the gyrations of a cosmic dance in which, as Naṭarāja, or Lord of Dancers, Śiva ecstatically creates and sustains and destroys. The elaboration of the idea of *līlā* into a studied doctrine has been primarily the work of the Vaiṣṇava tradition; in particular, the cult of Kṛṣṇa as Gopāla, the young cowherd, carried the teaching of *līlā* to its most advanced development. This later Kṛṣṇaism was shaped decisively by the idea of *līlā* in almost every aspect of its religious system—in its theology, its mythology, its mysticism, and its conception of salvation.

The Theology of *Līlā*

The first appearance of *līlā* as a theological term is apparently a use of the word in the *Vedānta Sūtra* of Bādarāyaṇa (third century C.E.?). In 2.1.33 of that work the author defends belief in a personal Creator against an objection that the God of monotheistic belief who is all and has all cannot be credited with creation, because persons create only in order to come into possession of something that they do not already have. The author replies that, even in the ordinary world, some people carry out creative acts not for the satisfaction of any wants, but merely sportively, for the sheer joy of the activity itself. Faith in a personal Creator is thus reasonable and possible.

The theological literature on *līlā* consists primarily of the commentarial writings on this passage that have been written by the founders and other recognized scholars of the various Vaiṣṇava sects. In the twelfth century, for example, Rāmānuja illustrates the meaning of *līlā* by the example of a great monarch who, though he has no unsatisfied desire, sports enthusiastically on the playing field just for the amusement of the game. The Caitanyaite commentator Baladeva compares the Creator's activity to that of a healthy man just awakened in the morning from deep sleep, who breaks into a dance simply to express his own exuberance.

Since all schools of Vedānta accept the *Vedānta Sūtra,* in some fashion they must accept also its teaching on divine sportiveness. The adherents of the illusionist school of Advaita Vedānta have been obliged, of course, to understand the sports of God to have only such reality as belongs to the personal God himself. For them, the absolute being is not in truth a person, nor in reality has any world been created, nor have any sports been performed. The teaching of *līlā* is provisional only, expressing how unenlightened persons must understand the course of the apparent world so long as they remain under the influence of the deluding cosmic ignorance (*māyā*) that creates the appearance of a world that is false. Over against this illusionist cosmology those who fully embraced the *līlā* teaching were able to maintain that the creative process is real and that the creation is not an obscuration but a manifestation of the nature of God. Indeed, some Hindus have been able to use the *līlā* doctrine to support appreciation of the world in a spirit of religious wonder and to sustain a joy in living. But the general world-weariness of medieval India did not encourage such positive applications. It was more common to use the idea of divine sportiveness to domesticate the tragedies of life by reflecting that wealth and poverty, health and sickness, and even death itself are apportioned to creatures of God in his mysterious play. The reasons for such fateful interventions are beyond human comprehension, but devotees who understand their fortunes to be the sport of God will know that it is not blind fate that controls their lot, and hence they will accept their condition as providential.

Some tension exists between the conception of God's sportiveness and the older picture presented in the *Bhagavadgītā* (3.21–25, 4.5–14) of God as acting in order to assist devotees, to maintain righteousness, and to preserve the integrity of the world. Thinkers of the school of Caitanya (1486–1533) have gone so far as to insist that God acts solely for his own sport and without thought of benefiting his creatures; creatures are in fact benefited by God's sportive acts, but only because those acts are the pleasure of a supreme being whose nature includes compassion. In other Vaiṣṇava circles it has been more common to see no difference between the two explanations of the divine motivation: God's sportive acts and his supportive acts are one because both are done without calculation of any selfish gain that might be made through them. Both are therefore desireless (*niṣkāma*) in terms of the ethical ideal of the *Bhagavadgītā,* and between God's *līlā* and his grace there is no inconsistency.

Līlā Mythology

Although such Vaiṣṇava reasonings could reconcile the old and new views of the divine motivation to each other at the level of theological doctrine, a lavish new mythology was arising in the same period that could not be reconciled so easily with the narratives of earlier forms of Kṛṣṇa worship. The theological development of the *līlā* idea was overshadowed in mass and influence by a profuse literature that expressed the new conception of the deity in myth. A diversion of attention away from the earnest Kṛṣṇa of the *Bhagavadgītā* is evident in the *Harivaṃśa Purāṇa,* composed about 300 C.E. Chapters 47 to 77 of that work relate for the first time a famous set of tales about how Kṛṣṇa as a child disobeyed his parents, played tricks on his elders, spread lighthearted havoc in his cowherd village, disposed of demons with jocular nonchalance, and flirted with the cowherdesses with a daring naughtiness. About a century later these whimsical stories were retold in the fifth book of the *Viṣṇu Purāṇa,* where Kṛṣṇa's antics are called *līlās* and the whole of his earthly career is described as his *manuṣyalīlā,* or human sport (5.7.38). About the ninth century C.E. these pranks were fully elaborated in the tenth book of the *Bhāgavata Purāṇa,* a text that remains the foremost scripture of the family of Vaiṣṇava sects that worship Kṛṣṇa in the form of Gopāla. The stories contained in the *Bhāgavata Purāṇa* have been retold endlessly in dependent literature in the regional languages of India. The major poets of Hindi, of whom Sūrdās was the greatest, have created in the Braj dialect an especially honored literature on the sport of the child Kṛṣṇa. The attractiveness of these myths has made the worship of Gopāla Kṛṣṇa one of the most prominent forms of Hinduism throughout the past thousand years.

In the Gopāla cult's portrayal of Kṛṣṇa's childhood behavior, the flouting of Hindu moral codes was a prominent element already in the *Viṣṇu Purāṇa,* and the antinomian tendency increased steadily thereafter. The stories of the god's infancy have remained relatively innocent in spirit, but the tales of his childhood and youth soon focused particularly upon his lying, stealing, violation of sexual taboos, and other mischievous tricks. His nocturnal flirtations in the *rāsa* dance with the *gopīs*, or cowherdesses, and in particular with a *gopī* named Rādhā, became more and more explicitly sexual. In recent centuries a major stream of Bengal Vaiṣṇavism has insisted that Kṛṣṇa's amours must be construed as adulterous. At the same time the story of Kṛṣṇa's dance with the *gopīs* has become ever more important, a central and revelatory mystery of the faith. The lesson that Kṛṣṇa worshipers have drawn from this myth has been purely devotional, however: the ideal devotee must surrender the self to God with a passion as total as that of the straying Hindu wife who, love-mad, sacrifices reputation and home and security in her ruinous devotion to a paramour.

Līlā in Meditation

The myths of Kṛṣṇa's *līlās* provide the mental material for most of the religious observances of the Gopāla cults. The purpose of their characteristic practices is to preoccupy the consciousness with visionary perception of the *līlās* of Kṛṣṇa. Simple conditioning begins with participation in assemblies where the stories are presented in dance, drama, the singing of narrative poetry, or the chanting of sacred texts. Brahman actors called *rāsdhārīs* enact the sports of Kṛṣṇa in a Hindi drama called the *rāslīlā*. Professional declaimers called *kathakas*, *purāṇikas*, or *kathāvācakas* read out the scriptural tales and explain them publicly. Devotees move toward a more inward absorption in the *līlās* by quiet and reflective reading of mythological books. Aspiration to yet deeper Kṛṣṇa consciousness leads some further into elaborate meditational practices analogous to yoga, carried out under the spiritual direction of a sectarian teacher. Because yogic instruction has traditionally been confidential, and particularly because meditation in this tradition focuses upon matter that is shockingly erotic by usual Hindu standards, the pattern of these disciplines has remained secret to an exceptional degree. A little can be learned from manuscript works of early scholastic writers of the Bengal school, however.

One plan of meditation requires the devotee to follow in imagination the erotic interplay between Rādhā and Kṛṣṇa through all the eight periods of the traditional Hindu day, from their arising in the morning to their retiring at night. Another requires long focus of the inner imagination upon one or another mythical meeting of the divine lovers in the bowers, the meditator assuming the role of one of the female attendants (*sakhīs*) whose names are mentioned in late Vaiṣṇava legends. The hope of the meditator is to perceive his chosen *līlā* no longer merely in his imagination but in its ongoing celestial reality. By meditating on the manifested (*prakaṭa*) *līlās* that are known to all because Kṛṣṇa performed them in the light of history when he descended to earth as an *avatāra,* it is possible to develop a spiritual eye and to attain vision (*darśana*) of the same sports as they are being played eternally in Kṛṣṇa's transcendent paradise in unmanifested (*aprakaṭa*) form. It helps one's meditation to take up residence in the holy region of Mathurā because that earthly city stands directly beneath the celestial city of that name where Kṛṣṇa sports unceasingly, and is its shadow and a point of special contact between the two. Such contemplations focus upon divine acts that have the form of human sexual activities, and success in meditation involves the deliberate arousal and sublimation and use of the meditator's own erotic sensibility. However, the divine love-sports that meditators sometimes see are not understood to be acts of lust (*kāma*), but acts of spiritual love (*prīti*). It is believed that they will remain forever invisible to those who cannot rise above longings that are carnal.

The religious experience that is idealized by this tradition is exemplified in Narsī Mehtā, a Kṛṣṇa devotee of sixteenth-century Gujarat. His career as a major poet sprang from a vision in which he found himself in a celestial region at night, an attendant holding a blazing torch in his hand and privileged to see the heavenly sports of Rādhā, Kṛṣṇa, and the *gopīs*. So fascinated did he become as he witnessed their eternal dance that his torch burned down through his hand, he said, without his having taken any notice. In visions such as this, intense devotion to Kṛṣṇa is produced and devotees receive assurance of divine assistance and of final liberation.

Līlā in Salvation

The idea of Kṛṣṇa's eternal sport dominates the Gopāla worshipers' understanding of the nature of ultimate blessedness also. They do not expect a merging with the deity but participation forevermore in his celestial sports. It is a state of liberation that can be achieved by attaining on earth a state of total mental absorption in the *līlā*s. The schools of Vallabha and of Caitanya hold that such raptness of attention is not a mere means of liberation but is the state of liberation itself, and say that those who truly attain this ecstatic state do not care whether they shall be taken into transcendency on death or shall be reborn forever into the world. The usual anticipation, however, is mythological in its imagery. According to the *Brahmavaivarta Purāṇa* (4.4.78ff.), the sainted visionary will rise not merely to Vaikuṇṭha, the paradise of Viṣṇu, but to its highest level, Goloka, the paradise of Kṛṣṇa. There the liberated become cowherdesses belonging to the sportive entourage of Kṛṣṇa. As delighted observers and helpers, they attend forever upon the love sports of Rādhā and Kṛṣṇa, expressing through their joyful service their love for Kṛṣṇa as the center of all existence.

Hindu critics of the notion of *līlā* have felt that it trivializes God's motives and obscures his active benevolence as savior. Rāmānuja avoids the use of the word when not obliged to explain it in his role as a commentator on a sacred text, and never mentions the mythology of the *Bhāgavata Purāṇa,* which was already widely known in his day. The Śaiva theologian Umāpati in section 19 of his *Śivap Pirakācam* declares that all five classes of divine activities recognized in the system of *Śaiva Siddhānta* must be understood to spring from God's gracious concern for the deliverance of souls, and that it is not permissible to say that Śiva's acts of creation, preservation, destruction, and so forth, are his sports. Nor have the chief spokesmen of modern Hinduism been attracted generally by the conception of *līlā* or by its myths. Swami Dayananda in his *Satyārthaprakāśa* denounces the sportive Kṛṣṇa and his supposed acts as immoral human fabrications. Moved by their social and civic concerns and influenced by the ethical stress in Christian theology, most modern Hindu leaders have preferred the morally earnest Kṛṣṇa of the *Bhagavadgītā* to the pleasure-seeking Gopāla. Yet a few have responded to the world-affirming implications of *līlā* as a cosmological idea and have used it in interpreting the natural and human realms. In his book *The Life Divine,* Aurobindo teaches that the Lord as a free artist creates real worlds and real beings, and sports with souls and in souls in order to lead his creatures to ever-higher levels of consciousness. Rabindranath Tagore uses the language of traditional *līlā* teaching in testifying to his intuitions that a joyful, ever-creative God is continually revealing himself in the play of natural forces and in the interactions of human beings (see his *Gītāñjali,* poems 56, 59, 63, 80, and 95).

Appraisals of the *līlā* doctrine have usually recognized its contribution to theology in providing a solution to an important question in cosmology and in supporting a positive appreciation of the world and of life. On the other hand, the *līlā* idea has been condemned widely as a negative development in Hindu ethics. The judgment assumes that thinking about God arises necessarily out of moral concern and must be applied immediately to the governing of the moral life. The *līlā* literature is entirely separate, however, from the *dharma* literature that is the repository of moral guidance for Hindus. The worshipers of the young Kṛṣṇa have never understood the sports of the god to be models for their own actions. Indeed, the *Bhāgavata Purāṇa* itself in 10.33.32f. admonishes ordinary mortals never to behave as Kṛṣṇa does, not even in their minds. The Kṛṣṇa cults have been orthodox in their submission to the social patterns prescribed in the Dharmaśāstras and the folk codes. Their sportiveness has manifested itself in cultic matters that are marginal to social ethics: in the exuberance of their religious assemblies, in the easy emotionality of their pathway of salvation through devotion, in the madcap behavior that they tolerate in their saints, and in the spirit of abandon that pervades their fairs and pilgrimages and a few saturnalian festivals like the licentious Holī. The great problem with which this religion deals is not a chaotic world's struggle for order, but the struggle for emotional freedom in a world already firmly and tryingly regulated. There is a clear correlation between the religion of sportiveness and the closed world of caste, as confirmed by the contemporaneity of their historical origins.

Fascination with Kṛṣṇa's *līlā*s became strong in the fourth century C.E., when the writing of mature Dharmaśāstras had become a full tide and the rules of caste were being systematically enforced for the first time by brahmanical dynasties after centuries of foreign rule. Thereafter Hindus found little meaning in the *Bhagavadgītā*'s call to save an anarchic world from disintegration; instead, they sought release from bondage, and found it in new tales about Kṛṣṇa as an irresponsible and irrepressible child. Seeking in the supernatural what was most desperately lacking in their lives, what they now cherished most in Kṛṣṇa was the spirit of sport. For many centuries, imaginative participation in the frolics of a boy–god helped them to endure the restrictions of the life of caste.

REFERENCES

Banerjea, Akshay Kumar. ''The Philosophy of Divine Leela.'' *Prabuddha Bharata* 49 (1944): 275–81, 311–16.

———. ''The Conception of the Sportive Absolute.'' *Prabuddha Bharata* 56 (1951): 170–73, 216–18, 258–61, 290–96. Banerjea's articles provide the beginner with a useful philosophical introduction to the concept of *līlā*.

Bäumer, Bettina, ''Schöpfung als Spiel: Der Begriff līlā im Hinduismus, seine philosophische und theologische Bedeutung.'' Ph.D. diss., Ludwig-Maximilians-Universität, Munich, 1969. This work is the sole monograph on the theological conception of *līlā*. In her conclusion, the author provides a comparison with Christian cosmogonies.

Coomaraswamy, Ananda K. ''Līlā.'' *Journal of the American Oriental Society* 61 (1941): 98–101. An inconclusive etymological study of the word *līlā* and the associated verbal root *krīḍ-* or *krīḷ-*, 'play'.

Kinsley, David R. *The Divine Player: A Study of Kṛṣṇalīlā*. Delhi, 1979. A loose survey of the concept of *līlā* and of some of the Hindu narratives in which it finds expression. Includes notes on related extra-Indian materials.

3

Līlā in Early Vaiṣṇava Thought

CLIFFORD HOSPITAL

My initial interest in the place of *līlā* in Vaiṣṇava thought was occasioned by an attempt to investigate the understanding of God's activity in the *Bhāgavata Purāṇa.*[1] This investigation happened to coincide with a development among Christians of a theology of play, and I went so far as to suggest that if Christians were seeking an appropriate mythical base for such a theology, they would do well to look to Kṛṣṇa rather than to Jesus for that base.[2] It is important to remind ourselves that this attempt among Christians to rediscover the playfulness of their own heritage was almost certainly a response to the widespread protests in the late sixties and early seventies against the drivenness of American culture.[3] It may well have been this cultural milieu that sensitized me—and others who were working on related materials about that time[4]—to the playfulness of Kṛṣṇa and thence to the importance of *līlā* as a concept in materials related to Kṛṣṇa. In my own case the frame of reference was a little broader in that I was aware of how frequently the idea of play was invoked in the *Bhāgavata* in association with a variety of Bhagavān's activities.

In addition, I was most struck by the fact that in this text—in contrast with what occurs, for example, in the *Brahmasūtras*—the identification of Bhagavān's activity as *līlā* was articulated most strongly not in relation to the cosmic processes of creation, preservation, and destruction but in relation to the *avatāras*. I was particularly interested in the attempt in *Bhāgavata* 2.6 and 2.7 to place the *avatāras* in the context of the Lord's other manifestations. In this section there are three basic kinds of manifestation: the primordial *avatāra*

(2.6.41: *adyo 'vatāra . . . parasya*), his manifestation as the cosmic Puruṣa, and the universe deriving from Puruṣa; the *māyāvibhūtis*, which include principles characteristic of, and the beings associated with, the different phases of the cosmic process—including Brahmā, Viṣṇu, and Śiva (2.7.39); and twenty-four *avatāras*, called *līlāvatāras* (2.6.45).[5]

In this earlier work I was content to limit myself primarily to trying to understand the theological implications of the idea of play presented implicitly and explicitly in the *Bhāgavata.* In this paper I am attempting to understand more adequately what is happening in the *Bhāgavata* by seeing it against the background of the development that gave rise to the ideas articulated in the *Bhāgavata*.

In order to understand this development it is useful to develop a theoretical framework in which we can think about the nature of theological statements in various major texts that are representative of the background to the *Bhāgavata.* Initially I find helpful a discussion by Peter Berger concerning different levels in relation to the legitimation of human activity:

> On the pretheoretical level there are to be found simple traditional affirmations of which the paradigm is "This is how things are done." There follows an incipiently theoretical level (hardly to be included, though, in the category of "ideas") in which legitimation takes the form of proverbs, moral maxims and traditional wisdom. This type of legitimating lore may be further developed and transmitted in the form of myths, legends and folk tales. Only then may one come upon explicitly theoretical legitimations, by which specific sectors of the social order are explained and justified by means of specialized bodies of "knowledge." Finally, there are the highly theoretical constructions by which the nomos of a society is legitimated *in toto* and in which all less-than-total legitimations are theoretically integrated in an all-embracing *Weltanschauung.*[6]

Although Berger focuses on legitimation, the differentiations he is making are applicable to a discussion of various levels of theological expression. (This is not to say that the question of the way in which divine activity legitimates human activity is unimportant, and we shall want to keep this question before us as we proceed.) As I see it, the texts that form a background to the *Bhāgavata*—from the Vedic *Saṃhitā*s, through the *Brāhmaṇa*s, *Upaniṣad*s, texts related to *dharma,* epics, *Purāṇa*s, and the *Sūtra*s related to the *darśana*s—contain a variety of Berger's levels, from incipiently theoretical to explicitly theoretical to highly theoretical (though Berger's example of the most highly theoretical, the "all-embracing *Weltanschauung,*" is evident, at least in explicit form, only in the commentarial traditions of the *darśana*s, most significant examples of which postdate the *Bhāgavata*).

Having said that I find Berger's levels helpful, I also believe it necessary to develop some refinement of them in relation to the understanding of divine activity in the texts we shall be considering. Since all imaginings of divine—or perhaps more broadly superhuman—reality are speculative and analogical, none would fit into Berger's category of pretheoretical. Within the spectrum from incipiently theoretical to highly theoretical we would want to differentiate between the mediation of abstract ideas implicitly in stories or myths and the explicit statements of those ideas. In the texts under discussion, as in most religious literature, the implicit and the explicit are intertwined (the only exceptions to this are in some highly theoretical texts that have been subsumed under such terms as theology, philosophy, and *darśana*—though even here the mythical is often used as illustrative, and ideas that the writer finds implicit in the myths are made explicit).

Before moving to the central task at hand, we need to remind ourselves of one other fact—that, as recent studies of Hindu mythology have made clear, what is implicit in the stories of superhuman beings is subject to very different interpretations on the part of those who attempt to explicate the implicit. Let me try to demonstrate what I mean by some reflections on Western scholarly interpretations of Hindu mythology over the last hundred years or so. As I see it, the earliest serious attempts at understanding followed essentially a developmental–historical approach, in which various broad periods were differentiated—Vedic mythology, epic mythology, and so forth—and in which what was implicit in the myths was understood on the basis of explicit expressions in associated materials.[7] There was, however, a problem. It was obvious that there was a great deal implicit in the myths of which the traditional commentators appeared unaware, and this approach offered little help in elucidating these hidden elements. What, to use perhaps the most obviously problematic example, was one to make of the strange, violent, horrific figure of Kālī? The traditional interpretations of the Tantras did not really seem to do justice to the psychological impact of Kālī; as a result, the writings of Sir John Woodroffe / Arthur Avalon, based in these interpretations, strike one as rather flat, a whitewashing of something that is inherently quite shocking.[8]

Enter the depth psychologists, of both Freudian and Jungian varieties. Working in various ways from Freud's celebrated idea of the unconscious, scholars utilized these theories to find much more that was implicit in the myths than earlier scholars had realized, and made it explicit. In general, what they did was to identify symbols embedded in the myths, and to interpret these in terms of a cross-culturally based theory of the human psyche.[9]

Whether what they made explicit was really there, implicit in the myths, has, of course, been subject to considerable debate. In particular, scholars more recently have doubted that a symbol necessarily has the same meaning in different cultures, so they sought and found other theoretical tools to elucidate what is implicit. Much present thinking is informed, rather, by structuralist approaches—or some form of eclecticism informed by structuralism—that attempt by an exhaustive examination of the entirety of Indian culture to unveil what is implicit— in the more extreme sense of "deeply hidden," "deep structures"—in myths, as well as in ritual and other forms of human activity.

What I have been saying thus far is by way of prolegomena. I have introduced this discussion for two reasons. First, I believe that in trying to understand the application of the idea of play to the activity of superhuman beings in Hindu thought—and ultimately to the activity of the Supreme Person, the Lord, in Vaiṣṇava thought—it is necessary to be quite nuanced in our treatment of texts, in order to understand what is implicit and explicit. The second reason is that many of the essays in this collection raise important questions about the ramifications of the use of Sanskrit terms, such as *līlā,* which approximate the English word *play*. For example: With respect to the subjects of our investigations, is play delineated centrally by contrast with work, as it appears to be in our culture? Is the use of the idea of play in relation to divine actions intended to say something substantive about a contrast between them and human actions? Is there implicit a special relation between play and childhood? When words for play are used in relation to a deity's activity in a particular text, is this merely a use of conventional imagery, or is it the author's intention to evoke a generic quality of playfulness for all of that deity's activity?

In a foundational article on *līlā* Ananda Coomaraswamy notes that "the notion of a divine 'playing' occurs repeatedly in RV."[10] He mentions twenty-eight occurrences of *krīḷ,* 'to play', and proceeds to give details related to Soma and Agni. He argues that the idea of divine play is fully represented in the Upaniṣads and the *Bhagavadgītā,* though the only actual use of a word meaning play is in *Chāndogya Upaniṣad* 8.12.2, where the disembodied *ātman* is described as "laughing, sporting, having enjoyment with women or chariots or friends, not remembering the appendage of this body."[11] Coomaraswamy goes on to argue that "we might as legitimately speak of a Soma-*krīḍā* or Agni-*krīḍā* or Ātma-*krīḍā* or Brahma-*līlā* as we do of a Buddha-*līḷhā* or Kṛṣṇa-*līlā.*"[12]

I must admit to not being quite convinced. The description of the *ātman* in the *Chāndogya* appears to be a piece of speculation akin to the account in the *Kauśītaki Upaniṣad* 1.4 of the (presumably liberated) person in the world of *brahman.* Both mix quite abstract concepts with concrete descriptions—though the latter is the more concrete. But the milieu does not appear at all similar to that of the activity of the Devas in the *Ṛgveda.*

Further, it seems to me that to apply a generic play to, say, the activity of

Agni, on the basis of occasional associations, is to push things too far. In the *Ṛgveda* we have many examples of poetry containing vibrant imagery—what we would identify as similes and metaphors—in descriptions of natural phenomena, and such imagery appears to be in effect in the uses of *krīḷ* noted by Coomaraswamy.

Admittedly, there is a further complicating factor for our attempt to decide whether there is any general sense of divine activity as play implicit in this use of imagery. There are many examples of the use of imagery in Ṛgvedic poetry where it is more than that, in that it is actually assimilated to the form of the deity being hymned. Thus, for example, in relation to *uṣas* (the dawn), we find descriptions that suggest it / she is like a mother of a young woman, drifting into a personification of Dawn—not, however, the mere use of a poetic technique of personification but a personification that includes the praise of Dawn as a deity.[13]

The clear lack of differentiations that we would make when considering such poetry makes it difficult for us to think our way into the kind of religious consciousness evident in these hymns. If we attempt it, however, we *might* conclude that a generic identification of divine activity as play is implicit in the *Ṛgveda*.

Nevertheless, given that the association is relatively rare, I am more inclined to the view that, if such an idea is implicit, it is so only for a few deities whose natural form specifically evokes an imagery of playing. (Although it is not quite clear from the article, it may be that Coomaraswamy is not arguing more than this.) But even of this I am doubtful. For an occasional use of imagery suggesting play does not seem to me to warrant the judgment that there is a generic quality of playfulness implicit in all of the deity's activity. That is, I am not convinced of an implicit, generic Agni-*krīḍā* or Soma-*krīḍā*.

Such reflections are helpful when we turn to consider the developments in early to middle Purāṇic texts associated with Viṣṇu that form a background to the ideas of the *Bhāgavata*. In a variety of texts, words for play are associated with three different modes of Viṣṇu's activity: the creation of the universe (in some cases, the entire process of creation, preservation, and destruction); the activity of Viṣṇu in the form of the boar; and his form as Kṛṣṇa (or the combined forms of Kṛṣṇa and Balarāma).

The earliest association of creation with the idea of play appears to be that in *Mānavadharmaśāstra* 1.80,[14] where the subject is Brahmā:

> The Manvantaras, creations and destructions are innumerable; playing, as it were, the Supreme One performs this again and again.
>
> (*krīḍanniva etat kurute parameṣṭhi punaḥ punaḥ*)

This statement occurs at the end of a long account of the creation of the world by Brahmā. This takes a form that later became standard for Purāṇic authors, where quite abstract early Sāṃkhya ideas are used to account for the evolution of the elements of the universe, and in which the origin of various living beings is portrayed in much more concrete mythical terms. In this context play provides an evocative image of the idea, developed around this time, of an ongoing process of evolution of the universe into the discrete forms in which we know it, its remaining with relative stability in that form for countless aeons, and its eventual return to an undifferentiated form—and this repeated endlessly. The image suggests as background the ability of children in play to repeat their imaginative adventures with toys, tirelessly, without being bored—creating a world, destroying it, and creating it again.[15] Whether we should infer from this imagery an implicit idea of the creative process as the play of God in this text is unclear.[16]

In a number of early and middle Purāṇas, however, this idea becomes explicit. Thus, in *Vāyu* 5.30 we read:

> The Lord of Yoga, who in his play manifests various creations, activities, forms, names, and conditions, creates and effects changes in bodies.
>
> (*yogeśvaraḥ śarīrāṇi karoti vikaroti ca /*
> *nānākṛtikriyārūpanāmavṛttiḥ svalīlayā //*)

An almost identical statement is found in *Kūrma* 1.4.54:

> The Lord of Yoga in his play creates and effects changes in bodies of diverse shapes, activities, features, and names.
>
> (*yogeśvaraḥ śarīrāṇi karoti vikaroti ca /*
> *nānākṛtikriyārūpanāmavanti svalīlayā //*)

In these cases there is an explicit identification of the activity of God in the cosmic process as in some sense *līlā*. It is no longer a matter of imagery, and what may or may not be implicit in that. We are still left with some difficulty in determining the sense implied in the use of the instrumental case. Are we to understand true instrumentality, "by means of," or is it an expression of occasion or reason, "by reason of," or "in virtue of," more commonly expressed with the use of the ablative?[17] The point is not a crucial one, since either way the universe is seen as the result of God's play.

Agni 17.1 is more direct:

> Listen: I shall now describe the play of Viṣṇu, which is the creation and so on of the universe.
>
> (*jagatsargādikāṃ krīḍāṃ viṣṇor vakṣye 'dhunā śṛṇu /*)

In trying to understand the background to the *Bhāgavata* ideas provided by these earlier examples, a number of points should be made. First, there are a number of occasions in the *Bhāgavata* where a similar link is made between *līlā* and the cosmic process (e.g., 1.10.24, 2.4.12, 3.9.14, 7.8.40).[18]

Second, in none of these examples in the *Bhāgavata* or earlier are there any clues about what it means in theological terms to talk about the universe as the play of God. That is, while the idea of play is explicit, the theological implications of the idea are not. Thus, there is no suggestion of the interpretation given by commentators of the celebrated phrase in the *Brahmasūtra* 2.1.33—"But as in ordinary life, creation is mere sport" (*lokavat tu līlā kaivalyam*)—on the analogy of a great king who is completely self-fulfilled, that the creation does not involve any motive on God's part other than to amuse himself—that it is a purely spontaneous act.[19]

Third, one should note that this association with play is quite rare in these early and middle Purāṇas. And when it does occur, it does not seem to be of great importance. Virtually all Purāṇas of this period are interested in describing the evolution of the cosmos, and they do it in similar fashion, with more or less detail. Almost always the accounts are given in response to a request like "Tell us how this world came to be." In general there appears to be a widespread interest in cosmogony. If there is anything implicit in these accounts that is of prime theological import it is that all finds its origin in the Supreme Person (however that person is identified).

The second example of divine activity where the idea of play recurs with some frequency is that of the Varāha *avatāra*. Thus *Vāyu* 6.11: "He called to mind the form of a boar, happy in water sports" (*jalakrīḍāsu ruciraṃ vārāhaṃ rūpam asmarat*). The *Brahmāṇḍa* is almost identical (1.1.5.11): *jalakrīḍāsamucitaṃ vārāhaṃ rūpam asmarat*. In both cases this occurs at the point in the story where Viṣṇu takes the form of the boar, and the same link with aquatic play is also found at this point in *Matsya* 248.64 and *Kūrma* 1.6.8. (In *Viṣṇu* the link is not made, though in a later hymn of the *yogī*s there is a verse [1.4.38] that Wilson translates as follows: "The orb of the earth is seen seated on the tip of thy tusks, as if thou hadst been sporting amidst a lake where the lotus floats, and hadst borne away the leaves covered with soil."[20] However, the word that Wilson translates as "sporting" is *vigāhataḥ*, from *vi* + $\sqrt{}$*gāh* 'to bathe', which appears to be not the same as aquatic play.)

If one attempts to understand what is happening in these texts where the idea of aquatic play is introduced, one should note that prior to the *Bhāgavata* this is the only association of the idea of play with an *avatāra* other than the pair of Balarāma and Kṛṣṇa, so there does not appear to be any concerted attempt to link the idea of play with this form of divine activity. Indeed, throughout this period, as scholars have long been aware, the central common idea running implicitly through the *avatāra* stories—and often made explicit—is the overcoming of *adharma,* the reestablishment of *dharma* in the world.[21]

The further important point is that quite early the myth of Varāha's raising of the earth is presented in a fairly standard form: at the beginning of this present *kalpa,* the *vārāhakalpa,* the earth is submerged in the primordial waters. The Lord becomes desirous of lifting her up. He assumes the form of an enormous boar (described in great detail, and identified with the Vedas; or the sacrifice; or Speech, further designated variously as *dharma* or *brahman*)[22] and sets the earth firmly on the waters. This action is frequently set as the final stage of the story of the creation of the world as we know it. In this context it picks up on very old creation accounts of the raising of the earth from the primordial waters by Prajāpati.[23]

We might wonder, then, whether this relating of the boar form to aquatic play was associated with the idea of creation as God's play. It seems unlikely since the former idea is rather more widespread than the latter. More likely is that the picture of the boar plunging into the water naturally evoked the image of water sports (and thus we might understand the origin of such an image as similar to what had happened in relation to a few Ṛgvedic deities).

The other pre-*Bhāgavata* texts where play is associated with the Lord's activity are, as I have indicated, related to Balarāma and Kṛṣṇa. Perhaps the earliest example of such an association is in the *Mahābhārata* 3.187.52:

> That primeval person, the ubiquitous lord, is Kṛṣṇa Vārṣṇeya, the strong-armed Hari of unimaginable soul, who sits here as though at play.[24]
>
> (*sa eṣa kṛṣṇo vārṣṇeyaḥ purāṇapuruṣo vibhuḥ /*
> *āste harir acintyātma krīḍanniva mahābhujaḥ //*)

This is a particularly tantalizing example since it is quite unlike any we have encountered so far. In all of these earlier examples we have seen that the activity described is naturally evocative of an image of some form of play. But Kṛṣṇa's sitting does not in itself evoke the simile "as though playing" (*krīḍanniva*). What does evoke it is the paradoxical relation between the primeval person, the ubiquitous lord, and the human form of Kṛṣṇa. What is suggested is a game of pretense, a kind of charade.

In other examples related to Balarāma and Kṛṣṇa the relation to play is much more direct (though, as we shall see, this element of paradox / pretense is also in evidence). In both the *Harivaṃśa* and the *Viṣṇu Purāṇa* there are extensive treatments of the childhood of Balarāma and Kṛṣṇa, and references to their childhood play are frequent. Both texts have descriptions of their playing, just before and after the account of the move from Vraja to

Vrndavana, and in the introduction to the story of Pralambha; and generic words for play are often included.[25]

There are some specific uses of words that merit attention. In the *Harivaṃśa, śiśulīlā* is used in relation to the overturning of the cart by Kṛṣṇa (50.5: *śiśulīlāṃ tataḥ kurvan*) and his climbing into a Kadamba tree and jumping into the Yamuna to tame Kāliya (55.57: *śiśulīlayā . . . damayiṣyāmi kāliyam*). In both examples there are both the actuality of the childish play of Kṛṣṇa and, as in our example from the *Mahābhārata,* the suggestion of pretense, the assumption of the forms of childish play for a particular purpose.

The most tantalizing reference in the *Harivaṃśa,* however, is in the description of the Gopīs at the time of the *rāsa* dance as "imitating the play of Kṛṣṇa" (63.26: *kṛṣṇalīlānukāriṇyaḥ*). I believe this is the earliest occurrence of the compound *kṛṣṇalīlā,* and one naturally wonders what is implied by the term. This is not made explicit, though the following verses indicate that they imitated him by striking their palms (presumably a reference to the young Kṛṣṇa's playing at being a warrior), and that they imitated his songs and dances. There is the further question about the implications of such imitation. Can we infer some devotional practice behind this, for example, dramatic presentations of Kṛṣṇa's *līlā*s? Or are we to see that at least the Gopīs are being portrayed as devotees? Or, again, are these just the actions of young girls infatuated with the young hero Kṛṣṇa? From within the text there is no strong evidence. On the whole I am inclined to agree with Sheth[26] that the milieu of the *Harivaṃśa* account reflects a heroic background rather than an emphasis upon Kṛṣṇa's divinity, although there are occasional references (including those I have mentioned in the preceding paragraph) that do suggest the latter. But in contrast to what we find in the *Viṣṇu,* and especially the *Bhāgavata,* an aspect of devotional response to Kṛṣṇa's activity does not seem to be incorporated into the text.

In the *Viṣṇu* there are some additional occurrences of *līlā* that tie in with a more explicit contemplation of Kṛṣṇa's divinity. When Balarāma reminds Kṛṣṇa of his divinity—that he is eternal (*śāśvataḥ*)— in order to encourage him to overcome Kāliya, he says (*Viṣṇu* 5.7.39): "The gods are all here, O Blessed One, sharing with you in human play [*manuṣyalīlām*], imitating your play [*viḍambayantas tvallīlāṃ*]."

Later it is said (5.11.16) that Kṛṣṇa lifts Govardhana "in play" (*līlayā*). And in parallel with the *Harivaṃśa,* at the time of the *rāsa* dance one of the Gopīs is described as "imitating the play of Kṛṣṇa" (5.13.29: *kṛṣṇalīlānusāriṇī*) in calling the cows. This is the last in a series of various imitations of Kṛṣṇa, recalling his singing, his taming of Kāliya, his raising of Govardhana, his killing of Dhenuka (and thus a more extensive and specific list than in the *Harivaṃśa*).

I have been attempting to review this background in the context of which we might see the rise of the specific ideas of the *Bhāgavata*. I can now outline more fully what constitutes the specific originality of the *Bhāgavata:* first, as I have already mentioned, that the *avatāras* are called collectively *līlāvatāra*s; second, that the listing of *līlāvatāra*s culminates in three references to the idea of play in relation to the life of Kṛṣṇa;[27] third, that in the accounts of a number of the major *avatāra*s (and not just Varāha) the idea of play is explicit;[28] and fourth, that correspondingly the *Bhāgavata* account of Kṛṣṇa expands imaginatively the portrayal of Kṛṣṇa's childhood playfulness.

In my previous study of *līlā* in the *Bhāgavata* I was struck with the complex interweaving of a number of frequently recurring motifs in relation to the life of Kṛṣṇa in Vraja and Vrndavana: the paradox of the Lord as baby and child; the activity of Kṛṣṇa as play—including heroic acts (*vikramalīlā*) such as the overcoming of demonic and / or dangerous beings, which are performed "in play" or "with ease" (*līlayā*); the identification of certain of Kṛṣṇa's deeds as the product of his *māyā;* the responses of those around Kṛṣṇa to his *līlā* and *māyā:* wonder, love, joy, and—in the case of the inimical beings killed and thus saved by him—the negative responses of enmity and fear; the further suggestion that what is salvific is the obsessive response, positive or negative, evoked by Kṛṣṇa's *līlā;* that all of this is a product of the Lord's grace.[29]

My initial interest in the activity of the Lord in the *Bhāgavata* was evoked by the frequent description of Bhagavān as the one "of marvelous acts" (*adbhūtakarmaṇaḥ*)[30] and by possible parallels and contrasts to the idea of God's mighty acts in the Hebrew scriptures. But I eventually became convinced that the central focus of God's activity in the *Bhāgavata* is Kṛṣṇa, and the key term in relation to his marvelous acts is *līlā*.

But what kind of scenario does our background provide for this development in the *Bhāgavata*? As I see it now, it appears that certain accounts of divine activity naturally evoked the idea of play: the continual creation and dissolution of the universe, the plunging of the prodigious boar into the primeval waters; and, in somewhat different fashion, the picture of the Lord manifest in the form of the human hero Kṛṣṇa. But the tales of Kṛṣṇa's heroic childhood lent themselves to a massive development in which God is seen as embodying his grace in the form of a playful child whose acts—marvelous as those of any small child, but how infinitely more so—call forth a response of devotional attachment that is transformative, liberative.

We might ask a further question about what is implicit in these developments: that is, what in Indian consciousness of this period gave rise to this focus on play? Are we to understand it, as Norvin Hein does in his concentration on the child Kṛṣṇa, via an interplay between Sudhir Kakar's interpretation of childhood in India, and the triumph of *dharma* under the Guptas (of which the early views on *avatāra*s are a reflection)—and hence, one might say, the interest in play as an imaginative release from restrictive order?[31] A comparison with the theology of play makes this attractive, in that one can see in that movement a similar, though thus far not very successful, attempt on the part of Christians to find release from the combination of puritanism and heroic (?) drivenness. Or can we better understand it, via an extension of Daniel Ingalls's treatment of the *Harivaṃśa,*[32] as an incorporation of the Indian pastoral tradition into Hindu religious life? Or should we understand it in terms of more general application, via an extension of McKim Marriott's treatment of Holi[33]—perhaps informed by Victor Turner[34]—in which the playfulness of the festival, its *communitas,* revitalizes and humanizes the structures of society? Or is it all three?

A final point. I have continually throughout my thinking about these materials wondered about the specific implications of words such as *krīḍā* and *līlā.* Like their English counterparts, *sport* and *game* and *play,* they are extraordinarily imprecise. I have found myself highly resistant to using the first two of these English words because in their recent history they represent the worst of human drivenness. The Ben Johnson scandal at the 1988 Olympic Games in Seoul, and the subsequent Dubin inquiry in Canada into the use of anabolic steroids, make us acutely aware of an economically driven pathology of modern sports. Sport now seems to have virtually nothing to do with "play," with *līlā.*

In seeking some further evocation of *līlā* in English, I have found myself informed by my wife's novel, *Charades.*[35] Any of the Australians represented there might characteristically say, "The universe! Life! What a bloody charade!" And if pushed a bit, perhaps, "What a magnificent charade!" To which the *Bhāgavata* might evoke a further response: "And most wonderful of all, the Kṛṣṇa-charade."

NOTES

1. See my Ph.D. dissertation "The Marvellous Acts of God: A Study in the *Bhāgavata Purāṇa,*" Harvard University, 1973.

2. Clifford G. Hospital, "Kṛṣṇa and the Theology of Play," *Studies in Religion/Sciences Religieuses* 6, no. 3 (1977), 285–91.

3. This can be observed from a perusal of major contributions to this movement: Sam Keen, *Apology for Wonder* (New York: Harper and Row, 1969); idem, "Manifesto for a Dionysian Theology," in Herbert W. Richardson and Donald R. Cutler, eds, *Transcendence* (Boston: Beacon Press, 1971); Robert W. Neale, *In Praise of Play*

(New York: Harper and Row, 1969); Harvey Cox, *The Feast of Fools: A Theological Essay on Festivity and Fantasy* (Cambridge, Mass.; Harvard University Press, 1969); David Miller, *Gods and Games: Towards a Theology of Play* (New York: World, 1970).

4. See, for example, David R. Kinsley, *The Divine Player: A Study of Kṛṣṇa Līlā* (Delhi: Motilal Banarsidass, 1979); John Stratton Hawley, *At Play with Krishna: Pilgrimage Dramas from Brindavan* (Princeton, N.J.: Princeton University Press, 1981); idem, *Krishna, the Butter Thief* (Princeton, N.J.: Princeton University Press, (1983); and Kenneth E. Bryant, *Poems to the Child-God: Structures and Strategies in the Poetry of Surdas* (Berkeley: University of California Press, 1978).

5. For further details, see Clifford G. Hospital, "Līlā in the Bhāgavata Purāṇa," *Purāṇa* 22, no. 1 (1980), 7–8.

6. Peter L. Berger, *The Sacred Canopy: Elements of a Sociological Theory of Religion* (New York: Doubleday, 1967), pp. 31–32.

7. This approach is evident in such classical texts as A. A. Macdonell, *Vedic Mythology* (Strasbourg: Trubner, 1897), and E. Washburn Hopkins, *Epic Mythology* (Strasbourg: Trubner, 1915).

8. See, for example, Arthur Avalon, *Shakti and Maya* (Bombay: Oxford University Press, 1917), p. 14; and idem, *Shakti, or the World as Power* (London: Women's Printing Society, 1920), p. 3.

9. See, for example, Heinrich Zimmer, *Myths in Indian Art and Civilization* (New York: Harper and Row, 1946).

10. Ananda K. Coomaraswamy, *"Līlā," Journal of the American Oriental Society* 61 (1941), 99.

11. Robert Ernest Hume, *The Thirteen Principal Upanishads: Translated from the Sanskrit,* 2nd rev. ed. (London: Oxford University Press, 1931), p. 272.

12. Coomaraswamy, "Līlā," p. 99.

13. See, for example, the hymns to Uṣas cited in Ainslie L. Embree, ed., *The Hindu Tradition* (New York: Random House, 1966), pp. 16–17 (*Ṛgveda* 1.113); and in Sarvepalli Radhakrishnan and Charles A Moore, eds., *A Source Book in Indian Philosophy* (Princeton, N.J.: Princeton University Press, 1957), pp. 13–15 (*Ṛgveda* 1.48).

14. Editions of Sanskrit texts cited in this essay are listed separately following the notes. Unless otherwise indicated, all English translations are my own.

15. For a similar image of creation as *līlā,* see the citation from Tagore in Edward C. Dimock, Jr., *"Līlā," History of Religions* 29, no. 2 (1989), 159.

16. The issue is somewhat related to that with respect to our discussion of the *Ṛgveda* materials. However, it appears that in general by this time there is a less direct relationship between such imagery and the characterization of a deity.

17. See William Dwight Whitney, *Sanskrit Grammar* (Cambridge, Mass.: Harvard University Press, 1889), p. 94.

18. Thus *Bhāgavata* 7.8.40:

> I bow down to the endless one, of enduring power, of wonderful prowess, of pure deeds, of imperishable self—who, in his play, executes the creation, preservation, and destruction of the universe by means of the *guṇas*.

nato 'smyanantāya durantaśaktaye vicitravīryāya pavitrakarmaṇe /
viśvasya sargasthitisaṃyamān guṇaiḥ svalīlayā saṃdadhate 'vyayātmane //

19. See Sarvepalli Radhakrishnan, *The Brahma Sūtra* (New York: Harper, 1960), p. 362.

20. H. H. Wilson, trans., *The Vishnu Purana: A System of Hindu Mythology and Tradition* (1840; reprint, Calcutta: Punthi Pustak, 1972), p. 28.

21. Thus in this period the *avātara* stories appear to be primarily consonant with the statement of Kṛṣṇa in *Bhagavadgītā* 4.7–8.

22. See *Agni* 4.2; *Matsya* 248.67–78; *Brahmāṇḍa* 1.1.5.16–22; and *Bhāgavata* 3.13.22–23, 34–39.

23. See *Taittirīya Brāhmaṇa* 1.1.3.5.

24. J. A. B. Van Buitenen, trans., *The Mahābhārata* (Chicago: University of Chicago Press, 1973–78), vol. 2, p. 593.

25. See, for example, *Viṣṇu* 5.6.31 (*bālalīlayā*), 5.6.49, 51 (*krīḍantau*), 5.9.6 (*krīḍābhir*), 5.9.12 (*harinakrīḍanaṃ nāma bālakrīḍanakaṃ*); and *Harivaṃśa* 52.6–8, 55.24–25, 58.8–9.

26. Noel Sheth, S.J., *The Divinity of Krishna* (New Delhi: Munshiram Manoharlal, 1984), p. 41.

27. *viharan* (2.7.28), *salīlam* (2.7.32), and *krīḍan* (2.7.33).

28. See *Bhāgavata* 3.13.32, 47, 3.19.37, 3.20.8 (*varāha*); 7.9.13, 7.10.24 (*nṛsiṃha*); 8.6.17, 38 (*kūrma*); 8.24.31, 54, 2.7.12 (*matsya*); 8.22.20 (*vāmana*); 9.11.20 (Rāma).

29. For a more detailed exploration of these themes, see Hospital, "Līlā in the Bhāgavata Purāṇa," 12–22.

30. *Bhāgavata* 1.18.1, 8.23.29, 8.24.1, etc. Similar phrases occur at 8.23.27, 8.4.13, 8.5.12, and 12.12.2.

31. See Norvin Hein, "A Revolution in Kṛṣṇaism: The Cult of Gopāla," *History of Religions* 25 (1986), 296–317.

32. Daniel H. H. Ingalls, "The *Harivaṃśa* as a *Mahākāvya*," in *Mélanges d'Indianisme à la mémoire de Louis Renou* (Paris: Éditions E. de Boccard, 1968), pp. 381–94.

33. McKim Marriott, "The Feast of Love," in Milton Singer, ed., *Krishna: Myths, Rites, and Attitudes* (Honolulu: East-West Center Press, University of Hawaii, 1966), pp. 200–212.

34. Victor Turner, *The Ritual Process: Structure and Anti-Structure* (Chicago: Aldine, 1969).

35. Janette Turner Hospital, *Charades* (New York: Bantam, 1989).

SANSKRIT TEXTS CITED

Agni Purāṇa. Ānandāśrama Sanskrit Series, 41. Poona, 1900.

Bhagavadgītā, with commentary by Śrī Śaṅkarācārya. Edited by D. V. Gokhale. Poona Oriental Series, 1. Poona, 1950.

Bhāgavata Purāṇa. Bombay, 1950.
Brahmāṇḍa Purāṇa. Banaras, 1983.
Harivaṃśa. 2 vols. Edited by P. L. Vaidya. Poona, 1969–71.
Kūrma Purāṇa. Translated by A. S. Gupta. Varanasi, 1972.
Mahābhārata. Edited by V. S. Sukthankar et al. Poona, 1933–69.
Mānavadharmaśāstra. Edited by J. Jolly. London, 1887.
Matsya Purāṇa. Anandāśrama Sanskrit Series, 54. Poona, 1907.
Taittirīya Brāhmaṇa, with commentary by Sāyaṇa. Bibliotheca Indica. Calcutta, 1859.
Vāyu Purāṇa. Ānandāśrama Sanskrit Series, 49. Poona, 1905.
Viṣṇu Purāṇa. Gorakhpur, 1967.

4

The Play of the Three Worlds: The Trika Concept of *Līlā*

BETTINA BÄUMER

Human activity, whether secular or religious, is mostly governed by binding conditions, motives, rules, and prescriptions. In play and artistic creation man is liberated from the laws of ordinary action and thus they become an expression of freedom. Divine activity springs from absolute freedom (*svātantrya*), and in order to distinguish it from the limited human action, the metaphor of play (*līlā, krīḍā,* etc.) is used to describe it. This may be the general background of the idea of *līlā* in Hindu religions, which becomes colored by the particular theology, spirituality, religious, and artistic practice of each tradition, whether Vaiṣṇava or Śaiva.[1]

General Śaiva Background

In Śaivism, whether Śaiva Siddhānta or Kashmir Śaivism, the divine activity has five phases, called *pañcakṛtya,* which correspond to a frequent fivefold division: *sṛṣṭi, sthiti, saṃhāra, tirodhāna,* and *anugraha* (creation, preservation, dissolution, veiling, and liberating grace). All these activities of Śiva have been related to *līlā,* though sometimes one or the other activity has been particularly linked with playful spontaneity. In the *advaita* of Kashmir Śaivism, these five phases also occur in any conscious being, not only the Supreme. It may suffice to give examples from the Śaivāgamas, both Siddhānta and Kashmiri. Thus the *Mataṅgapārameśvara* speaks of Śiva's acts as *krīḍā:*

> All-mighty Śrīkaṇṭha created the universe by his will of play and similarly in order to withdraw it within himself He proceeds playfully.
>
> (MPĀ VP XXV.4)

> *krīḍato'sya jagat kāryaṃ śrīkaṇṭhasyamitadyute,*
> *jagadātma-vaśaṃ kartum atha tasmāt sa līlayā.*

The *Svacchanda Tantra,* one of the main sources of Kashmir Śaivism, also describes the Lord's activity as playful:

> Oh Shining One (Goddess), the producer of creation and dissolution has issued forth from the heart of Bhairava, the great God, as he plays.
>
> (SvT IX.2)

> *mahābhairava-devasya krīḍamānasya bhāmini,*
> *sṛṣṭisaṃhārakartāram hṛdayāttu vinirgataḥ.*

The quality of the play is brought out by Kṣemarāja in his commentary on the word *krīḍā* in this context: it is absolutely free from obstacles (*niḥśeṣavighna praśamana*), bestower of fulfillment (*siddhi*), and it implies the desire to bestow grace (*anujighṛkṣā*). Śiva's heart is of the nature of the Energy of his own freedom (*svasvātantrya śaktyātmaka*). Here he also hints at the fact that the ultimate motive for the divine activity is that of bestowing grace and liberating the bound souls.

This general background need not be expanded here, but has to be kept in mind when we deal with the specific understanding of *līlā* (*krīḍā*) in Kashmir Śaivism. The Śaivāgamas being the common basis of both, Śaiva Siddhānta and Trika, there are many common theories and practices, as, e.g., the cosmology of the thirty-six *tattva*s. Apart from differences in philosophy and spirituality, Kasmir Śaivism has not been interested in the mythological aspects of *līlā,* nor do we have any evidence for a popular religious performance. However, classical Sanskrit drama has been a very important paradigm for Trika theology. Dramatic metaphors are frequently found in the texts where Śiva is described both as actor and stage-director.

Līlā is not a separate doctrine in Kashmir Śaivism nor is it a simple metaphor, as in Vedānta. In the *Brahmasūtra*s *līlā* occurs in the context of the motive of creation, following immediately after the Sūtra: *na prayojanavattvāt* (II.1.32), "(Creation is not possible for Brahman) on account of his having no motive." It is understood that there is no activity—human or divine—without any motive (*prayojana*). The reply is: *lokavattu līlākaivalyam* (BrSū II.1.33),

"As in the world (creation) is only a play." We cannot be sure about Bādarāyaṇa's philosophy of *līlā,* but Śaṅkara has clearly given an illusionistic interpretation of *līlā. Līlā* is no metaphysical category, it is simply a metaphor to defend the freedom of the Absolute from any motive of action. The metaphysical category is *māyā,*[2] which has no ontological reality. No doubt, the idea of freedom is also in the background of the Trika conception of *līlā,* but there is no trace of illusionism, and this is the basic distinction between the two *advaita* schools. In Trika, as we shall see, even the seeming illusion is real as a manifestation of the divine freedom. In a simplifying way we could say that the Vedāntic idea of the divine freedom is exclusive, whereas the Trika understanding is all-inclusive.

The conception of the divine playfulness pervades the whole system like salt is mixed with food. To isolate it from the whole theological and spiritual context is as difficult and meaningless as taking out salt from a cooked dish. The fact that *līlā* is not a concept but a pervasive attitude is also clear from the use of a number of synonyms and related terms, all expressing the same general idea.[3]

Trika shares some basic meanings of the idea of *līlā* with other philosophical and religious traditions, and it is not possible to discuss, much less to solve, here the historical question of the "origin" of the idea. The direct sources of Trika are clearly the Āgamas, and unless it can be proved that they have taken the idea of *līlā* from Vaiṣṇava sources (e.g., Pāñcarātra Saṃhitās), there is no reason to believe that the Śaivas have borrowed it from the Vaiṣṇavas.[4] *Līlā* is not the only common idea among the striking parallels between Śaivāgamas and Vaiṣṇava Saṃhitās. The conception may have belonged to a common substratum of popular ideas which have been assimilated in various ways. Thus it is difficult to decide which was the original context—Vaiṣṇava, Śaiva, or any other. I can only try to bring out the specific connotations of *krīḍā* in the Trika system, based on the main sources before Abhinavagupta and on Abhinavagupta's works.

The idea of *krīḍā,* or divine play, is operative at three levels: the theological and cosmological, the aesthetic, and the mystical. At the first level it is connected with the doctrine of absolute divine freedom, *svātantrya,* that is so central to this school that it has even been used to designate it as *svātantryavāda.* It is also related to the interplay between Śiva and Śakti. At the second level it is related to connotations of beauty and joy, also in the erotic meaning, and to the metaphor of drama, i.e., acting and dancing. Since the aesthetic experience serves here as a model and precursor of the mystical experience, this metaphor has far-reaching implications. At the third or mystical level the *jīvanmukta* shares in the divine freedom, spontaneity, and bliss overflowing in an ecstatic playfulness.

Pre-Abhinavagupta Sources and Commentators

In pre-Abhinavagupta sources we find two basic metaphors for the divine activity. Somānanda in his *Śivadṛṣṭi* explains the manifestations of the Lord in various forms and bodies with the simile of the king: ''Just as a king over the whole earth, in the joyous and startled intoxication of his sovereignty can play at being a simple soldier, imitating his behaviour, so, in His beatitude, the Lord amuses Himself by assuming the multiple forms of the whole'' (ŚD I.37b–38 tr. R. Gnoli). His assumption of human bodies even descends to the lowest possible forms of existence: ''(Without any object and, therefore), as a game, Parameśvara takes on the form of the bodies abiding in the gulf of the oceans of hell . . .'' (ibid., I.36). The simile of the monarch had been used by Śaṅkara in explaining the *Brahmasūtra* (see above), and Somānanada uses it throughout,[5] but it has not exercised much influence on later Kashmir Śaiva thinkers. However, the main point in this simile is the freedom of act and to assume other roles, which brings it close to the second simile of the actor.

Utpaladeva in his Vṛtti on *Śivadṛṣṭi* I.38 gives a beautiful definition of *krīḍā: tathā parameśvaraḥ pūrṇatvāt svata ānandaghūrṇitaistaistairbhūta-bhedātmabhiḥ prakārair evam etat sadṛśaṃ krīḍati. harṣānusārī spandaḥ krī-ḍā.* ''In the same way the highest Lord, due to his fullness plays spontaneously by imitating the ways of the separate beings, having become each of them due to his reeling under the intoxication of bliss. (For) play (*krīḍā*) is the vibration accompanying joy.'' And before he had paraphrased *krīḍā* by *nirargalatā,* unrestrained freedom. Though the simile of the king acting or playing is the same as in Vedānta, its explanation leads directly into the central themes of Trika which are those of *pūrṇatā, svātantrya, ānanda,* and *spanda.* The term *ghūrṇi* used here for the Lord is one of the five ''signs'' of the ecstasy of a yogi, when he is shaking or reeling under the impact of his inner bliss.[6] It is so to say a gross form of *spanda,* inner vibration.

The Micro-Macrocosmic Drama

The *Śivasūtras*, one of the main sources of Trika, contain a series of Sūtras on the simile of the actor/dancer (both being the same in Indian theatre), starting with: *nartaka ātmā,* ''The Self is an actor'' (ŚSū III.9). According to the commentator Kṣemarāja, this is said of the self-realized yogi who becomes one with the Lord. Kṣemarāja explains his action as being *svaparispanda līlayā,* ''playful by his own inner vibration,'' which manifests itself in movements of dance, a dance that is far from being a merely external movement, for ''it is based on his being established in his innermost hidden essential nature'' (*antarvigūhitasvasvarūpāvastambhamūlam*). Now all the terms used assume a double meaning, a yogic meaning and a technical meaning of the elements of drama. Thus the various parts played by an actor are the stages of consciousness like waking, dream, etc., i.e., *bhūmikā* (*tattajjāgarādinānā-bhūmikāprapañcam*).

In this context Kṣemarāja quotes a verse of Bhaṭṭa Nārāyaṇa's *Stavacintāmaṇi*(59):

> O Śiva, you have produced the drama of the three worlds containing the real seed of all creation and the germ within it. Having performed its prelude, is there any other artist but you who is capable of bringing it to its conclusion?

Śiva is here the artist (*kavi*), both author and stage-director of the universal drama in which he is also the actor. All the parts of a Sanskrit drama are also parts of the world-drama. For instance, *bīja,* the 'seed', is in drama the source of the plot contained in some allusion, while in the world the seed is *māyā,* the sorce of manifestation. *Garbha,* 'germ' or 'womb', is the schema of the dramatic action, while in the created world *garbha* corresponds to *prakṛti,* the womb of all existence. *Prastāva* is the introductory part of the play corresponding to creation, and *saṃhāra* its completion, corresponding to the reabsorption or dissolution of the universe.

Adding another quotation from Utpaladeva's *Īśvarapratyabhijñā* (probably *vivṛti,* since it is not traceable), Kṣemarāja concludes by saying that the Lord is the producer of the world-drama who remains awake even when the whole world is asleep, i.e., at the stage of *saṃhāra.* The verse of *Stavacintāmaṇi* following the one quoted by Kṣemarāja (v. 60) adds to the meaning of the divine actor and stage-director, for there Śiva is praised as the one who makes the real unreal and the unreal real, being both, free and unfree (*namaḥ sadasatāṃ kartum asattvaṃ sattvam eva vā, svatantrāyāsvatantrāya vyayaiśvaryaikaśāline,* v. 60).

The *Śivasūtra* further identifies the stage of the (inner or outer) drama with the inner Self or individual soul: *raṅgo'antarātmā* (ŚSū III.10), because: "The place where the self takes delight with the intention of exhibiting the play of the world drama is the stage, i.e., the place where the Self adopts the various roles" (*rajyate'smin jagannāṭya krīḍāpradarśanāśayenātmanā iti raṅgaḥ tattadbhūmikā grahaṇasthānam,* Kṣemarāja on the above). The three levels of meaning are here the external theater stage, the universal stage of the world-drama, and the yogic stage of the inner Self (*bhūmikā* again in the double meaning of stages in yoga and roles of the actor). The purport of the simile is the spiritual or yogic level, as also in the following Sūtra, where the senses are called the spectators: *prekṣakāṇīndriyāṇi* (III.11). Kṣemarāja comments: "The senses like eyes, etc. of the yogi witness inwardly their inmost Self full of the delight in exhibiting the world-drama. By the development of the performance of the drama, they provide to the yogi fullness of aesthetic rapture in which the sense of difference has disappeared'' (III.11; tr. Jaideva Singh).

Here it becomes clear that the simile is not merely a pretext for explaining the inexplicable (as in Vedānta), because the play is a real play of delight even for the yogi. The senses are here not denied, but they assume the role of spectators of the world-drama that is reflected in the inner consciousness, on the interior stage. Interiority (*antarmukhatā*) is not opposed to playful manifestation, it is rather the condition for the fullness of aesthetic delight (*camatkāra-rasasaṃpūrṇatā*). Since the world-drama is really enacted by the Lord himself, the yogi can enjoy its beauty and, instead of being distracted by external multiplicity, dissolve any sense of separateness due to this experience of joy (*vigalita vibhāgān*). Here the aesthetic and the mystical rapture become identical, the yogi being able to enjoy things more fully due to his rootedness in interiority.

If we summarize the idea of the Sūtras, the three main elements of the world-play are: (1) the actor and author/director of the drama, being the *ātman* or Śiva, (2) the stage, being the individual soul, and (3) the spectators, being the sense-organs.

To view the multiplicity of the universe as a divine play (*krīḍā*) is really the prerogative of the *jīvanmukta,* as the *Spanda Kārikā* also emphasizes: ''He who has this realization (viz. identity of his Self with the whole universe), being constantly united with the Divine, views the entire world as the play (of the Self identical with Śiva), and is liberated while alive. There is no doubt about this'' (SpKā II.5; tr. Jaideva Singh) (*iti vā yasya saṃvittiḥ krīḍātvenākhilaṃ jagat, sa paśyansatatāṃ yukto jīvanmukto na saṃśayaḥ*). This is the aspect of the liberated one who sees reality in the light of the divine. The other aspect is the divine, Śiva himself assuming multiplicity due to his play. Kṣemarāja (*Spanda Nirṇaya* on SpKā II.3–4) quotes from *Śrī Jñānagarbha* (source not traced) the following verse: ''Thy sport (*vihāra*) becomes in this world the cause of the diversity of the knower, knowing, knowledge and the knowable. Since on thy play being over, that diversity disappears somewhere, thou art seldom seen in that light and only by some''(p. 117; tr. Jaideva Singh).

Multiplicity and manifestation are in Trika often explained in two ways, involving two similies, both taken from art-forms: the play or drama, where the performance appears on the stage and is again withdrawn when the play is over, and a painting which produces manifold forms and colors on a plain white canvas. In both cases Śiva is the author, producer, and artist of the world-drama or world-picture. The artist produces forms out of his inner fullness and overwhelming joy, and the logical question about the why of his creation is a wrong question. This applies as much to the divine author of the five acts as to the human artist, for in both cases creation is a spontaneous outpouring, only comparable to play.

The Festival of Worship

Utpaladeva brings out the playful nature of the divine in a context of *bhakti* in his *Śivastotrāvalī*. Here *krīḍā* is neither a philosophical simile nor a replica of classical drama, but it is part of the delight of the festival of worship (*utsava, mahotsava*). The devotee who realizes that the whole manifestation is but the play of the Lord, himself shares in the joy of this play even in the midst of the world of suffering.

> O Lord of the universe!
> How blessed are your devotees,
> praiseworthy in the world!
> For to them even this ocean of (fearful) transmigratory existence
> is nothing but a great pleasure-lake
> for their entertainment!
>
> *Śivastotrāvalī* III.15

It is the Lord himself who out of his own fullness makes the whole world dance, and the devotees are those who consciously share in this dance (cf. III.11).

> Being self-luminous
> You cause everything to shine;
> Delighting in your form
> You fill the universe with delight;
> Rocking with your own bliss [*nijarasena ghūrṇase*]
> You make the whole world dance with joy.
> (XIII.15; tr. C. Rhodes Bailly)

In another implication, *krīḍā* refers to the whole of manifestation:

> When the whole universe
> Honours just this much of your splendor—
> The mere play in the world—
> How infinite indeed
> Must be your bliss!
> (XX.5; tr. C. Rhodes Bailly)

The creation is his recreation (*sṛṣṭivinodāya*), preservation is his comfortable seat (*sthitisukhāsane*), and dissolution is his contentment after swallowing the three worlds (XX.9).

Abhinavagupta and Commentators

Abhinavagupta (10th–11th cent.) carries all the ideas of the tradition further and systematizes them. For him too, *krīḍā* is the characteristic of divine activity, because it springs from spontaneity, total freedom, and bliss. It is related to the Energy of Will (*icchā*), and generally to the Śakti of the Lord who carries out the various functions of creation. He also uses the hermeneutic device of etymology to connect divine activity with play, since the root *div-* underlying *deva* or *devī,* also has the meaning 'to play'.[7] In this context, he explains *krīḍā* in his *Tantrāloka:*

> The upsurge of one's own intense bliss without any purpose like rejection or acceptance is play. This is the Will of the Lord to set in motion, because of excelling everything, and this is his freedom.
>
> (I.101; tr. H. N. Chakravarty)
>
> *heyopādeyakathāvirahe svānandaghanatayocchalanam,*
> *krīḍā sarvotkarṣeṇa vartanecchā tathā svatantratvam.*

Jayaratha comments on this verse: "Due to the greatness of his own freedom the play of the Lord is nothing but the delightful manifestation (*ullasanam*) of the entire universe from Śiva down to the earth, it is his will to set in motion because he excels everything, and his action is freedom, so that, though there is no difference, he differentiates within himself, and this is his play, for *devyati* means 'to play' (*krīḍati*), hence he is called *deva* (God). And here (in the case of the Lord's manifestation) there is no other efficient cause except play (*na krīḍātiriktaṃ nimittam*) . . ." (KSTS, vol. 1, p. 144).

I have quoted this commentary more extensively because it summarizes very well the basic ideas of *krīḍā* in their proper context. Play is related to freedom from all obligations and limitations by social or religious rules (*heyopādeya*). It is also clear that Trika theology refuses to accept any cause for creation except the free will of the Lord.

The relation between *krīḍā* and *icchā*, 'will' in the sense of the spontaneous first upsurge of creativity, not in any psychological sense of willpower, is already contained in the *Śivasūtra*s, in the context of the Sūtra: *icchāśaktir umā kumārī* (ŚSū I.13). Kṣemarāja comments on *kumārī,* 'virgin': "The supreme Goddess (Śakti) who is of the nature of Freedom, she is Kumārī, i.e., intent on the play of manifesting the universe and (finally) withdrawing it (within Herself) (*viśvasargasaṃhāra krīḍāparā*). This interpretation is based on the root '*kumāra*' meaning to play'' (cf. Jaideva Singh, translation modified, p. 53). This freedom to play is precisely *icchāśakti,* the Energy of spontaneous upsurge of will. The other implication of *kumārī* as young girl also implies that the first Śakti to manifest is *icchā,* innocent like a young girl. The other two Śaktis, *jñāna* and *kriyā,* belong to a developed stage.

Let us consider another verse from the *Tantrāloka* in the context of pure consciousness which is complete in itself (TĀl IV.9):

> By his difficult creatorship and by his immaculate freedom the highest Lord is clever in the game of hiding his own Self.
>
> *kiṃ tu durghaṭakāritvāt svacchandyannirmalādasau*
> *svātmapracchādanakrīḍā paṇḍitaḥ parameśvaraḥ.*
>
> (TĀl IV.10)

Here the aspect of play points to the self-concealing aspect of the Lord's activity (*tirodhāna*). Jayaratha paraphrases *krīḍā* here as ''the concealment of his own Self, i.e., the appearance in the form of each, subject, object, etc., because of playful manifestation, that is verily play'' (*svātmanaḥ pracchādanaṃ grāhyagrāhakadyullāsāt tathātvenābhāsanam saiva krīḍā,* (KSTS, p. 10). In the following verse Abhinavagupta connects this self-veiling of the Lord with *māyā* as Śakti, being the source of differentiation (IV.11).

In fact, the self-veiling of the Lord in the individual souls is more mysterious and difficult to explain than creation, hence *krīḍā* and *svātantrya* are the only possible motives.

In the chapter on *śāmbhava upāya* Abhinavagupta describes the light-nature (*prakāśatvam*) of the Lord, thus:

> Therefore he is the highest Lord (Parameśvara) who manifests unrestrained the play of creation and dissolution in the space of his own self.
>
> (TĀl III.3)

He concludes the first chapters of both *Tantrāloka* and its abridged version *Tantrasāra* with highly poetical verses, summarizing the chapter that is itself a summary of the whole text. We may first read the easier verse in the *Tantrasāra:*

> The Self whose body is Light, Śiva, the independent one, hides his own nature by the impetuous play of his freedom, and again he reveals himself fully, either successively or immediately, or in threefold manner.
>
> (TS I, p. 7)

The *Tantrāloka* verse addresses in an ironical way not the Lord but the totality of the limited existence, *bhāvavrāta,* the multitude of external things.

> Oh things of this world! You take possession forcefully of the hearts of people like an actor, and you playfully hide your real self under many disguises!
>
> Those who call you insentient are themselves insentient (stupid), believing themselves to be sensitive [*sahṛdaya*], they are not learned. I believe that their stupidity (insentience) is a praise for them, since it makes them similar to you!
>
> *bhāvavrāta! haṭhājjanasya hṛdayānyākramya yannartayan,*
> *bhaṅgībhirvividhābhirātmahṛdayaṃ pracchādya saṃkrīḍase,*
> *yastvamāha jaḍam jaḍaḥ sahṛdayaṃ manyatvā duḥśikṣito,*
> *manye'muṣya jaḍātmatā stutipadaṃ tvatsāmyasaṃbhāvanāt.*
>
> (TĀl. 332)

This verse is full of suggested meaning (*dhvani*), and we are fortunate to have Abhinavagupta's own exegesis in his *Dhvanyāloka Locana,* where he quotes it as an example of *vastudhvani.*[8] Here he compares the misunderstood and despised 'things of the world'(*bhāvavrāta*) with a great saint (*mahāpuruṣa*) who hides his real being by behaving like a fool or an ordinary man: "Some great saint who is concealing himself among ordinary people, although he has overcome all attachment, even though he has removed the far-spread darkness due to his being steeped in the light of true discrimination, he makes people gossip, without manifesting his real self, therefore those very people call him a crazy man, and while he is being despised, his transcendental character (*lokottaraṃ caritam*) rather reveals itself through hints (allusion or suggestion)." Pretending to be afflicted with love, he amuses the people and makes them dance according to his will. His depth, intelligence, and selfless nature are not recognized by the people, and if they call him a fool (*jaḍa*), this only shows that they are much greater fools than he. There is a play on the words *jaḍa* and *hṛdaya,* as opposites, and the two meanings of *jaḍa* as insentient (for the things) and stupid (for the person) have to be kept in mind.

This simile has some very deep implications. In relation to play it means that the self-concealing nature is a dominant feature of *krīḍā*. But instead of comparing it with the actor, as Jayaratha does, Abhinava's comparison with a great saint goes much deeper. First of all, his 'play' presupposes a real inner freedom and detachment, not caring for his image or reputation. Second, his very play of behaving like a crazy man cannot completely conceal his real nature. Those who are sensitive (*sahṛdaya*) are able to recognize his heart (*hṛdaya*) by means of hints (*vyaṅga*) or suggestions. Ultimately, the term of comparison is *bhāvavrāta,* the collection of things, taken by everybody to be insentient (*jaḍa*). In reality even the external things are nothing but the playfully assumed garb of the "great person," Śiva himself, and nothing in this world is insentient. Calling it insentient only reflects back on the insensitivity or stupidity of the one who utters such words, since he cannot grasp the hints contained in the play itself which point to the underlying perfection or fullness.

Jayaratha's explanation is much more straightforward than Abhinava's own exegesis. He explains *nartayan yat saṃkrīḍase* by: "you appear playfully like an actor who assumes unreal forms" (*naṭavat atāttvikena rūpeṇa samullasasi,* KSTS, p. 307), and he equally stresses the nature of play as the hiding of one's real nature. The meaning of the verse is that, though the whole world and even the apparently insentient things participate in the nature of the Lord being pure light of Consciousness, those very things hide his real nature by attracting the heart of people to their separate existence. Because they are opaque, that is, not transparent to their real being, they are like an actor who assumes a disguise and takes pleasure in beguiling an audience without disclosing his real identity. Though it is ironically addressed to the world, this verse really refers to the *tirodhāna* aspect of Śiva's activity, his self-veiling.

Again, in his *Paramārthasāra* Abhinavagupta relates play with the circle of Śaktis, whereas Śiva remains the still center, the pure "I": "In this way the God sets the machine of the wheel of Energies in motion by his play, being the 'I' alone in its purity who stays at the place of the driver of the great wheel of Energies" (v. 47: *iti śakticakrayantraṃ krīḍāyogena vāhayan devaḥ, ahameva śuddharūpaḥ śaktimahācakranāyakapadārthaḥ*). Here we have another comparison of the Lord's play, where he is compared to the driver setting the wheel in motion while remaining himself still. The whole manifestation and reabsorption is brought about by the divine Śaktis who, taken together, form a circle or wheel (*cakra*). Here *krīḍā* is related to movement, whereas the agent of this movement is eternally at rest (*viśrānti*). Expressed mythologically, it means the eternal play of God and Goddess, of Śiva and Śakti, as expressed in the *Bodhapañcadaśikā:*

This God is ever intent on enjoying the essence of play with this Goddess.
Being all pervading, he brings about simultaneously these manifold creations and dissolutions.

(v. p.6)

eṣa devo'nayā devyā nityaṃ krīḍārasotsukaḥ,
vicitrān sṛṣṭisaṃhārān vidhatte yugapad vibhuḥ.[9]

Conclusion

The metaphor of play is based on various human activities and experiences which are figuratively used for the divine action. In all cases, whether it is the king, the child, the actor/dancer, the lover, or the saint, playfulness presupposes a sense of freedom. An action, even if it has the appearance of a game, that does not spring from freedom, cannot be called *līlā* or *krīḍā*. Modern sport based on strict rules and self-interested competition does not share this characteristic of freedom and spontaneity, whereas artistic activity comes much closer to the idea of play implied in *līlā*.

Each comparison used for the divine play has its own implications. The most elaborate metaphor in Kashmir Śaivism is the one of the actor/dancer, which does not entail a theory of illusionism: Even the disguise of the Lord in the world is real, in the same way as is his inner essence. In the metaphor of the drama we have found all the five acts of Śiva, but the dominating aspect is that of self-veiling. But because of the blissful nature of manifestation, and the wonder of aesthetic delight (*camatkāra*), the same action that conceals also finally reveals, in an act of grace (*anugraha*).

We can find a certain complementarity underlying the idea of play in the context of Trika theology, with *krīḍā* on the one side, on the side of manifestation, appearance, activity, and *viśrānti* on the other, on the side of the divine essence, pure I-being (*ahaṃbhāva*), resting in pure Consciousness (*saṃvit*).

The subtle aspect of *krīḍā* is contained in the concept of *spanda,* 'vibration', and it is experienced in the yogic state of *ghūrṇi,* the shaking of the body under the impact of blissful rapture. Here, 'play' means purely the outflow of the inner fullness in the body, and not any conscious action. It is an action, if at all, of the subject without any object, whereas the dramatic and the erotic forms of play require an object and a material, a partner, a stage, even spectators. *Spanda* is the origin of *krīḍā*.

Summarizing, we could again try to reduce the various aspects of *krīḍā* to two basic meanings: (1) play as an explosion of bliss, wonder, freedom, and unlimited fullness; (2) acting as concealment of the real nature, as creation of appearance (*ābhāsa*), having its phases of creation, withdrawal, etc. Both aspects apply equally to the great Artist (*kavi*), the creator of the three worlds, who is simultaneously engaged in the drama of creation and resting in his own blissful nature.[10]

Let us consider the question to what kind of performance, if at all, these metaphors and similies refer. First of all, from the *Śivasūtra*s and from Abhinavagupta it is clear that the classical Sanskrit drama is the basis of comparison, and not a popular performance. On the other hand, the advaitic interpretation of the divine *līlā* in the context of drama leads to conceiving dramatic forms in which the stage-director and the actor/dancer enacting several roles are one and the same person. Whether we can draw any conclusion from this theological interpretation with regard to particular forms of performance[11] is a matter of discussion and further investigation. Apart from Sanskrit drama, at least Utpaladeva suggests a link between the concept of *krīḍā* and *utsava,* 'religious festival'. Nowhere do we have any evidence of popular *līlā*-performances comparable to Kṛṣṇalīlā or Rāmlīlā, for the reason mentioned earlier, i.e., that the mythological aspects of Śiva are entirely secondary in this school.

Not by chance has Kashmir Śaivism made the greatest contribution to the aesthetic theory of the classical Sanskrit tradition, a theory that is embedded deeply in Trika metaphysics. The concept of *krīḍā* also belongs to this sphere of aesthetics, the *rasa*-experience being the core of any art-form. The divine play leads to a spiritual *rasa*-experience, and just as a human drama can only be enjoyed by a *sahṛdaya,* the divine 'drama of the three worlds' equally requires the spiritual sensibility of *sahṛdayatva.* The whole aesthetic theory could be applied here.[12]

Finally, we are coming back to the three levels of meaning which can be distinguished, but not separated, in Kashmir Śaivism: At the philosophical/theological level *krīḍā* serves as the only motive of divine activity, being intimately linked with Śiva's characteristics of freedom, bliss, fullness, and with his Śaktis or dynamic Energies. At the aesthetic level, as we have seen, the art-forms, drama in particular as embracing all the arts, are the fit model for a free, creative activity which entertains and at the same time liberates the spectator form the burden of everyday existence.[13] Ultimately, all these dimensions have their meaning only in a spiritual context. The divine play is meaningful and transparent only to the yogi or *jīvanmukta,* for others are misled by outward appearances. He not only understands the divine play in the world, in his ecstasy he becomes an active participant in the Lord's delight of self-manifestation and self-concealment, both being nothing but an instrument of liberating grace.

NOTES

1. Cf. my thesis: Bettina Bäumer, "Schöpfung als Spiel. Der Begriff līlā im Hinduismus, seine philosophische und theologische Bedeutung," München, 1969.

2. Cf. my thesis chapter on Līlā und māyā," pp. 89–101

3. The following are some of the verbs and nouns used: *ullas-, ullāsa, vilāsa, vihāra, vinoda, nartaka, naṭaka, narman, moda, pramoda, utsava, div-, spanda,* besides, of course, *krīdā* and *līlā.*

4. This has frequently been suggested, e.g., N. Hein, "A Revolution in Kṛṣṇaism: The Cult of Gopāla," *History of Religions* 25 (1986): 296–317.

5. Cf. ŚD IV.4.ff

6. Cf. *Mālinivijaya Tantra* 18.35; *Tantrāloka* V.107–11.

7. Cf TĀl I.101; in the *Parātrīśikā Vivaraṇa,* Abhinavagupta defines *devī* in one of the meanings in this way: "Because in the succeeding order of creation from *paśyantī* down to external manifestation like blue etc., she sports with the creative delight of her

consciousness (*svavimarśānandātmanā krīḍanena*), for the root '*div*' from which the noun *Devī* is derived means 'to sport''' (p. 10 tr. Jaideva Singh).

8. On *Dhvanyāloka* I.13 (reprint of Kāvyamālā ed. 1983, pp. 51–52). I owe the hint to this reference to R. Gnoli's note to his Italian translation of *Tantrāloka,* p.111, note 130. There are a few variants in the quotation in *Dhvanyāloka Locana: yat krīḍase* for *saṃkrīḍase, tataḥ* for *jaḍaḥ, jaḍātmanaḥ* for *jaḍātmatā*. After completing this article I received the translation of "The Dhvanyāloka of Ānandavardhana with the Locana of Abhinavagupta" by D. H. H. Ingalls, J. M. Masson and M. V. Patwardhan (Cambridge Mass.: Harvard University Press, 1990). It is interesting that the three translators have not traced the source of this verse in the *Tantrāloka.* Thus their interpretation is purely aesthetic and literary. Compare their translation:

> Troop of delights, who storm the hearts of men
> and make them dance in many an antic step;
> concealing your own intention as you play;
> men call you brute and stupid, in their ignorance
> thinking themselves intelligent thereby.
> That title of stupidity, I think,
> if given to them would be honorific
> for it would seem to liken them to you.

These different interpretations are but a proof for the manifoldness of *dhvani*.

9. Cf. also *Paramārthadvādaśikā,* v. 11 *krīḍāḍambaram*. Cf. also Kṣemarāja, *Spandanirṇaya* on SpKā I.1, where the expressions *krīḍāḍambara* and *jagatsargādi-krīḍā* occur in the context of the manifestation of the *śakticakra*.

10. Cf. Bettina Bäumer, "The Divine Artist" in *The Indian Theosophist.* Jaideva Singh Felicitation Volume, Varanari, 1986.

11. E.g., Pāṇḍavāni in Madhya Pradesh.

12. Cf. R. Gnoli, *The Aesthetic Experience According to Abhinavagupta*, (Varanasi: Chowkhambha Sanskrit Series Office, 1968). It is not possible to discuss in detail the technicalities of Abhinavagupta's aesthetic theory, which would require a study of his *Abhinava Bhāratī* on *Nāṭya-Śāstra*.

13. The relationship between *krīḍā* and ritual should be investigated: ritual is on the one hand a "purposeless" and hence free activity, on the other it is regulated by precise rules. Cf. the Christian conception of liturgy as a play (cf. R. Guardini). Again it is only the *jīvanmukta* who is beyond the ritual restrictions, who can deal with ritual in a playful way. Ritual has been fulfilled in him, and yet he may perform it freely, comparable to the divine freedom to create.

ABBREVIATIONS AND BIBLIOGRAPHY

Bodhapañcadaśikā of Abhinavagupta. Ed. by J. Zadoo. KSTS, no. 86. Bombay, Nirnaya Sagar press: 1947.

BrSū *Brahmasūtra*

Dhvanyāloka Locana of Abhinavagupta: The Dhvanyāloka of Ānandavardhanāchārya.

Ed. by Durgaprasad and Kasinath Pandurang Parab. Reprinted from 1935 ed. of Nirnaya Sagar Press, Bombay, Kavyamala, no. 25 (rpt. Delhi, 1983).

The Dhvanyāloka of Ānandavardhana with the Locana of Abhinavagupta. Tr. by D. H. H. Ingalls, J. M. Masson, M. V. Patwardhan. Cambridge, Mass.: Harvard University Press, 1990.

Guardini, Romano. *Vom Geist der Liturgie.* Munich, 1939.

KSTS Kashmir Series of Texts and Studies.

Īśvarapratyabhijñā Kārikā by Utpaladeva with Vimarśinī by Abhinavagupta (2 vols.). Vol. 1, KSTS, no. 22, Srinagar 1918 (ed. M. R. Sastri); Vol. 2, KSTS, no. 33, Srinagar 1921 (ed. M. S. Kaul).

Mālinīvijayottara Tankra. Ed. by Madhusūden Kaul Śāstrī. KSTS, no. 37, Srinagar: 1922.

MPĀ Mataṅgapārameśvara Āgama. Ed. by N. R. Bhatt. Pondicherry: Institut Français d'Indologie, 1982.

Paramārthadvādaśikā: Lilian Silburn, tr. Hymnes de Abhinavagupta. Publications de L'Institut de Civilisation Indienne, fascicule 31, Paaris: Editions de Boccard, 1970, pp. 65–69.

Paramārthasāra of Abhinavagupta with commentary of Yogarāja. Ed. by J. C. Chatterji. KSTS, no. 7, Srinagar, 1916.

Parātrīśikā Vivaraṇa of Abhinavagupta, The Secret of Tantric Mysticism. Sanskrit text ed. by Swami Lakshmanjee, English translation by Jaideva Singh; ed. by B. Bäumer. Delhi: Motilal Banarsidass, 1988.

ŚD *Śivadṛṣṭi of Somānanda, with the Vṛtti by Utpaladeva.* KSTS, no. 54. Srinagar, 1934.

Śivastotrāvalī of Utpaladevāchārya with the Sanskrit Commentary of Kṣemarāja. Chowkhamba Sanskrit Series. Ed. by Rajanaka Laksmana. Varanasi, 1964. English translation by C. Rhodes Bailly, *Shaiva Devotional Songs of Kashmir.* New York: SUNY Press, 1987.

ŚSū *Śiva-Sūtras Śiva Sūtras. The Yoga of Supreme Identitiy.* Sanskrit text and English translation by Jaideva Singh, Delhi: Motilal Banarsidass, 1979.

Spandanirṇaya of Kṣemarāja. Ed. by M. S. Kaul. KSTS, no. 25. Bombay, Nirnaya Sagar Press: 1925

SpKā *Spanda Kārikā. The Divine Creative Pulsation.* Sanskrit text and English translation by Jaideva Singh. Delhi: Motilal Banarsidass, 1980.

Stavacintāmaṇī: Lilian Silburn, tr., *La bhakti: le "Stavacintāmaṇī" de Bhaṭṭanārāyaṇa.* Paris: De Boccard, 1964.

Svacchandabhairavatantra with uddyota by Kṣemarāja (7 vols.), ed. M. S. Kaul. KSTS 21, 1921; 38/1923; 44/1925; 48/1927; 51/1930; 53/1933; 56/1955. Bombay: Nirnaya Sagar Press.

TĀl *Tantrāloka of Abhinavagupta* (12 vols.), with commentary by Rājānaka Jayaratha. KSTS, 1918. Italian translation by Raniero Gnoli, Luce delle Sacre Scritture (Tantraloka) di Abhinavagupta. Torino: UTET, 1972.

TS *Tantrasāra of Abhinavagupta.* KSTS, no. 27, Bombay, 1918. Italian translation by Raniero Gnoli. Essenza dei Tantra (Tantrasara). Torino: Edizione Boringhieri, 1960. Hindi translation with English introd. by H. N. Chakravarty, Tantrasāra by Abhinavaguptācārya. Varanasi: Varanaseya Sanskrit Sansthan, 1986.

5

The Play World of Sanskrit Poetry

ROBERT E. GOODWIN

The object of this essay is to examine a prominent—perhaps *the* prominent—Sanskrit drama, Kālidāsa's *Śakuntalā,*[1] for a practical understanding of aesthetic play (*līlā, krīḍā*). We find certain theoretical or programmatic models of *līlā* in Ānandavardhana, Mammaṭa, and other poeticians, which depict the poet as a creator who fashions an autonomous *rasa* world for his own and the *rasika-sahṛdaya*'s (the poetically educated "man of feeling's" delight. This picture, in turn, reminds us of metaphysical *līlāvāda* in Vedānta and in Kashmir Śaivism, the latter being of particular importance because it provided the philosophical background for theoretical aesthetics, which was largely a Kashmiri phenomenon. We notice in the theoretical picture two major features. One I would call the trend to solipsism, which brings up the question of the status of the aesthetic object and beyond that the much larger issue of subjectivity and objectivity in the human relations that *kāvya* depicts. The other is an emphasis on creative freedom and autonomy. The *rasika,* according to the expressed ideal, experiences the poetic world as a playful exercise of freedom, whose sole purpose is delight. Here he knows the laws of karmic causality (fate or *niyati,* etc.) in the guise of the poetic structuration the supports *rasa.* Only in the creative experience can one know law as play, that is, a creative means of freedom. Thus, for Ānandavardhana and the rest, the poet becomes his own lawgiver: there is no higher authority. But it is the special concern of this paper to look at the way this exhilarating perspective is realized and problematized in *kāvya* itself. We shall see that we cannot speak of aesthetics in the Indian context (perhaps any context) without bringing in the erotic. In a practical sense this means that aesthetic questions take on a more human dimension, inasmuch as they come to focus on the issue of an ideal relationship between lovers. It is here that the play world of poetry begins to appear less than autonomous and free, for it serves to express hopes and fears that remain rooted to real-life concerns despite sui generis (*alaukika*) aesthetic claims. *Śakuntalā,* like many other dramas, has an idealized *rasika* as its hero, who, though given to *līlā,* finds himself confronted with dilemmas that in effect thematize the whole complex of *rasa* aesthetics. In feeling out the implications of *līlā* in a thematic, narrative realization, we test its viability as an emotional ideal without imposing external judgments.[2]

The Metaphysics of Play

I deal here only with the monistic version of the play idea, leaving alone, for example, the dualistic literature of Vaiṣṇava *bhakti,* where God's sport with the world is typified as Kṛṣṇa's play with the Gopīs (personifying the *jīva*s, or human souls). I do this because I am approaching *kāvya* through mainstream Indian aesthetic theory, and it is the monistic tradition of both Śaivism and Vedānta that is pertinent to this. The dualistic model—with its adulation of Kṛṣṇa as child, master, companion, and lover—would also afford insight into kāvyic patterns, since we see almost every *nāyaka* (protagonist, hero) adulated in the same ways in the poems and plays. And, as we shall see, the monistic bias of the aesthetic play ideal cannot be sustained. But the subject—which would entail a scrutiny of *bhakti* aesthetics—is beyond the range of this essay.

I further restrict myself to three monistic models: the Vedāntic conceptions of Śaṅkara and Rāmānuja and Trika Śaivism.[3] The Vedāntic versions come out of *Brahmasūtra* 2.1.33, the *līlā-sūtra,*[4] which solves the problem of the Absolute's relation to the world by making it sport. Only a play relation to the world can save God's transcendence, since play assumes freedom from the need to act. Both Śaṅkara and Rāmānuja point to courtly amusements as the probable referent of the sūtra's *lokavat* ("as in the world"), which is of interest to us in view of the predominantly courtly atmosphere of *kāvya* and its status as a court poetry. Already we have hints of the pleasure garden and its erotic charms. For Śaṅkara, however, the play doctrine can only be figurative, part of the "lower knowledge" (*aparā vidyā*) that helps us make the leap into the unfathomable. He is led to the position, doubtless, because he knows that play represents a genuine paradox. It must be absorbing, in order to bring delight. But whatever absorbs the attention is obviously a threat to the autonomy and transcendence of consciousness. Even an imaginary object tends to reify, causing forgetfulness of Self. So Śaṅkara stoutly maintains that *saṃsāra* is the superimposition of a false vision on the absolute ground of being. The result is another paradox, which critics like Rāmānuja[5] delight in pointing out: how error or illusion can arise in the first place, since there is only Ātman, transcendent consciousness without a second, to serve as its subject. Nevertheless, Śaṅkara's negation of *saṃsāra* is instructive. He is probably right to see that the psychological implications of aestheticizing metaphysics are more of a threat to monism than logical paradox. The valorization of *līlā* and its delights introduces the problematics of Eros and the living ghost of the Other.

The genteel asceticism of Śaṅkara's Vedānta, its conversion of renunciation (*tapas* or *saṃnyāsa*) into objectless knowledge (*jñāna*), made it very prominent among educated Brahmans, with a prestige that is felt strongly even today. For this reason, and also because he is a less sophisticated thinker than Śaṅkara, we tend to discount the Upaniṣadic roots of Rāmānuja's Vedāntic system, with its ontological validation of *saṃsāra*. For Rāmānuja, however, transcendence does not preclude immanence. God not only creates the world, He *is* the world—along with the individual *jīva*s or souls it forms his body. When the liberated soul realizes its paradoxical identity as Ātman (paradoxical because it remains separate from Ātman in the full sense) the *māyā* world does not disappear, as it does in Śaṅkara's system, but simply loses its power to bewilder and bind. It accordingly becomes a playground to be entered at will. Rāmānuja even accords the liberated soul the same power as Īśvara to create worlds out of its own power of imagination (*satyasaṃkalpatva*), though all these have to fit somehow into Īśvara's structure.[6] The soul may relish these worlds (*līlārasa,* ŚBh 3.2.12, 4.13–14), whether created by Īśvara or itself, either in a bodiless dream presence or by taking bodily form (the equivalent of divine *avatāra*). Where Śaṅkara draws his chief inspiration from the *neti neti* tenor of texts like BAU 4.3.21–22, 4.3.32–33, and 4.5.15, Rāmānuja draws his from ChU passages that affirm the liberated soul's delight in what is nevertheless continued sense-experience, though now purified and transformed into Self-achievement. Thus ChU 7.25.2 and 8.12.1–3:

> The Self (*ātman*) is this All. He who sees thus, thinks thus, understands thus is one whose pleasure is in the Self (*ātmarati*), whose sport is in the Self (*ātmakrīḍa*), whose intercourse is with the Self (*ātmamithuna*), whose happiness is in the Self (*ātmānanda*). He is autonomous (*svarāj*) and in all worlds he has movement according to his desire (*kāmacāra*). But those who know otherwise have others as their rulers (*anyrājānāḥ*), their worlds are perishable, and in all worlds they do not have movement according to their desires.[7]

> Verily, there is no freedom from pleasure and pain for one while he is incorporate. Verily, while one is bodiless, pleasure and pain do not touch him. The wind

> is bodiless. Clouds, lightning, thunder—these are bodiless. Now as these, when they arise from yonder space and reach the highest light, appear each with its own form, even so that serene one [the liberated soul], when he rises up from this body and reaches the highest light, appears with his own form. Such a one is the supreme person (*uttamapuruṣa*). There such a one goes around laughing, sporting (*krīḍan*), having enjoyment with women or chariots or friends, not remembering the appendage of this body. As a draft-animal is yoked in a wagon, even so this spirit (*prāṇa*) is yoked in this body.[8]

Such an idea of liberation—kinglike (*svarāj*) movement through the worlds according to one's desire—does not regard the sensuous manifold itself as a delusion, but rather only that bondage to action and desire that keeps the soul confused about its identity and confined within the cycle of rebirth. Note, too, the evocation of an aristocratic or courtly ethos even at this early stage (ca. sixth century B.C. when courts were very rudimentary compared to what they would be in Nanda times), complete with erotic idealization: *ātmarati* and *ātmamithuna* give suggestive meaning to *kāmacāra* in the first passage, and in the second, play with women and chariots is specifically mentioned as a mokṣic treat. *Līlāmokṣa* posits an experience of *saṃsāra* that is simultaneously transcendent and immanent, like a dream in which one is conscious of dreaming and so is both omniscient artist and spectator of a world in which one also plays the leading part and indeed all the parts (cf. BAU 4.3.7–38). No one who has experienced the conscious-dreaming phenomenon can doubt its power to confer an exhilarating sense of existential enlightenment.

But perhaps the most extensive development of this idea comes in Kashmir Śaivism. I quote *Śivasūtra* 3.9–11 with Kṣemarāja's commentary in extenso both because it and statements like it are still not very well known and because, as I said, Śaiva metaphysics formed the intellectual and religious background for India's mainstream aesthetic theory.

> *The self* (*ātman*) *is the actor*. He acts, i.e., in the mere sport of self-vibration (*svaparispandalīlayaiva*)[9] he manifests, in self-differentiation, the manifold world which consists of various roles in the waking and dreaming states—which world, however, is firmly based in the essential nature concealed within it. . . . Thus Bhaṭṭa Nārāyaṇa says (*Stavacintāmaṇi* 59):
>
> You have introduced the cosmic drama, Hara,
> into which you have released the seeds of all beings.
> Who then but you are the poet
> to bring it to a conclusion? . . .
>
> *The individual self* (*antarātman*) *is the theater*. He (Śiva) delights therein, by means of the self (*ātman*) that is the basis (*āśraya*) for the manifestation of the sport which is the cosmic drama. . . . Thus, having made his abode (in the

embodied self), he manifests the cosmic drama through the vibration of his own senses.

The senses are the audience. The eyes, etc., of the *yogin* witness, when they are turned inward, the absolute essence (or "identity," *svasvarūpa*) that is filled with delight by the manifestation of the drama of *saṃsāra*. As this performance develops (or "intensifies," *tatprayogaprarūḍhyā*), the senses produce a plenum of wondrous delight (*camatkāra*) and *rasa,* in which all division drops away.[10]

One could produce other passages along these lines,[11] but they would not add anything essential. The universe in the absolute perspective is a work of art, a play (in both senses), for it is nothing but transcendental consciousness taking form for its own delight. The sensuous manifold is the self-manifestation (*ābhāsa*) of Śiva, the absolute subject (our metaphysical "I"), arising spontaneously from him by the power of his *śakti* or *pratibhā* (= Māyā, Parā Vāc, Devī, et al.) and known-felt,[12] in an orgasmic shudder (*spanda*), as a blissful experience of Self in imaginary Other. This is far from Śaṅkara's notion of *māyā* as the inexplicable ignorance that leaves absolute consciousness—for which it does not exist any more than does the illusory snake for the rope—completely untouched. For Śaṅkara all self-consciousness is already false.[13] Monistic Śaivism is fundamentally an aesthetic mysticism, as we see in Kṣemarāja's reference to *rasa* and *camatkāra* in the passage cited previously. Thus Abhinavagupta's view of the aesthetic experience as a foretaste of the mystical experience, from which it does not differ in kind.[14] The adept's experience of *saṃsāra* is, therefore, one in which there is no bondage, no pain, no personal limitation.[15] All is, and is savored as, the "sport of self-vibration" (*svaparispandalīlā*).

What distinguishes monistic Kashmir Śaivism, Rāmānuja's qualified nondualism (*viśiṣṭādvaita*), and other systems that take the play doctrine seriously from those that do not is a reluctance to turn one's back completely on the world of experience. Instead we find what seems to be an impulse to recuperate the phenomenal world in the face of a radical ascetic drive to renunciation. Perhaps the guiding sense is the dread of loss. To repudiate the world entirely is to deprive the notion of bliss of any experiential ground. To sacrifice a vibrant sense awareness for an impersonal "knowledge" that does not even include self-consciousness (see note 13), to reject imagination and memory for a hope of bliss that rests in complete abstraction (*nirvikalpatva*)—there is something fundamentally impractical about such a Pascalian wager. We sense in the desire to be rid of desire the deep longing for rest that Freud has called the death drive. The model for such an idea of bliss is dreamless sleep rather than the conscious-dreaming phenomenon that seems to underlie the *līlā* ideal. The *līlāvādin*s, therefore, instead of finding play an aporia that threatens the self-repose of ultimate consciousness see in it the possibility of achieving that repose with eyes open onto a world of iridescent charm that reflects the mystery of self-identity. It is the repose of a mystical sensitivity to emotion, *rasāsvāda* (*rasa* savoring) on the highest possible level.[16]

On the other hand, we should not underestimate the force of submerged asceticism[17] even in what may strike us as an apotheosis of the leisure-class play ethos. We must remember, for instance, that the end result of Śaiva monism, for all its relish of the sensuous manifold, is a transcendental solipsism. The thrill (*camatkāra*) of cosmic vibration is, in crude but not I think misleading terms, onanistic. Śiva remains alone in his very fullness. Mystical absorption in the orgasmic bliss of union with his feminized *śakti*—as in the yogi's self-absorption in the ritual intercourse of the *kulayāga*—does not disguise a certain reductive impoverishment of affect implicit in any monism. Love loses its meaning when it dissolves into a self-absorbed ecstatic shudder. With the narcissistic appropriation of the Other, love ceases to be a site of vital disclosure. We see this also on the level of purely aesthetic doctrine. In the philosophical understanding of aesthetic delight (*rasāsvāda, camatkāra,* etc.) every emotional response, though engendered by an imaginative engagement in a virtual world, becomes nothing but the spectator's own blissful self-savoring. Aesthetic representation then exists only as a vehicle for an inner pleasure: not to arouse curiosity, to provide inspiration, to make us see better or marvel at the world itself. Not only is it completely without the referential function, it is ultimately, and paradoxically, not even a fascinating object in its own right. So we see that in the *līlāvāda* of Kashmir Śaivism and its associated aesthetics the ascetic impulse that characterized Śaṅkara's uncompromising nondualism reappears as the rejection of emotional engagement in the world, a reduction of all "You" to "It" and all "It" to a modality of "I".[18]

The mystical idealization of poetry has a profound general significance. Above all, it points to the great intensity with which the *rasika* felt his emotional response to poetry. It seems to me, therefore, that Bhaṭṭa Nāyaka, Abhinavagupta, and those who followed them had a genuine insight into the depth of the *rasika*'s longing for transcendence of affective limitation, that is, for a breakthrough into freedom-in-feeling. As we shall see in the next section, *rasa* afforded the "man of heart / feeling" (*sahṛdaya, rasika*) an entry—temporary, perhaps, but all-enveloping—into a different universe, in which personal feeling was atmospherically suffused (cf. *dravaṇa, rasa*'s melting sensation) and felt as bliss. *Rasāsvāda* is related to *brahmāsvāda* most importantly on the affective level because the *rasika* cannot accept a *mokṣa* that excludes sentiment. All the profound longing for deliverance that underlies the spiritual ideal in Indian culture is invested by him with a positive emotional significance. We have seen that *līlāmokṣa* gives us religious models of the convergence of these two domains. We shall see, however, that the *rasika*'s play world retains a human poignancy that we altogether miss in the monistic perspective we have examined.

Thus the real question for us, as we move from metaphysics to aesthetics, regards the status of affect in *kāvya*. Does the solipsizing *rasa* doctrine of Abhinavagupta accurately describe what really goes on in the *rasika-sahṛdaya*'s imaginative experience? It would be easy simply to answer no and go on with a more humanistic analysis. But this would be to ignore something essential in the aestheticizing consciousness. Does not connoisseurship in any tradition involve a certain reduction, whereby things become mere bearers of savor? All the Indian tradition does in this respect—though it is a major alteration—is add a mystical dimension to the paradigm. Inevitably, however, there is a tension between art and life, the savor and the vehicle, and it centers on the question of love—in aesthetic terms the *śṛṅgāra* theme—not only because it is the dominant theme of *kāvya* but because it is where the status of the "You" is most problematic. It is easy to abandon a world that is only a disturbance, but how can one abandon what one loves—or wishes to love—without destroying one's ability to savor anything? The *rasika,* however, is as much of an aesthete as he is a lover, and we see his plight dramatized in the *nāyaka*'s (protagonist's) erotic response to the *nāyikā* (heroine). That is to say, it is very difficult to decide whether love for him, the ideal projection of the *rasika-sahṛdaya,* is a surrender of emotional autonomy (qua self-dedication to the Radiant Female) or a detached savoring of affect, both in himself and in the woman who arouses his interest. Ultimately it is a question about *kāvya*'s human meaning.

The Woman in the Garden

I have to start by recalling certain passages from the literature in poetics that bring *kāvya* more directly in line with the *līlāvāda* we have already discussed. First we may mention *Nāṭyaśāstra* 1, in which the gods, desirous of a Veda for the Kali Age, seek a "plaything" (*krīḍanīyaka,* 1.11; cf. 1.104 [KSS ed.]) that will serve as an instructive model of life in the triple world. There is nothing in this innocent use of the term that need detain us. It is basically a formulation of the dual pleasure-instruction (*prīti-upadeśa*) function of poetry mentioned in surviving Indian texts first by Aśvaghoṣa (*Saundarānanda,* final two verses) and familiar as well in the Western classical tradition. But when Dhanaṃjaya uses the play paradigm in *Daśarūpaka* 4, the application is more significant: "Like children playing with clay elephants and the like, hearers of poetry, playing with characters like Arjuna, etc., savor their own energy."[19] These lines come just after the theoretical discussion of *rasāsvāda,* which follows the teaching of Bhaṭṭa Nāyaka,[20] and just before the descriptive treatment of the individual *rasas*. Thus it summarizes the doctrine of the subjective nature of aesthetic delight (consciousness savoring itself through irreal appearances)[21] in a trope that gives emphasis to the "hearer's"—that is the *rasika*'s or *sahṛdaya*'s[22]—imaginative automony.

To flesh out the meaning of this aesthetic "child's play" we must move to Mammaṭa and Ānandavardhana. Let me take Mammaṭa (late 11th cen. A.D.) first, despite the anachronism, because *Kāvyaprakāśa* 1.1 gives us a cosmic perspective on the poetic play world without immediately introducing us to the *śṛṅgāra* theme.

> Triumphant is the word of the poet,
> which creates a world devoid of Fate's restrictions,
> consisting only of delight,
> utterly autonomous, and radiant with the nine *rasas*.[23]

Mammaṭa paints here the picture of a world of pure enchantment. Poetry is triumphant because it succeeds in delivering us from all the restrictions we associate with the law of *karman* but not at the price of banishing the sensuous manifold. The actual world undergoes a sea change: bondage becomes freedom, and painful emotions (fear, disgust, sorrow, etc.) are transmuted to *rasas*, whose essence is delight. Thus Mammaṭa explains his own verse:

> Such is the world created by Brahmā: essentially restricted by the power of fate; consisting of happiness, unhappiness, and delusion (*moha*); dependent on material and auxiliary causes such as atoms and activity (*karman*); having only six *rasas* (tastes), not all of them agreeable [the reference is to sweet, sour, salty, bitter, astringent, and pungent]. The poet's world is without these characteristics: that is why it is triumphant.[24]

In poetry we transcend the workaday fate-bound world of the Vedic creator figure Brahmā and distill from its experience what Rāmānuja calls the "savor of play" (*līlārasa*). Thus we are put on the plane of God or liberated soul in Rāmānuja's Vedānta and Kashmir Śaivism.

So, too, in a frequently cited passage of Ānandavardhana some two hundred years earlier (ca. 875 A.D.):

> In the boundless universe of poetry, the poet is the creator,
> and as it pleases him, so does this world come forth.
> If the poet is a man of passion (*śṛṅgārin*), the world in poetry is full of *rasa*.
> But if he is passionless (*vītarāga*), that world is devoid of *rasa* altogether.[25]

The poet creates the world according to the pleasure principle. If we combine this statement with Mammaṭa's, the implicit connection between poet and *rasika* becomes obvious. If the only law is that of *rasa*, then there can be no essential difference between the poet's and listener–spectator–reader's *experience* of the poetic universe.[26] But something else surfaces here. In metaphysical *līlāvāda* we have noted the inevitable ascetic accent, the reduction of play to a modality of self-savoring for a consciousness that remains fundamentally transcendent. Ānandavardhana's *rasika,* however, must already be a man of passion, that is, he is not ideally disengaged from the world. He creates a new world in order to give play to already existent feeling, to receive the surfeit that finds no adequate expression in his actuality. The model is perhaps the poetically familiar one of Prajāpati's creation of a beautiful woman out of the longing of his heart, through meditation or by bringing a picture to life (cf. Ś 2.10 [9], reading *citre*), a woman who embodies the disparate world's potential for ravishing charm. Here, though, is where the *līlā* ideal of autonomy begins to erode. If the *rasika* poet is already a man of feeling for whom the world as it is is insufficient, is not the new creation the echo of a desire for emotional fulfillment *in* life? In other words, are we talking here about entering a rarified world of aesthetic (self-)savoring, or is the poetic universe an attempt to realize a potential presence?

We can see what the presence is by paying attention to certain metaphors that describe poetic charm. Here first is Mammaṭa again, verse and commentary:

> *Kāvya* gives glory, attainment of wealth,
> knowledge of the world, an end to the inauspicious,
> sudden bliss, and counsel sweet
> as from the lips of a beloved consort.

> Bliss is its (poetry's) chief purpose and is immediate; it derives from the savoring of *rasa* and makes fall away all other objects of cognition. Poetry (*kāvya*), i.e. the activity of the poet skilled in depicting the supranormal world [cf. KP 1.1 *supra*], is different from learned texts (*śāstras*) such as the Vedas, whose words are like those of a master, and from epic and Purāṇa, which is like the advice of a friend—different by virtue of its prevalent function of rendering word and content subservient to *rasa*. Poetry gives instruction (such as ''One should act like Rāma rather than Rāvaṇa'') to poet and *sahṛdaya* alike in the manner of a beloved consort, addressing one directly and producing a state of being with *rasa*.[27]

Passages like this, which convey a standard trope, should convince us to what extent the *rasika* in general is assumed to be male. The metaphoric association of poetic and erotic seduction is not dismissable as a pedagogical device, the self-effacing vehicle of a purely aesthetic tenor, but gives us essential information about poetic reception in the Indian cultural context.[28] Any extensive reading of *kāvya* will establish beyond doubt that the poetic play world must have the Radiant Female, a Śrī-like principle of charm, at its center. It is by her magic that one enters into the poetic universe, which is to feel oneself and the world transformed by *rasa,* to feel suddenly free (Mammaṭa 1.1) in an atmosphere whose raison d'être is the elicitation of an emotional response described as both a melting (*dravaṇa, druti*) and a sprouting (*vikāsa, aṅkurībhāva*) sensation.[29] The ''state of being with *rasa*''—as in the use of that term in nontechnical language—is in the first instance a state of erotic excitement or captivation.[30]

Thus Abhinavagupta describes the inception of *rasāsvāda* (''savoring of sentiment'') in such a way that we cannot really distinguish the *rasika* outside the poem from the hero within it:

> The savoring of *rasa,* whose essence is a more-than-ordinary (*alaukika*) delight (''thrill,'' *camatkāra*) is different from memory or inference (of an emotional state) or ordinary self-consciousmess. Thus one (viz. the *sahṛdaya* or *rasika*) does not apprehend a beautiful woman, etc.,[31] in a state of indifference, as he would in ordinary inference, but rather in a state of germinating (*aṅkurībhāva*) *rasa*-savoring soon to reach fullness, because he is a *sahṛdaya,* which means that his heart is attuned (to such objects). He does not need to climb the ladder of inference, memory, etc., because the experience is essentially a savoring (*carvaṇā*) befitting utter absorption (*tanmayībhāva*) (in her *qua* object).[32]

This passage reveals that the hero's (*nāyaka*'s) response to the *pramadā* (''woman of intoxicating beauty'') within poem or play enacts a paradigm of aesthetic response in general.[33] The *rasika* is both in the poem as the woman's admirer, savoring his response to her, and outside savoring his response to the poem.[34] To extract some purely aesthetic (i.e., emotionally neutral, indifferent) essence from the total aesthetic–erotic response, as most critics have tried to do, is to deny the suggestive principle that Indian theory itself enshrines. Let us again cite the dictum of Bhaṭṭa Tauta (see note 26): ''The hero, the poet, and the listener (i.e., *rasika*) all have the same experience'' (*nāyakasya kaveḥ śrotuḥ sāmāno 'nubhavas tataḥ,* DhAL 1.6+). The *rasika* enjoys the play world of poetry as a *participant* who surrenders himself to it, as to a beautiful woman. In the passage cited earlier we have a much more vivid and telling use of *tanmayībhāva* (''identification, absorption'') than we get in Abhinava's famous definition of the *sahṛdaya* in the *Dhvanyālokalocana*.[35] Who else is the ideally seductive woman, then, but the *generic* heroine of all Sanskrit poetry?[36]

And were do we find her if not in the floral paradise that typifies *kāvya* as a whole? Even if the garden were not her actual setting, she would create it around herself, like a seasonal Śri, in metaphor or suggestion. In the third act of Bhāsa's *Pratijñāyaugandharāyaṇa* this is precisely what occurs: Vāsavadatta creates a pleasure garden out of Udayana's prison cell, casting a spell over his imagination. Instead of lamenting his fate, Udayana basks in the magical aura of the Radiant Female and devotes himself to the "royal sport of love."[37] This garden aura that surrounds the *pramadā* heroine is nothing other than the imagistic actualization or scenarioizing of the sprouting sensation (*aṅkurībhāva*) of *rasāsvāda*.[38]

But there is a further dimension as well, which invests the aesthetic–erotic paradigm of The Woman in the Garden with the suggestion of a venerable religious idea and gives special symbolic significance to the courtly ambience in which the erotic *līlā* of *kāvya* usually takes place. This is the Śrī concept, to which we have several times alluded. In Śrī–Lakṣmī seasonal fertility, wealth, and happiness are personified precisely in the figure of the voluptuous garden-world *pramadā* (typically associated with the lotus, but in fact with all kinds of flowering vegetation).[39] The king as ideal representative of the human community is regarded as wedded to the goddess (mythologically the consort of the god Viṣṇu), whose worship goes well back into Vedic times.[40] She is thus not only the goddess of seasonal beauty, fertility, and so forth, but the personification of victory and the sovereignty itself. The monarchy therefore becomes a conduit of divine radiance, representing or embodying the paradisal play world of divinity on earth. Notions of magical correspondence between the person of the king and the state of the kingdom—ofter remarked on in studies of Indian kingship[41]—make it possible for the king's dalliance with beautiful women, all auspicious representatives of the Śrī principle, to be taken as a "magical" inducement to social prosperity. We see similar auspicious symbolism in the *mithuna* motif in Indian art: the auspicious male–female pair (sometimes engaged in sexual intercourse, *maithuna*) that adorns religious structures ubiquitously.[42] The union of hero and heroine and the luxuriant heightening of erotic atmosphere in drama and poetry cannot be understood adequately without reference to these notions. The garden world of poetry with its synaesthetic allure (soft breezes, fragrant scents, low hums and warbles, etc., amid the opulence of florid vegetation) is thus the locus for the epiphany of Śrī and the auspicious transformation of her hero–consort and his world.

Let us recapitulate the themes of this section before moving into the *Śakuntalā*. We have seen that the poeticians celebrate poetry as a world constructed according to the demand of *rasa,* in effect an aesthetic parallel to *līlāmokṣa*. We have likewise seen that the central element in this play world is encounter with the Radiant Female who embodies its power (*śakti*) to captivate or entrance. Without her there would be no world nor any *rasa* for it to enshrine. And finally we have noted how the dream woman of poetry wears the aspect of Śrī, thus becoming a communal symbol of auspiciousness. The questions we posed at the end of the last section are still unanswered, but now we can better appreciate their implications. In the Abhinavagupta paradigm cited earlier, aesthetic and erotic perspectives mix, but in such a way that love is transformed into a connoisseur's savoring of *rasa*. In other words, it is a solipsizing *līlā*: the *rasika* enters into the poetic universe only to savor the rarified emotion aroused by stimulating images. This is not far from what on the purely secular plane would be a refined courtly hedonism. In Ānadavardhana's model, however, we seem to find something more poignantly human: the longing for love, for the utopian world that mirrors the heart's demand for sentimental response. For in both his and Mammaṭa's praise of poetry as ideal universe we glimpse a shadow of disappointment in the real world, which does not offer sufficient opportunity for that mingling of hearts that *kāvya* holds up as its ideal.[43] Yet the more *kāvya* takes on the dimensions of wish fulfillment, the less playlike it becomes. *Līlā*'s delicate balance of immanence and transcendence tilts here toward immanence. Courtly (or mystical) aestheticism begins to seem like a screen separating the *rasika* as lover from the dream woman who would deliver his heart from its isolation.[44] Which version is correct? Or are both?

Śakuntalā

We turn, then, to the *Śakuntalā*. I have treated the play in great detail elsewhere (see preceding note), so I will not linger here over points I have already made. The essence of the matter is the hero's crossover into the enchanting world of the hermitage and what it represents. I see it as an enactment of *rasa* transformation in terms that are consonant with entry into the poetic universe as Ānandavardhana and Mammaṭa describe it.[45] In the prologue the actress is induced to sing a song celebrating the summer season in which the first three acts of the play are set. The song has an entrancing effect on both audience and stage manager. The audience, in the stage manager's words, becomes "painted into the picture"[46] of the charming world her song describes: a summer scene featuring a group of young maidens with bees buzzing around their floral ear ornaments. Meanwhile the stage manager has so lost himself in the spell of the poetic evocation that he has forgotten what play they are going to put on. All this is very significant thematically. The young women with bees buzzing around their faces become Śakuntalā and her friends (the woman-and-bee motif appears at crucial unctures throughout the play). The mesmerized audience, painted into the magical stillness of the poetic world, becomes the play's hero, King Duḥṣanta. Awestruck by Śakuntalā's beauty, he observes her with mounting excitement from behind some shrubbery—like a sensitive spectator in a theater—until an incident with a bee allows him to step forth into direct participation in *rāgalīlā* with the heroine. The stage manager's obliviousness foreshadows both Śakuntalā's love revery, in which she neglects the arrival of the dangerous ascetic guest who curses her for her abstraction from the here and now, and the oblivion that overtakes Duḥṣanta, turning his rapture with Śakuntalā into a negative parody of itself: entrancement without charismatic focus, without the Śrī who turns daze to enchantment. And if this were not enough, the very deer that lures the king into the *āśrama* is explicitly likened to the actress's "ravishing" song by the stage manager himself.[47]

So the *rasika* has entered the enchanted world of poetic promise, led to the threshold by a wondrous animal that metaphorically embodies the charm of song. Once inside he finds himself in an ideally feminine atmosphere of lush vegetation, and so forth, with the nubile child–woman Śakuntalā as its focus, the virtual tutelary goddes of the place (*sādhidaivata iva śakuntalayā . . . āśramo,* 1.11+*). His first glimpse of her sends him into shudders of ecstasy: innocent and ripe for the plucking, her breasts pressing with the sap of youth against the confines of her barken garment (1.18[17] and preceding). This last detail could stand as a symbol of his expectations, for he wishes either to ignore as much as possible the ascetic character of the place or see it as a source of charm.[48] In his imagination it is the paradise he, as *rasika,* has encountered many times in poetry and song. His own palace pleasure garden is only an imitation of this lush primordial grove (1.16[15]). Here is the Golden Age (*kṛtayuga*) in all its alluring freshness, untainted by the vulgarity of hunting or farming economies. Śakuntalā seems to him like the embodiment of its vegetal abundance (1.20[18] and throughout act 1); a "recreation of woman" in the imagination of a *rasika* Prajāpati (2.10[9]); "an unsmelt flower, an unsnipped shoot, an uncut gem, new honey (wine?) yet unsavored (*madhu navam anāsvāditarasam*), the full fruit of (past lives') merit—whose lot will it be to enjoy her faultless beauty in this world?" (2.11[10]). The final question is the crux of the matter, but we know without a doubt that the lot is his, the *rasika*'s. Poetic theory is unanimous on this point. Only he has the cultivation (*vyutpatti, abhyāsa*) and imagination (*śakti, pratibhā*) capable of enjoying her.[49] What could an "oily-head ascetic (2.11[10]+)—think of the poeticians' scorn for the *ahṛdaya* pandit—do with beauty of such resonance? Duḥṣanta's lyric asides, which translate her charm into the figural language (*alaṃkāra*) of poetry, are the only adequate responses, for they alone present her in her imaginative dimension as an object of *rasāsvāda*. Sexual intercourse itself, which takes place offstage between acts 3 and 4, is an experience of the imagination as much as of the senses. It is only not so for those who have no aesthetic capacity.

Yet, in the terms we have set up, we can see a drift here toward the solipsistic consciousness of aesthetic hedonism: love paradoxically reduced through aesthetic enhancement to sensation. Śakuntalā has become simply the vehicle of her own ravishing charm, which the *rasika* can savor as a modality of his own subjective consciousness without reference to hers. In the terms of Kashmir Śaivism she is the play manifestation (*ābhāsa*) whose raison d'être is the savoring subject's "sport of self-vibration" (*svaparispandalīlā*). Even the glimpses we have into her mind in the first three acts, as desire disturbs her girlish innocence, seem designed to make her more erotically appealing, as fantasy object, to the *rasika*.[50] We could almost say that she is really no more than the concretization of a dreamily erotic atmosphere, an aphrodisiac to a refined, contemplative onanism. But in the end there is something terribly one-sided and unsympathetic about such a view, which distorts the *rasika* consciousness by stripping it of its psychological resonance. We have referred before to the principle of the "materiality of the signifier," and it applies here as well. Śakuntalā cannot be the merely transparent vehicle of a subjective experience. If the Radiant Female is necessary to the aesthetic–erotic consciousness, then she is an irreducible Other. This otherness, which is at bottom a subjectivity resistant to the *rasika*'s narcissism, can be suppressed but not overcome in *rasa* savoring. There is a trapdoor in aesthetic idealism. Śakuntalā attracts because she represents a promise, a promise that can never be fully defined or attained without ceasing to attract. Here is the abyssal pseudologic of Lacan's Imaginary level of consciousness: one seeks to appropriate the radiant fullness of the Other only to find that it can only reside elsewhere. The solipsizing aesthetic ideal contains an inescapable contradiction.

The fact is that the hero of the aesthetic–erotic play world needs the Śrī presence whose magic conjures it into existence. However pronounced the tendency to narcissistic appropriation of the heroine as savor-bearing appearance, there is an equally strong tendency toward submission to her transformative power. With the king's first appearance onstage we see him as a hunter who is being lured (*hṛtaḥ*, 1.5) by his prey into the garden world of the hermitage which will soon disclose Śakuntalā as its "virtual goddess." He is, in other words, as passive as he is active, captivated by a principle of female beauty that demands a response of him. Is there no symbolic resonance to the fact that he enters as a devotee—nominally to salute Śakuntalā as her father's proxy, but his "devotion" (*bhakti*, 1.12+) soon acquires more suggestive meaning—even divesting himself of the insignia of his worldly rank? The note of awestruck devotion and pained craving, maintained in numerous verses of acts 2 and 3, is of course a conventional feature of *kāvya,* but does this render it meaningless? Does not the convention itself require explanation? I do not suggest that such a posture is inconsistent with a narcissistic tendency (erotic idealization can be a form of domination),[51] but the very fact that it takes the form of an implicit plea makes us realize that the Other is a force undermining the autonomy of the subject's play fantasy. It is virtually inevitable on these grounds alone that the erotic tone of the first three acts will shift to one of pathos (*karuṇa rasa*), most prominent in acts 4 and 6 but underlying the anger (*raudra*) of act 5 and the wonder (*adbhuta*) of act 7 as well.

I think that we can best understand this pathetic accent in terms of the remarks made in the preceding section on the implications of Ānandavardhana's model of the aesthetic play world, namely, that it is not created out of some spontaneous play impulse as in the theological paradigms but rather to realize or fulfill a desire for something that is lacking in the real world. Thus in the latter part of the play the hero is in the position of having somehow to translate the elation of the first three acts into the actual world of the court, where despite panegyrical salutes that perpetuate the fiction of his charismatic dominance the pleasure principle is in fact subordinated to the reality principle. In act 5, in his déjà vu reaction to another wife's offstage song (5.9[2]), it strikes him forcefully that aesthetic response discloses a disturbing gap in ordinary emotional experience, which can only be bridged, as he comes to understand in act 6, by bringing the woman epiphanized in poetry—for him, Śakuntalā—to life. In the portrait scene of act 6 (6.15–24[15–22]) he tries to reenter the illusory aesthetic–erotic paradise, but he finds he cannot go backward. Śakuntalā must now be brought into his world, not the other way around. But this is precisely where he reveals his lack of autonomy. To enter the kāvyic dreamworld there are only two requirements: enchantment (*pratibhā, rasa*) and a cultivated sensibility (*sahṛdayatva*); but to bring its promise to life one must submit to certain demands, demands that accentuate the hero's vulnerability.

Again I must state that I have gone over much of this ground in another essay.[52] My treatment here will, therefore, be summary, except where I am breaking new ground. In the sixth act Duḥṣanta, the *sahṛdaya* hero, is reduced to making a sentimental display of himself in order to attract sympathy. He is onstage before a hidden observer, specifically Miśrakeśī (or Sānumatī), the *apsaras* from Mārīca-Kaśyapa's hermitage who represents the lost presence of Śakuntalā. In demonstrating his hurt confusion before her he is surreptitiously pleading for female understanding. The Śrī of his imagination is not his to conjure up at will (like Śiva playfully engaging his *śakti*). Rather, he appears in his pathetic posture like a disconsolate child, as if Śakuntalā were more his mother than his erotic ideal. Actually, this is not so far fetched, if we reflect on the nurturing feminine atmosphere of the hermitage in act 1. The gentle teasing laughter of three female companions, highlighted by the lushly sensuous world of soft hums and warm, fragrant breezes, might be the muffled echo of voices heard long ago in the "maternal cosmos" of infancy,[53] where the females of the extended family—mother, aunts, older sisters, cousins—had maintained an enveloping atmosphere of benign solicitude and indulgence. In entering the paradise of acts 1 through 3 the hero was in a sense reentering the predhārmic play world of early childhood, bringing its diffuse, subliminal eroticism into sharp adult focus in the image of a beautiful young woman whose sexual awakening is to him alone, a beautiful-and-distressed fairy-tale princess (Indian style), whose savior–hero he was always meant to be.[54] The curse that has exiled him from this paradise is, in this perspective, the fundamental No to the pleasure principle, the renunciation that is at the root of all Law and which marks the first stage of entry into the adult world of responsibility.

But why must there be a plea, and why, further, must it be conveyed indirectly through dramatics, that is, by making a spectacle of oneself? The answer has both ethical and psychological dimensions, both of which undermine the erotic–aesthetic autonomy of the play ideal. It is hard to avoid the impression that the curse is in some sense a concretization of a betrayal. Despite the numerous epistemological tropes that seek to ennoble the hero's confusion by placing it in a quasi-metaphysical context,[55] it is clear enough that the hero needs to expiate a sense of guilt. We could see this betrayal, with Tagore, as a simple matter of sexual exploitation.[56] But this, I think, is too literal and fails to appreciate the extent to which the hero represents the idealized *rasika-sahṛdaya* sensibility. The betrayal seems to me to be more a matter of attitude than of act. The aesthetic–erotic idealization of woman creates a barrier to love as an affective relationship. (I refer the reader back to my remarks on the onanistic implications of the Trika model of *līlā* in the first section.) The *rasika* hero oscillates between two idealizations of the heroine, neither of which leaves him any room for a genuine understanding with her. On the one hand she is the aesthetic–erotic object with all its solipsistic implications, on the other the sole access to a lost world of nurturing affection. But where is she herself, as subject in her own right? The problem is not exclusively a women's issue. The *rasika* himself does not escape the isolation that results from the failure of mutual engagement on a personal level. Ultimately one cannot love; or even bask in, an image or an atmosphere. One needs the vitality of another consciousness.

Whether the hero (or the *rasika* he represents) ever reaches such a realization in the play is impossible to decide, since the issue is never a conscious one for him. Nevertheless, we see him attempting to demonstrate the authenticity of his feeling for her across the abyss that separates them in act 6, presenting the *apsaras* who functions as Śakuntalā's representative with the pathos of his situation without her. While he thus displays his vulnerability—which comes to a peak first in the episode of the portrait, through which he achieves a brief, illusory reentry into the charmed garden world, and then again in his shame over his childlessness—she remains a hidden spectator, the female *rasikā* whose sympathetic response will validate his innocence. Is this a genuine call for recognition or a ploy by which the (male) *rasika* relieves himself of any sense of responsibility for the gap that divides him from his idealized beloved? Let us remember that the theme of a hero's betrayal of his wife is a major one in Sanskrit literature. We have only to think of Nala and Rāma. The former abandons his wife in the forest, leaving her to deal with all kinds of difficulties, while he seeks to comprehend the dark forces that inhabit him (he is literally possessed by a gambling demon); the latter humiliates Sītā (more than once) and makes himself miserable for the same reason he had gone into exile many years earlier, because he cannot choose pleasure over duty, personal inspiration over collective demand. None of these situations—Duḥṣanta's, Nala's, or Rāma's—is easy to judge. The texts that present them invite sympathy for both parties while—overtly, at least—insisting on the inevitability of the dilemma, thus establishing a tragic perspective on life in the world.

Nevertheless, we can see different levels of meaning here. In the context of *dharma* the wife is in most respects the last one to whom the householder has any obligations. The emphasis is all the other way around: she is to serve him, take him as her *guru,* and so on, while he fulfills his debts to the sages, the gods, his ancestors, guests, and even creatures at large (the *pancayajña*). Even the intimacy of sexual life is invaded by the dharmic *obligation* to have monthly intercourse, since constant pregnancy better ensures male offspring to perform the required rituals. The wife is on the whole a means, an instrument, for the householder's fulfillment of essential obligations, rather than being an object of his moral attention in her own right. If family disharmony develops, the overt blame is likely to fall on her (cf. the role of Kaikeyī in the Rāma story). Yet on the other hand, she is terribly idealized. She is held up as the Śrī of her husband's world, the locus and inspiration of his emotional life, even though she may be little more than a stranger to him.[57] Servant, mistress of his soul, and nurturing mother: how can she be all these things? and how can he bridge the gap on his side of the dilemma? How can he remove the veil that separates him from her, a veil for whose existence he denies personal responsibility, while nursing a sense of guilt and needing forgiveness?

What I am getting at here, obviously, is the way literary representations of love separation become mythical nuclei of real-life feelings. In the context of arranged marriage (and let us remember that most *rasikas* were in fact not princes) there is a greater barrier to the intimate sharing of emotion than there would otherwise be, greater potential for awkwardness between husband and wife, for a certain stiff formality that may well remain throughout the marriage. In these mythical paradigms—the stories of Nala, Rāma, Duḥṣanta—the male demonstrates his good faith, shows himself to be at the mercy of destiny, and yet discloses the hidden existence of his love. He can have it both ways, in other words. Acts 4 and 5 of the *Śakuntalā* show a genuine sensitivity to the plight of women. The former's almost cloying tenderness[58] combined with the latter's insults and accusations points not only to an awareness of the shock that awaited perhaps most Indian girls of high birth but an uneasy conscience about it. And not only about sending a precious daughter out into a colder, more impersonal milieu (all Kaṇva can really hope is that Śakuntalā will be treated with respect; the rest, he says, depends on fate, 4.19[17]), but about receiving her as a wife. Duḥṣanta betrays Śakuntalā in act 5, and in act 6 he acts out his incomprehension of his deed and the anguish he feels about it, all the while seeking to disclose a truer emotional self that defies appearances. "This is the real me," he says to the woman behind the barrier, which he cannot remove though he has acquiesced in its construction. "Please do not withdraw your love from me." If I have suggested that this might be a ploy, it is because it is difficult to avoid seeing such emotional demonstrations as evasions. But the truth is that here we are at the limits of Sanskrit poetry and perhaps classical Indian culture itself. We wish that it were possible for the hero to raise this problem explicitly to consciousness. We wish both he and the heroine could be more than idealized types, that they could think as well as feel. We wish the demand for *rasa* did not exclude a moral problematics *on the conscious level.* This would mean, however, an ideal of love that was something more than either quasi-mystical intoxication or mere dhārmic partnership.

For the *rasika* the dilemma—sentimental longing kept veiled by emotional reserve—is more charge than for the ordinary man, because he is naturally a sentimentalist. He cannot regard a world that does not place the demands of the heart first as a good world (see the second section of this essay). Yet he is forced to expiate an implicit sense of guilt, for the gap that exists between his actual relations with women and their sentimental ideal and the further gap existing within that ideal itself, that is, the mutual incompatibility of autonomous aesthetic–erotic *līlā* and the "cry from the heart" for mutual love and understanding. This latter shape of the dilemma is the tension between the first three acts of *Śakuntalā* and the final four. In the former *kāvya* is the play world of the erotic imagination; in the latter—like the portrait in act 6—it is a vehicle of pathos.[59] Thus we see that something like a curse is needed to mythicize a gap that already exists between the desire of the heart and the poetic dreamworld that represents it. The *rasika* knows that his poetry contains a promise of a true emotional breakthrough, but he cannot realize it in a poetry of idealized sentiment and high formal polish. The very conventional limits of *kāvya* ensure that it will always need to make the romantic hero a man of tears and swoons, seeking to demonstrate by self-display what he cannot communicate directly.[60] By giving us the *rasika* as uncomprehending victim and soliciting a gush of sympathetic feeling on his behalf the play shifts from an ideal of aesthetic–erotic transformation to one of tragic self-portrayal: the man of feeling as beautiful, childlike soul. If one cannot truly find one's Śrī, one can hope to attract her sympathetic smile from afar. The question is whether the appeal ever gets beyond self-pity.

The pathos works, to an extent, though the paradisal promise of the first three acts (the utopian world of emotional release) is never realized. The hero succeeds in recuperating female sympathy: the eavesdropping *apsaras* acts the part of a mother moved by her child's weepy protestations of innocence (act 6). Śakuntalā herself, however, remains reserved though docile (act 7). The bewitching goddess of the poetic imagination has become humble wife and mother, just as the hero is no longer the *rasika* but the obedient servant of destiny standing before the magnified dhārmic father Mārīca. The erotic magic of the first three acts, in other words, is not a part of the conclusion. The magical atmosphere of the second *āśrama* rings with the emotional tone of wonder (*adbhuta rasa*). Thus we move from eros to pathos and finally, as the great paternal figure of Mārīca is revealed, to awe.[61]

Conclusion: The Ambiguous Play World

But exactly what is the outcome for the *rasika*? Viewed positively, the conclusion represents reconciliation with male authority (note 61) and the recuperation of female indulgence. It is the stuff of all romance. We can even say that the shift from ecstatic eroticism to familial tenderness—the movement from Śakuntalā's breathtaking sexual allure to her chastened dignity as wife and mother—is all for the good, since it seems to represent a more balanced ideal of love between man and woman. But, as I have written elsewhere,[62] the problem is not so much with the outcome itself as with its implementation, which makes us suspicious of the value of the ideal. What we lack is a sense of the *rasika*'s conscious engagement of and dialectic with the larger-than-life male and female powers that dominate his imagination. Instead he succeeds through psychodrama, that is, through self-display, the taking of postures. While this is natural in an art form that sublimates posture to the condition of aesthetic cause (*vibhāva*) of *rasa* enchantment, it nevertheless evades the substantial issues that the art form raises. The hero never comes—nor apparently does the *rasika* in the audience—to any moral or intellectual insight into his situation. We might say that the issues are only accidentially invoked, but I think this is wrong. We are missing the point of the mythical paradigm we have explored if we think it is not fundamentally about the hope of realization of the love ideal and the tensions that surround it. There is nothing accidental about subliminal meaning: quite the contrary.

We have seen that the paradisal model of love incorporates many different facets of the *rasika*'s aspiration. First there is the intensity of longing for aesthetic transformation of the real world into something shimmering with intensified feeling, a feeling that Ānandavardhana identifies as *śṛṅgāra.*[63] We find here a yearning for escape from the strictures of necessity, especially from the ascetic spirit of *dharma* with its characteristic frown on spontaneous love—an escape readily invested with the emotional intensity of the longing for *mokṣa.*[64] Thus the aptness of the aesthetic model of world experience as *līlā,* with all its transcendental implications. Beyond this there is the socio-religious idea of Śrī, an idea that valorizes the fulfillment of desire as an auspicious force percolating through the whole society. Against the ascetic ideal of *dharma* as self-restraint (the impersonal ritualization of *pravṛtti* according to *nivṛtti* values) is set the model of an ordered society infused from within by a divine radiance: charismatic happiness versus depersonalized calm. Included in this idea is the further valorization of the courtly and aristocratic environment in which *līlā* was a lived ideal. Then there is the psychological dimension of the recaptured Golden Age, the bliss of play in the "maternal cosmos" of early childhood. But to achieve this multifaceted paradise one must evade reality—not only the paternal No to the pleasure principle but even the genuine needs of the heart. No art, no wish-fulfilling dream, can completely overcome reality, precisely because it is only in reality that the fantasy desire has a chance of being satisifed. Even for the most radical escapist the ideal leads surreptitiously back to the real. Thus one is brought to the point of psychological, ethical, even ontological revelations concerning the subjectivity of the Other. The very intensity of longing creates a paradoxical effect, and *kāvya* moves in two directions at once: toward a purely autonomous world of "sport" insulated by the coy excellences of poetic form (*alaṃkāra, guṇa,* etc.) and toward an epiphany that holds out the promise of happiness for which an autonomous aesthetic world is an inadequate vehicle, a defacto constraint.

In the first section we found that the paradox of play is precisely its indecision between transcendence and immanence. What we have found, I believe, is what Śaṅkara seems to have known when he rejected *līlā* on the level of the Absolute, namely, that play inevitably tilts toward the immanent because of its necessary erotic component,[65] which contains sub rosa a humanizing plea. The aesthetic–erotic ideal of *kāvya* as thematized in the mythical framework of the *Śakuntalā* seems to prove likewise that any flirtation with Eros inevitably subverts *līlā*'s transcendent claims. A curse hangs over the solipsistic garden world of the first three acts, which can be lifted only when the *rasika* seeks to translate the Śrī of his imagination into the real world with its social and practical limitations. The *Śakuntalā* moves to the side of desire for *fulfillment* of the promise enshrined in the erotic paradise: the utopian hope of happiness in love supported by a social system that honors the sentimental ideals of the heart. It has to be this way, or else even erotic play becomes paradoxically ascetic by virtue of its solipsistic detachment from affect. The question is whether or not the hero has actually learned that this must be the case. If there were an act 8 to this play, would we not find the hero again dazzled by another Śakuntalā, with the original reduced to the offstage role of Haṃsavatī? The lure of the play-world paradigm of emotional release never lost its force in *kāvya,* or religion for that matter. Nevertheless, this play of Kālidāsa's (and it is emblematic rather than unique in this regard) gives us reasons for doubting the psychological viability of the ideal. The hero as self-possessed connoisseur of emotion, sporting in the feminized garden of Eros, becomes a child pleading for understanding from hidden authorities who, he fears, may be indifferent to his affective needs.

Appendix

The editor of this volume has asked me to include a plot summary of *Śakuntalā* for readers who may not be very familiar with it. Since I have often referred to the play by act, I shall indicate these divisions here.

In act 1 there is a prologue wherein the stage manager introduces the play and then asks the actress to sing a song celebrating the summer season. He is so mesmerized by the beauty of her evocation that he has to ask the actress what play they are going to perform, thus introducing us to the thematic heart of the play, which has to do with the significance of the lovers' mutual entrancement. He then compares the song's charm to a deer, which is even now leading the protagonist, King Duḥṣanta, into the precinct of the sage Kaṇva's hermitage. In this way we segue into the play proper. After a few verses by the king and his charioteer marking the wondrous character of their deer-led transition from the mundane sphere into a world of unusual possibilites, the king is met with a stern reminder from two hermits (reminding us of the pair Śārṅgarava and Śāradvata in act 5) that hermitage deer are off-limits to hunters. In fact, they say, the king's role is to protect tender life, not injure it—words that suggestively comment upon the worldling king's soon to be aroused sexual interests. The king immediately quivers his arrow and soon divests himself of his royal insignia, in order to enter the *āśrama* and pay his respects to "Father Kaṇva," or rather to his daughter Śakuntalā, whom Kaṇva has designated his proxy while he travels to a pilgrimage spot for the removal of a mysterious "adverse fate" that now hangs over her (the maiden-in-distress motif). As Duḥṣanta makes his way, alone, into the hermitage, he is stopped in his tracks by the pleasant voices of three young women who have come to water some trees and shrubs. He decides to conceal himself in order to eavesdrop. It is at this point that he becomes awestruck by the beauty of one of them, Śakuntalā herself, who seems the embodied charm of the enchanting floral atmosphere that envelops him. He rehearses to himself a number of *kāvya* verses on her breathtaking allure, until he finds an opportunity to reveal himself—though not fully, since he lets it be understood that he is only a royal official. After some charming conversation, in which he finds out that she is only Kaṇva's foster daughter, in fact a *kṣatriya* like himself by birth (thus suitable for marriage), and we discover that Śakuntalā in her shy maiden's way is as taken with him as he is with her, an alarm is raised offstage. One of the elephants in the king's hunting party has broken loose and is causing panic in the hermitage. The three young women leave the stage in a hurry, and we are led by the technique of suggestion (*dhvani*) to the notion that the love that has arisen between the two protagonists is, from the point of view of her virgin state and the hermitage that is a spatial extension of it, a serious and even violent disruption,

In act 2 what is notable, aside from the idealizing quality of certain verses in which the king declares his love for Śakuntalā in the presence of his friend (the comic *vidūṣaka*), is that he is offered the perfect excuse to remain away from the capital. In Kaṇva's absence the hermits request that he act his royal role as protector of sacrifice by remaining with them to ward off the demons who wish to ravage it. Duty thus, although only superficially, coincides with pleasure.

In act 3 we have the courtship. The king comes upon Śakuntalā in another eavesdropping scene: she is lying in a bower on a bed of freshly picked blossoms in an attempt by her friends to assuage her love fever. Once he hears from her own lips that she is waning from desire of him, he reveals himself as her savior. Her friends elicit from him an avowal of his honorable intent (to include her among his numerous wives) and then leave the two of them alone on a fabricated pretext. Śakuntalā is initially very bashful. The king tries to reassure her, claiming that their physical love constitutes a dhārmic form of marriage (*gāndharva* marriage) and at one point reaches out to restrain her when she wishes to go. She reminds him then that they have come out into a clearing and are visible to chance onlookers. At this he quickly retreats to the bower. But now it is her turn to eavesdrop. Satisfying herself by this method that he indeed loves her to distraction, she discloses her presence (an anticipation of the testing and disclosure of acts 6 and 7). Their passion is finally on the verge of satisfaction (she awaits his kiss with eyes closed in one of those heightened kāvyic moments that seems to stand still) when another interruption occurs: the ascetic "mother" Gautamī calling the time of evening prayers. Then the king himself, voicing his regrets at the missed opportunity, is summoned to guard the sacrifice again.

Act 4, in effect, has two prologues. In the first, which is so named (the other is part of the act proper), occurs the curse. Śakuntalā, Kaṇva's proxy as receiver of guests, fails to notice the arrival of the irascible ascetic Durvāsas because she is caught up in love revery. The curse takes homoeopathic form: her lover will be as oblivious of her as she has been of the ascetic. Śakuntalā herself is unaware of the curse, though it is overheard by her two companions, who are able to secure from its author a certain abatement: when Śakuntalā reveals to the king the ring he has given her, inscribed with his name, the fog of amnesia will lift. In the next de facto prologue a young hermit comes onto the stage (it is the dawn of another day) and utters lines on the cyclic vicissitudes of life (the mention of the deer in the fourth stanza effectively evokes the opening of the play, as we prepare for the phase of love-in-separation in the total love cycle). It is worth mentioning, in this respect, that the play as a whole moves from the summer of act 1 to the spring of acts 6 and 7—the curse and its effects thus suggesting the falling away and (relatively, in India) barren repose of winter. The rest of the act is concerned with the celebration of Śakuntalā's rite of passage from protected girlhood into the world of a wife's duties. Kaṇva, thanks to a divine voice, has learned of and accepted the lovers' union as a legitimate marriage, and he imparts his blessing upon her as she takes her leave. It is a very sentimental scene—father and daughter both tearful, and the virginal forest itself waving farewell—acclaimed in the received judgment of pandits as the very height of *kāvya*.

The prologue to act 5 contains the déjà vu scene, in which a chance song by one of his queens alerts Duḥṣanta to the immanent presence of some great happiness that eludes consciousness. After this Śakuntalā's entourage is announced, and we have enacted for us a painfully ironic scenario in which the king cannot remember having seen before the pregnant woman now being presented to him as his wife. Śakuntalā, unfortunately, has dropped her ring into a river they had forded on the way to the capital and is powerless to awaken him (she herself, like him, is still ignorant of the curse). Angry words are exchanged all around. Śakuntalā accuses him of being a hypocrite, he accuses her of being a wily woman wishing to entrap him into touching another man's wife, and the two escorting ascetics (Śārṅgarava and Śāradvata) are scornful of both of them. Rejected by the king, Śakuntalā turns to the ascetics for consolation but is rebuffed as a sinner who has forfeited her foster father's care. It is clear that these ascetics extend symbolically the austere wrath of Durvāsas rather than the benignity of Kaṇva, whom they ostensibly represent. At this moment Śakuntalā's divine mother appears in a flash of light and swoops her daughter away. We learn in the next act that she has taken her to another hermitage, presided over by the mystical sage figure Mārīca (a Prajāpati, or World Creator). The king retires in bewilderment.

In act 6 comes the awakening to sorrow and confused remorse. The ring is discovered in the belly of a fish and brought to the king, who in his grief puts a ban upon the celebration of the spring festival to the god of love (thus acting out the part of Śiva as destroyer of desire). With his companion the Vidūṣaka he gives repeated expression to his love anguish, enough to convince an eavesdropper—the celestial nymph Miśrakeśī, who has been sent to check on him by Śakuntalā's mother—that his love is genuine. The full force of his subliminal "argument" comes with his vain attempt to recapture the happiness of his encounter with Śakuntalā in Kaṇva's *āśrama* via the medium of a painting: his tragic sorrow leaves the nymph no room for doubting his sincerity. Also notable in this act is a new emphasis on the dharmic theme. Just after the painting sequence, news comes to him that a rich merchant has died with no heir. Finding out that the merchant's wife is pregnant with what promises to be a male child, the king vows to preserve the inheritance and declares himself the protective kinsman of all his subjects. But the event has also reminded him of his own loss of a son, for it is beyond doubt that Śakuntalā must have been pregnant with the male heir none of his hundred or so other wives has been able to give him. He swoons in embarrassment and shame before the imagined specters of his male ancestors, who face the extinction of the prescribed family rites. But shortly an alarm is raised offstage. The Vidūṣaka (who had earlier gone off with the painting to protect it from a jealous wife) is being attacked by a demon who mocks aloud Duḥṣanta's power and authority. This is enough to rouse the king's anger, at which point the demon reveals himself as an emissary from Indra, who needs him as his general in cosmic warfare with demons. The emissary, Mātali, knew of no other way to rouse him to an eagerness to perform his duty.

In act 7, the battle over, Mātali touches down with the king, savoring the accolades of Indra and the other celestials, in the marvelous hermitage of Mārīca, high on a mythical mountain peak. There in a cleverly milked recognition scene the hero discovers first his lost son and then Śakuntalā herself. The lovers' reencounter is somewhat subdued. The mood that prevails now is one of wonder rather than love, wonder whose focus in the figure of the great sage Mārīca himself. It is he who blesses the united family standing before him, assigning them allegorical, sacrificial identities, and reveals the secret of the curse. Only now do the king and Śakuntalā understand what has befallen them. The play ends with the conventional auspicious prayer for the play's success to radiate out into the world in the form of general prosperity and happiness.

NOTES

ABh	*Abhinavahbāratī* of Abhinavagupta
AEAG	R. Gnoli, *The Aesthetic Experience According to Abhinavagupta*
AG	Abhinavagupta
AO	*Acta Orientalia* (Hungary)
ĀV	Ānandavardhana
BAU	*Bṛhadāraṇyaka Upaniṣad*
BhN	Bhaṭṭa Nāyaka
BORI	Bhandarkar Oriental Research Institute
BOS	Bhandarkar Oriental Series
BS	*Brahmasūtra* (*Vedāntasūtra*) of Bādarāyaṇa
ChU	*Chāndogya Upaniṣad*
CSS	Chowkhamba Sanskrit Studies
DhĀ	*Dhvanyāloka* of Ānandavardhana
DhĀL	*Dhvanyālokalocana* of Abhinavagupta
DR	*Daśarūpaka* of Dhanaṃjaya
HSP	S. K. De, *History of Sanskrit Poetics*
IA	K. C. Pandey, *Indian Aesthetics*
IPVV	*Īśvarapratijñāvivṛtivimarśinī* of Abhinavagupta
JAOS	*Journal of the American Oriental Society*
JIP	*Journal of Indian Philosophy*
JRAS	*Journal of the Royal Asiatic Society*
JSAL	*Journal of South Asian Literature*
KP	*Kāvyaprakāśa* of Mammaṭa
KSS	Kashi Sanskrit Series
KSTS	Kashmir Series of Texts and Studies
MuU	*Muṇḍaka Upanisad*

NŚ	*Nāṭyaśāstra*
PEW	*Philosophy East and West*
PICI	Publications de l'Institut de Civilisation Indienne
PTV	*Parātriṃśikāvivaraṇa* of Abhinavagupta
PY	*Pratijñayangandharāyaṇa* of Bhāsa
Ś	*Śakuntalā* of Kālidāsa
ŚBh	*Śrī-Bhāṣya* of Rāmānuja (comm. on *Brahmasūtra*)
SBE	Sacred Books of the East
SD	*Sāhityadarpaṇa* of Viśvanātha
SOR	Serie Orientale Roma
ŚR	J. L. Masson and M. V. Patwardhan, *Śāntarasa*
TĀ	*Tantrāloka* of Abhinavagupta

1. Cf. the pandits' dictum given to Sir William Jones two centuries ago and reported in his preface to the first translation of *Śakuntalā*:

> *kāvyeṣu nāṭakaṃ ramyaṃ tatra ramyā śakuntalā /*
> *tatrāpi ca caturtho'ṅkas tatra ślokacatuṣṭayam /*
> *yāsyaty adyeti tatrāpi padyaṃ ramyatamaṃ matam //*

> Of *kāvya* drama is the most attractive form, and *Śakuntalā* the most attractive drama. In it the 4th Act, in that a group of four verses, and of those the most attractive verse is "She will depart today . . ." (4.8[5])

My version cited from Edwin Gerow ("Plot Structure and the Development of *Rasa* in the Śakuntalā," parts 1 and 2, JAOS 99, no. 4 [1979]: 559–72; 100, no.3 [1980]: 267–82), 564. I agree with Gerow that "such traditional verses exaggerate a point that nevertheless deserves our attention: in discussing the Śakuntalā as drama, we are also at the center of the Indian poetic problem. By the judgment of the tradition itself, the Śakuntalā is the validating aesthetic creation of a civilization" (*ibid.*). A word about my numbering of the *Śakuntalā* verses. The first numbers cited are those found in the Bengali recension, while those that follow in parentheses or square brackets are according to the Devanagari recension, if different. An asterisk means that the passage is not in the Devanagari. A "plus" sign indicates prose (often commentary) following verse. The editions I use are (Bengali) *Kālidāsa's Śakuntalā,* 2nd ed., ed. Richard Pischel, Harvard Oriental Series 16 (Cambridge Mass., 1922); (related Maithili) *Abhijñāna-Śakuntalam of Kālidāsa,* with commentaries of Śaṅkara and Narahari, ed. Ramanath Jha (Darbhanga: Mithila Institute of Post-Graduate Studies and Research in Sanskrit Learning, 1957); (Devanagari) *The Abhijñāna-Śākuntala of Kālidāsa*, with commentary of Rāghavabhaṭṭa, ed. N. B. Godabole, 5th rev. ed. by W. L. Shastri Fanasikar (Bombay: Nirnaya Sagar, 1909). Michael Coulson translates the Bengali recension in *Three Sanskrit Plays* (Harmondsworth, Eng.: Penguin, 1981), as does Chandra Rajan in *Kālidāsa: The Loom of Time* (Harmondsworth, Eng.: Penguin, 1990). Barbara Stoler Miller translates the Devanagari in *Theater of Memory* (New York: Columbia University Press, 1984).

2. A word of methodological explanation. What validity can there be in treating the *Śakuntalā* in the light of aesthetic ideas developed at least four hundred years later? The basic answer is: heuristic. If Kashmiri aesthetics is irrelevant to actual aesthetic creations we will only find out by using it in practice. But, in fact, I think that the *līlā* aesthetic I outline in the second section is implicit in *kāvya* from the start, and that Ānandavardhana, Abhinavagupta, Mammaṭa, and others who glorify poetic *pratibhā* are only translating *kāvya*'s impulse toward emotional transcendence, both thematically within the poem and as the audience's *rasa* response, into mythic or metaphysical language. *Rasa* delight easily lent itself to comparisons with *mokṣa* because it was felt from the start with an intensity that suggested a transcendence of ordinary emotional experience. The emotional release portrayed in and felt in response to *kāvya* resonated with utopian implications.

3. Alexis Sanderson, who has generously commented on this essay, has noted that Kashmir Vaiṣṇava nondualism is more pertinent to Kashmiri aesthetics than Rāmānuja's *viśiṣṭādvaita*. I include Rāmānuja primarily as a check on Śaṅkara, whose version of Vedānta was and still is unduly generalized, to show that even within the sober Vedāntic tradition there is an ''aesthetic'' understanding of play. The relation of both to Indian aesthetics is quite indirect, despite S. K. De and others who have read Śaṅkara into AG's theory. In this paper they serve as foils, and to underline the Upaniṣadic roots of the play idea.

4. *lokavat tu līlākaivalyam.* ''Play only, as in the world.''

5. As in Śbh 2.1.15.

6. ŚBh 4.14. (For the notion of *satyasaṃkalpa* see ChU 3.14.2, 8.1.4–6.) The principal Rāmānuja texts on *līlā* are his commentaries on BS 1.4.27, 2.1.15, 2.1.33, 3.2.12, and 4.4.13–14. These are discussed by Bettina Bäumer, Schöpfung als Spiel: Der Begriff līlā im Hinduismus, seine philosophische und theologische Deutung, Ph.D. diss., München, 1969, as are all the Upaniṣadic passages and much more. See also Olivier Lacombe, *L'Absolu selon le Vedānta,* Annales du Musée Guimet 49 (Paris, 1937); and George Thibaut's translations of the BS with Śaṅkara's and Rāmānuja's commentaries (*Vedānta-Sūtras,* SBE 34, 38, 48 [Oxford, 1904], reprinted several times since 1962 by Motilal Banarsidass).

7. ChU 7.25.2. To save space I shall keep from citing long passages in Sanskrit but will indicate key terms in parentheses or in notes. There is an echo of this passage in MuU 3.1.4. See Bäumer, pp. 13–23, for all Upaniṣadic passages.

8. ChU 8.12.1–3 (translation Hume: R. E. Hume, *The Thirteen Principal Upanishads,* 2nd rev. ed. [London: Oxford, 1931; reprint, 1979], p. 272). Of the numerous passages one could compare, the most important are ChU 8.1.4–6; BAU 2.1.17–20; 4.3.7–38; 4.4.22; 4.5.15. On the whole the *mokṣa* doctrine of BAU 4.3–5 supports a Śaṅkaran *advaita* interpretation relegating the *līlāvāda* of ChU to the level of figurative meaning. See also Śaṅkara's treatment of BS 4.4.8ff. as teaching only the ''lower knowledge'' (*aparā vidyā*).

9. In Vibration Doctrine (*spandavāda*), adopted by AG in his Trika synthesis of

the monistic strains of Tantra, self-knowledge is an orgasmic ecstasy. The *ābhāsa* world is mediated by the feminine *śakti,* and Śiva's relation to it calls to mind the iconographic representation of the Androgyne Śiva (*ardhanārīśvara*), in which orgasmic self-awareness is internal and constant. This experience is ritually reduplicated in the *kulayāga,* in which the initiate achieves gnosis through sexual intercourse amid wine, meat, incense, flowers, etc. See *Vijñānabhairava* 69–75 (*Le Vijñāna Bhairava,* ed. and trans. Lilian Silburn, PICI 15 [Paris: Brocard, 1961], pp. 111–16); AG, *Tantrāloka* 29.115–16 (and throughout chap. 29); AG, *Parātriṃśikā-* or *Parātrīśikāvivaraṇa* (KSTS ed.), pp. 46–51 (found in R. Gnoli, ed., *Il Commento di Abhinavagupta alle Parātriṃśikā* (*Parātriṃśikātattvavivaraṇam*), SOR 58 [Roma: Instituto Italiano per il Medio ed Estremo Oriente, 1985], pp. 201–3; Italian trans. pp. 45–50). See also L. Silburn, *Kuṇḍalinī: Energy of the Depths,* trans. Jacques Gontier (Albany: State University of New York Press, 1988; French ed., 1983), pp. 177–205; L. Silburn, ed., *La Mahārthamañjarī de Maheśvarānanda,* PICI 29 (Paris: Brocard, 1968), pp. 54ff.; K. C. Pandey, *Abhinavagupta: An Historical and Philosophical Study,* 2nd ed. (Varanasi: Chowkhamba, 1963), pp. 542–732. For the general subject of *spandavāda,* see Mark S. G. Dyczkowski, *The Doctrine of Vibration* (Albany: State University of New York Press, 1987), which among other things is an invaluable bibliographic guide. The most concentrated treatment of Trika's orgasmicism can be found in Alexis Sanderson, "Trika Śaivism," in M. Eliade et al., eds., *The Encyclopedia of Religion* (New York: Macmillan, 1987), 13:15–16. See also Sanderson, "Purity and Power Among the Brahmans of Kashmir," in M. Carrithers et al., eds., *The Category of the Person* (Cambridge University Press, 1985), pp. 190–216, esp. pp. 203–6.

10. Kṣemarāja, *Śivasūtravimarśinī,* ed. J. C. Chatterjee, KSTS 1 (Srinagar, 1911). It is important to cite the Sanskrit here (*sūtra*s marked off by double lines beginning paragraphs).

> *nartaka ātmā// nṛtyati, antarnigūhitasvasvarūpāvaṣṭambhamūlaṃ tattajjāgarādinānābhūmikāprapañcaṃ svaparispandalīlayaiva svabhittau prakaṭayatīti nartaka ātmā/ . . . bhaṭṭanārāyaṇenāpi* [*tad uktam*]—
>
> *visṛṣṭaśeṣasadbījagarbhaṃ trailokyanāṭakam/*
> *prastāvya hara samhartuṃ tvattaḥ ko'nyaḥ kaviḥ kṣamaḥ// . . .*
>
> *raṅgo'ntarātmā// rajyate'smin jagannāṭyakrīḍāpradarśanāśrayenātmanā iti raṅgaḥ. . . . tatra hi* [i.e., *dehāpekṣayā antare jīve*] *ayaṃ kṛtapadaḥ svakaraṇaparispandakrameṇa jagannāṭyam ābhāsayati/ . . . prekṣakānīndriyāṇi// yoginaś cakṣurādīni indriyāṇi hi saṃsāranāṭyaprakaṭanapramodanirbharaṃ svasvarūpam antarmukhatayā sākṣāt kurvanti, tatprayogaprarūḍhyā vigalitavibhāgaṃ camatkārarasasampūrṇatām āpādayanti/*

11. See the essay by Bettina Bäumer in this volume.

12. In *spandavāda* knowledge is essentially feeling. Thus we can understand AG's compression of Bhaṭṭa Nāyaka's *bhāvaka* and *bhojaka* functions of language: perception and enjoyment merge when self-consciousness is *camatkāra.* Cf. Raniero Gnoli, AEAG, 2nd rev. ed. (Varanasi: Chowkhamba, 1968), pp. 10–11.

13. I am speaking here of consciousness of self in the objective genitive sense. Śaṅkara's Ātman cannot even be aware of itself: it is pure, objectless awareness.

14. The difference is one of degree. Aesthetic experience is *tatkālika*, that is, temporally limited to the duration of aesthetic stimuli (AEAG, p. 20). Nor does it completely eliminate the *saṃskāras* (traces of desire and action) that bind us to the karmic world. The locus classicus is IPVV, vol. 2 (KSTS 62), pp. 178–79, which is extracted in full by K. C. Pandey, *Indian Aesthetics,* 2nd ed. (Varanasi: Chowkhamba, 1959), pp. 631–32, and in part by J. C. Masson and M. V. Patwardhan, *Śāntarasa and Abhinavagupta's Philosophy of Aesthetics,* BOS 9 (Poona: BORI, 1969), p. 44. For translations see the latter, pp. 44–45, and Gnoli, AEAG, pp. xlii–xlv. I cite the final sentences in Gnoli's translation: "The so-called supreme bliss [*paramānanda,* i.e., mystical experience], the lysis [*nirvṛti*], the wonder [*camatkāra*], is therefore nothing but a tasting, that is, a cogitation, in all its compact density, of our own liberty. This liberty is *realissima* (that is to say, not metaphorical [*anupacaritasya*]) and inseparable from the very nature of consciousness. We must not, however, forget, that in the tasting of a juice of sweet flavor, etc., there is between this bliss and us the separating screen [*vyavadhāna*], so to say, of the exterior reality. In poetry, in drama, and so on, this screen is actually missing [since the aesthetic world is virtual or irreal], but it remains in a latent state. Also in these forms of limited bliss, however, those people whose hearts are carefully devoted to cancel out the part which performs the function of a screen, succeed in reaching the supreme bliss. 'Supreme bliss,' it has been said, 'may even take place disclosed by drinking and eating.'" "Those whose hearts," and so forth, are the so-called *yogins* of the Tantra tradition, who cultivate the savoring of mystical bliss in complete *tanmayībhāva* with the world appearance, that is, complete identification with Śiva consciousness itself, since the world is, as certain Buddhists say, "mind only" (*vijñaptimātra*) (cf. AEAG, p. xxiv). Cf. the Bhaṭṭa Nāyaka verse by which the *sahṛdaya* achieves bliss watching the cosmic drama created by Śiva, cited in Masson and Patwardhan, ŚR, p. 23. Gerald J. Larson, "The Aesthetic (*rasāsvāda*) and the Religious (*brahmāsvāda*) in Abhinavagupta's Kashmir Saivism," PEW 26 no. 4 (1976): 371–87, makes useful distinctions, but the crux of the matter is on p. 382, where Larson puzzles over the identity of *vikalpa* and *nirvikalpa* experience on the ultimate level (I thank my colleague Donna M. Wulff for this reference—see her "Religion in a New Mode: The Convergence of the Aesthetic and the Religious in Medieval India," *Journal of the Academy of Religion* 54 no. 4 [1988]: 673–88).

15. Utpaladeva, *Śivastotrāvalī* 20.12:

> *duḥkhānyapi sukhāyante viṣam apyamṛtāyate/*
> *mokṣāyate ca saṃsāro yatra mārgaḥ sa śāṅkaraḥ//*
>
> Pains become pleasures, poison turns to nectar,
> the world becomes deliverance: this is Śiva's path.

This conversion of pain into pleasure is one of the central elements of *rasa* theory, which must take into account how the aesthetic subject can experience delight in the representation of sorrow. Cf. BhN in AEAG, p. 10; DhĀ 1.5 (with *Locana*); Viśvanātha, SD 3.6–7 (for more see S. K. De, *History of Sanskrit Poetics*, 2nd ed. [Calcutta: Firma KLM, 1960], 2:132).

16. Cf., for example, AG's *viśrānti* in AEAG, p. 15, with the reference to *spanda* on the preceding page. The notion that *rasāsvāda* is a repose of consciousness free of

obstacles, that is, generalized (*sādhāraṇīkṛta*), is found earlier in Bhaṭṭa Nāyaka (AEAG, p. 10). For a discussion of the philosophical idea see AEAG, pp. xxxvi–vii.

17. Cf. the interesting observation of Lacombe, *L'Absolu,* p. 253: "Il y a comme une ascèse souriante et suave, une incantation salvatrice en ce thème du jeu magique du Seigneur." He is speaking about Śaṅkara's doctrine here, but it applies to all monistic *līlāvāda*.

18. The case is not much better in Rāmānuja's system: the world as such is a charming playground, but no more. The only true affective relationship is between Īśvara and the *jīva*s who are never fully absorbed in him. One can love God but not man or woman.

19. DR 4.41cd–42ab:

> *krīḍatāṃ mṛnmayair yadvad bālānāṃ dviradādibhiḥ/*
> *svotsāhaḥ svādate tadvac chrotṛṇām arjunādibhiḥ//*

20. BhN flourished ca. 900 A.D. in Kashmir. To be more accurate, it is Dhanika, Dhanaṃjaya's contemporary commentator (and brother, it seems), who uses BhN's *bhāvakatva* terminology. Cf. George C. O. Haas, ed. and trans., *The Daśarūpa: A Treatise on Hindu Dramaturgy by Dhanaṃjaya* (New York: Columbia University Press, 1912; reprint, New York: AMS Press, 1965), introduction, pp. xxi–xlv. Dhanaṃjaya and Dhanika (living in Malwa) were contemporaries of AG and seem not to have been aware of his work.

21. This doctrine is more typically associated with AG, who developed it in great detail after receiving it from BhN, doubtless through his own teacher Bhaṭṭa Tauta. BhN's only known work—*Hṛdaya-* or *Sahṛdayadarpaṇa*—has not survived. See AEAG, pp. 10–11, for a summary of BhN's position. For AG's own classical formulations, see idem, pp. 13–15, 20–23.

22. *Rasika* ('person of taste', 'savorer of *rasa*') is the term used in the DR and by many later writers (e.g., Bhoja), while *sahṛdaya* ('person of heart', 'sympathetic listener') is favored by the Kashmiri poeticians, such as AV, BhN, and AG.

23. KP 1.1:

> *niyatikṛtaniyamarahitāṃ hlādaikamayīm ananyaparatantrām/*
> *navarasarucirāṃ nirmitim ādadhatī bhāratī kaver jayati//*

AG too uses this trope in ABh 1.1: "The poet is like Prajāpati from whose desire (*kāma*) the world is produced. He possesses the power (*śakti*) of creating the marvelous and unprecedented, a power which arises through the favor of the goddess Parā Vāc (Supreme Speech), termed *pratibhā,* and remains always in the expanse of his own heart" (*kaver api svahṛdayāyatanasatatoditapratibhābhidhānaparavāgdevatānugrahotthitavicitrāpūrvārthanirmāṇaśaktiśālinaḥ prajāpater iva kāmajanitajagataḥ*).

24. Here and in the *vṛtti* on 1.2 (cited later) my translation sometimes echoes that of Ganganatha Jha, ed. and trans., *The Kāvyaprakāśa of Mammaṭa* (Varanasi: Bharatiya Vidya, 1967):

> *niyatiśaktyā niyatarūpā sukhaduḥkhamohasvabhāvā paramāṇvākyupadānakarmādisahakārikakāraṇaparatantrā ṣaḍrasā na ca hṛdyaiva taiḥ, tādṛśī brahmaṇo nirmitir nimāṇam/ etadvilakṣaṇā tu kavivāṅnirmitiḥ/ ata eva jayati/*

25. DhĀ 3.42+:

> *apāre kāvyasaṃsāre kavir eka prajāpatiḥ/*
> *yathāsmai rocate viśvaṃ tathedaṃ parivartate//*
> *śṛṅgārī cet kaviḥ kāvye jātaṃ rasamayaṃ jagat/*
> *sa eva vītarāgaś cen nīrasaṃ sarvam eva tat//*

It is difficult to know to what extent AV was relying on Tantric conceptions of *pratibhā*. Vasugupta, author (ostensibly the discoverer) of the *Śivasūtra,* is earlier by some decades (early to mid-9th cen. A.D.), so there is no chronological difficulty in assuming his familiarity with Śaiva "poetic" cosmogony. *Pratibhā* itself (or its synonym *śakti*) as the principal cause of poetic creation goes back to Bhāmaha and Daṇḍin and probably earlier, and in the latter, at least with regard to Speech (Vāc), we have a cosmogonic dimension. The seminal source is Bhartṛhari's sublimation of *vāc* and *pratibhā*. The relation between them is problematic; See Elizabeth Christie, "Indian Philosophers on Poetic Imagination (*Pratibhā*)," *JIP* 7 (1979): 164ff., on cosmogonic principles, an idea already developed in the late *Ṛgveda* for Vāc. For passages on *pratibhā*, see ŚR, pp. 17–20; Christie, "Indian Philosophers"; and K. Krishnamoorthy, "The Sanskrit Conception of a Poet," in *Essays in Sanskrit Literary Criticism,* ed. Krishnamoorthy (Dharwar: Karnatak University, 1974), pp. 167–86. I have not seen Gopinath Kaviraj, "The Doctrine of *Pratibhā,*" in *Aspects of Indian Thought* (Burdwan, 1966).

26. As the poet is himself a *rasika*, so the *rasika*'s imaginative capacity makes him a virtual poet. Cf. Rājaśekhara's elevation of the *rasika*'s role to that of creative *pratibhā* (*bhāvayitrī* as distinct from the poet's *kārayitrī*) in *Kāvyamīmāṃsā* 4. Also AG citation of his teacher Bhaṭṭa Tauta in DhĀl 1.6+: "The hero (of a poem or drama), the poet, and the listener all have the same experience" (*nāyakasya kaveḥ śrotuḥ sāmāno 'nubhavas tataḥ*). In plain terms we may say that the poet articulates the vision of the community of taste in which he functions, as is the case generally in conventional poetry.

27. KP 1.2:

> *kāvyaṃ yaśase 'rthakṛte vyavahāravide śivetarakṣataye/*
> *sadyaḥ parinirvṛtaye kāntāsammitatayopadeśayuje//*

> *sakalaprayojanamaulībhūtaṃ samanantaram eva rasāsvādanasamudbhūtaṃ vigalitavedyāntaram ānandaṃ prabhusammitaśabdapradhānavedādiśāstrebhyaḥ suhṛtsammitārthatātparyavatpurāṇāditihāsebhyaś ca śabdārthayor guṇabhāvena rasāṅgabhūtavyāpārapravaṇatayā vilakṣaṇaṃ yat kāvyaṃ lokottaravarṇanānipuṇakavikarma tat kānteva sarasatāpādanenābhimukhīkṛtya rāmādivad vartitavyaṃ na rāvaṇādivad ity upadeśaṃ ca yathāyogaṃ kaveḥ sahṛdayasya karoti. . . ./*

Mammaṭa appears to be following AG (DhAL 1.1 toward end), where the same analogies are made:

> But pleasure (*prīti*) or bliss (*ānanda*) is the chief thing. For this is what makes poetry, which provides instruction (*vyutpatti*) as if coming from a woman, differ-

ent from the Vedas, etc., which provide it as if coming from a master, and from epic, etc., which provides it as if coming from a friend. For bliss is far and away the principal reward of poetry, more so even that instruction in the four ends of life.

tathāpi tatra prītir eva pradhānam/ anyathā prabhusammitebhyo vedādibhyo mitrasammitebhyaś cetibāsādibhyo vyutpattihetubhyaḥ ko' sya kāvyarūpasya vyutpattihetor jāyāsammitatvalakṣaṇo viśeṣa iti prādhānyenānanda evoktaḥ/ caturvargeṣvutpatter api cānanda eva paryantikaṃ mukhyaṃ phalam/

See also DhĀl 2.4, where he cites BhN to the same effect. The same image is present also in Ānandavardhana, who compares *dhvani* ('suggestion''), the soul of poetry (*kāvyātmā*, DhĀ 1.1–5), to the 'charm of beartiful women' (1.4 and commentary) and later (4.7+) quotes from one of his own poetic works to the same effect:

No limit is set for them, nor are they ever repeated:
the charms of beautiful women and the meaning of poetical expressions.

na ca teṣāṃ ghatate 'vadhir na ca te dṛśyantekatham api punaruktāḥ/
ye vibramāḥ priyāṇām arthā vā sukavivāṇīnām//

(Sanskritized from the Prakrit.)

28. Cf. the Derridean principle of the materiality of the signifier.

29. It seems to have been BhN who codified the three facets of aesthetic response as melting, expansion, and sudden sprouting (*drutivistāravikāsātmanā . . . bhogena*: AEAG, p. 10), but thereafter it is general. For *aṅkurībhāva*, see next quote and the passage of DhĀL cited by J. L. Masson and M. V. Patwardhan, *Aesthetic Rapture* (Poona: Deccan College Postgraduate and Research Institute, 1970), 2:37–38.

30. *Rasa* is often a word for love itself qua delicious feeling. It is no accident that the handbooks' treatment of *śṛṅgāra rasa* is always the longest and most detailed: how could it be otherwise given the overwhelming importance—and ubiquitous presence—of the erotic theme in *kāvya*? It is doubtful that the *rasa* aesthetic could have evolved in any other circumstances, since it is only when a fictional subject—a necessary feature of *rasa* theory—is in love that we get the slow, nuanced buildup of emotion with full attention to landscape, and so forth (the *vibhāvādi*) that the theory demands for all *rasāsvāda*.

31. The "etc." here refers to the full complex of aesthetic presentation demanded by *rasa* theory. The woman herself is an *ālambana vibhāva*, or "basic cause" of an emotional response in a fictional character. Various elements of landscape, and so forth, such as sweet breezes, flowering vegetation, and her jewelery, are "excitatory causes" (*uddīpana vibhāva*). Certain effects such as horripilation or sighing show themselves in the hero gazing at her (called *anubhāva*). And finally subsidiary emotional states (*saṃcāri-* or *vyabhicāribhāva*), such as joy or contentment, accompany the hero's basic emotional response, namely, love (*rati*). For the reader–spectator the whole complex taken together transmutes *rati* into *śṛṅgāra rasa* (the erotic sentiment). In practice, however, it is not so easy to distinguish fictional and actual subjects. The erotic hero of drama, such as King Duḥṣanta of *Śakuntalā* (acts 1–3), is in fact a savorer of his own emotional state. Abhinava usually avoids the question of the status of

characters within a play or poem, regarding them as mere vehicles of emotional response for the *rasika* spectator, though in at least one place (AEAG pp. 89–90, 96–98) he speaks of identification in the sense in which we use the term today. Ordinarily, as in the passage being cited here, *tanmayībhāva* for him refers to the *rasika*'s absorption in the fictional object (here the woman being apprehended by the hero) not the fictional subject (the hero himself).

32. AEAG, p. 21:

> *tenālaukikacamatkārātmā rasāsvādaḥ smṛtyanumānalaukikasvasaṃvedanavilakṣaṇa eva/ tathā hi laukikenānumānena saṃskṛtaḥ pramadādi na tāṭasthyena pratipadyate, api tu hṛdayasaṃvādātmakasahṛdayatvabalāt pūrṇibhavisyadrasāsvādāṅkurībhāvenanumānasmṛtyādisopānam anāruhyaiva tanmayībhāvocitacarvaṇāprāṇatayā/*

For the germinating sensation as typical of *śṛṅgāra*, see DR 4.44

33. This passage contrasts with another famous example of aesthetic experience. In that passage (AEAG, p. 13) the aesthetic object (the deer pursued by Duḥṣanta in Ś 1. 7) and the emotion (fear) that becomes universalized as the fearful sentiment (*bhayānaka rasa*) are in the same locus, and there is no fictional character with whose gaze we are identified, save the king, who speaks the verse but whose emotional response is one of detached wonder rather than sympathetic fear. (One could argue on this basis that the true *rasa* here is *adbhuta* rather than *bhayānaka*. This is one of many problematic areas of AG's thought that await careful exploration.) In the present case our response is felt through a fictive subject who is himself a *rasika*, that is, whose emotion is aroused by what is for him simultaneously an aesthetic and an erotic object. Thus *tanmayībhāva* has to be understood in a very different sense in the two cases. There is no way that the deer can stand as a symbol of poetry the way the beautiful woman can.

34. No truly critical analysis of Abhinavagupta's aesthetic theory has yet been made. Gnoli, Masson and Patwardhan, and Pandey (so far our best guides) are exegetes who avoid troubling theoretical inconsistencies (which seem to center on the issue of identification) in order to present an overall picture. Since this was written, Daniel H. H. Ingalls has made thoughtful comments on a number of passages in the DhAl. I would not, however, say that the basic *problems* of AG's aesthetics have been examined. *The Dhvanyāloka of Ānandavandhana with the Locana of Abhinavagupta*, trans. Daniel H. H. Ingalls, Jeffrey Moosaieff Masson, and M. V. Patwardhan (Cambridge, Mass.: Harvard University Press, 1990).

35. DhĀl 1.1 (toward end): "The *sahṛdaya* is one who participates in a 'concordance of heart,' that is, one who has a capacity for identification with what is described (in poem or play), an identification which takes place in a mirrorlike mind made clear by familiarity with and practice of poetry" (*yeṣāṃ kāvyānuśīlanābhyāsavaśād viṣadībhūte manomukure varnaṇīyatanmayībhavanayogyatā te svahṛdayasaṃvādabhājaḥ sahṛdayāḥ*). We should note that although *tanmayībhāva* seems to have come into prominence as a theoretical concept only with AG (or BhN, judging from the title of his lost work: *The Mirror of the Heart* [*Hṛdayadarpana*]), it was already being used by Kālidāsa as a technical term in the fourth or fifth century, A.D.: see *Mālavikāgnimitra*

2.8 (*tanmayatvaṃ raseṣu*). For *tanmayībhāva* in the metaphysical context see TĀ 4.207–9, 3.240 (mistranslated by Masson and Patwardhan, ŚR, p. 49), and 28.373ff., comparing the use of "mirror" and "heart" with the definition just quoted. In PTV, in a passage describing the yogi's susceptibility to mystical *camatkāra,* AG give us another definiton of *sahṛdaya*:

> Those who are not nourished by this force (*vīrya*), who do not experience the intoxicating bliss that consists of the arousal of such force, are like stones, and for them neither the sight of a beautiful women nor the sound of the song that comes from her mouth results in complete bliss. *Camatkāra* is limited according to the degree of (presence or) absence of that which nourishes it (i.e., *vīrya*). The complete absence of *camatkāra* indicates an insensate state, whereas a high degree of immersion/absorption (*āveśa*) in *camatkāra*—which is nothing but the arousal of *vīrya*—is termed the state of sensibility (*sahṛdayatā*, i.e. being a *sahṛdaya*). The person whose heart is nourished by the infinite nourishing force (*vīrya*) and given over to (*niveśita*) constant practice in such enjoyments, such a person possesses *camatkriyā* in the highest degree. (KSTS ed., pp. 46–48 [= Gnoli, PTV, p. 202])

It is impossible to maintain there is no *intrinsic* connection in AG's thought between the three domains of aesthetic, erotic, and mystical experience.

36. Barbara Stoler Miller ("Kālidāsa's World and His Plays," in B.S. Miller, ed., *Theater of Memory,* [New York: Columbia University Press, 1984], pp. 27–31) is certainly right to identify the heroine of drama in some sense with Vāc–Sarasvatī, the goddess of poetry, as well as with Śrī. ĀV's final verse in DhĀ identifies the sweet instructress as Sarasvatī, though he says nothing about the kāvyic heroine as such. Maria Christopher Byrski (*Concept of an Ancient Indian Theatre* [Delhi: Munshiram Manoharlal, 1974], pp. 76–90) also sees the heroine of drama as Vāc, for entirely different reasons. F. B. J. Kuiper (*Varuṇa and Vidūṣaka: On the Origins of Sanskrit Drama* [Amsterdam: North Holland, 1979], pp. 236–41) sees her as both Vāc–Sasrasvatī and Śrī from a cosmological–ritual point of view.

37. PY 3.5+: "He has now imagined his cell as a pleasure garden and is all ready for the royal sport of love" (*bandhanam idānīṃ pramadavanaṃ sambhāvya pravṛtto rāga-*[or *rāja-*]*līlāṃ kartum*). The Prakrit *rāalīlaṃ* admits both *rāja* and *raga*, and it seems restrictive to adopt one at the other's expense. A modern version of Udayana can be found in Stendhal's Fabrizio del Dongo (*The Charterhouse of Parma*).

38. Cf. the organic imagery of DhĀ 4.4: "Inclusion of *rasa* makes the trite subjects of poetry seem new as trees in Spring."

dṛṣṭapūrvā api hy arthāḥ kāvye rasaparigrahāt/
sarve navā ivābhānti madhumāsa iva drumāḥ//

39. Cf. *Mālavikāgnimitra* 3.4–5, where mention of Śrī as goddess of spring leads directly to the epiphany of Mālavikā, whose role is the Śrī-like one of inducing an *aśoka* tree to flower.

40. I. Scheftelowitz, *Die Apokryphen des Ṛgveda* (1906; reprint, Hildesheim:

Georg Olms, 1966) p. 3, dates most of the *khilas* (including the *śrīsūkta*, or Hymn to Śrī, 72ff.) to the Yajurvedic period (ca. 800 B.C.). In general, see Gerda Hartmann, Beiträge sur Geschichte der Göttin Lakṣmī, Ph.D. diss., Kiel, 1932, pp. 1–16. Alf Hiltebeitel, *The Ritual of Battle* (Ithaca, N.Y.: Cornell University Press, 1976), has much to say about Śrī from a Dumezilian structuralist position. For some early Buddhist references, see T. W. Rhys Davids, *Buddhist India* (New York: G. P. Putnam's, 1903), pp. 216–19. See John M. Rosenfield, *The Dynastic Arts of the Kushans* (Berkeley: University of California Press, 1967, for iconographic information (particularly foreign influences); likewise A. S. Altekar, *Catalogue of the Gupta Gold Coins in the Bayana Hoard* (Bombay: Numismatic Society of India, 1954).

41. For example, J. Gonda, *Ancient Indian Kingship from the Religious Point of View* (Leiden: E. J. Brill, 1969), pp. 6–11. His treatment of Śrī (pp. 27, 46, 52, etc.) and the symbolism of wealth (pp. 13–15) is not very imaginative, however.

42. The *mithuna* is not the only religiously auspicious symbol of this type. The bright and sinuous sensuality of Buddhist sculpture at such sites as Sanchi and Amaravati reveals that the *līlā* world of the court in all its aspects itself functioned this way. The paradox of intoxicating sensuous depiction of the charms of embodied life in the context of a religious message that denies its validity is a commonplace of Indian art history.

43. See, for example, Kālidāsa, *Mālavikāgnimitra* 3.15. Thus, too, the ideal of *gāndharva* marriage in *kāvya*, since only this presupposes mutual love.

44. In "*Dākṣiṇya* and *Rasa* in the *Vikramorvaśīya*," JRAS 1988.2, pp. 288–304, and "Aesthetic and Erotic Entrancement in the *Śakuntalā*" AO 42, no. 5 (1988): 473–97, I have argued that we cannot simply think of the *rasika* as a courtier. Sociologically the range is broad among the educated class (extending into bohemian circles and the family library). But even beyond this the *rasika* is a sort of Everyman, representing in a refined sensibility the emotional aspirations of the whole culture, aspirations that existed in considerable tension with another cultural ideal, renunciation.

45. Let it be spelled out that I do not think Kālidāsa intended an allegory on the aesthetic experience, and in any case he was obviously not influenced by later theory (see note 2 in this section).

46. *asau hi rāgapahṛtacittavṛttir ālikhita iva bhāti sarvato raṅgaḥ* (1.4+).

47. Ś 1.5:

tavāsmi gītarāgeṇa hāriṇā prasabhaṃ hṛtaḥ/
esa rājeva duḥṣantaḥ sāraṅgenātiraṃhasā//

The deer is clearly a "white rabbit" figure leading the hero across a magical threshold; cf. the wondrous quality of the three verses that mark the transition (1.7–9).

48. Unfortunately, I lack the space in this format to expand upon the hero's subliminal encounter with ascetic authority. See the note at the end of this section on the Dharmic Father.

49. These are actually the three requirements for being a poet, but they apply just as much to the *rasika*, as argued in the second section of the essay. J. Nobel has assem-

bled numerous passages discussing these so-called *kāvyakāraṇas* (*The Foundations of Indian Poetry* [Calcutta: R. N. Seal, 1925], pp. 43–77).

50. Paul Thieme, "Das indische Theater," in H. Kinderman, ed., *Fernöstlisches Theater* (Stuttgart: A. Kröner, 1966), pp. 26–120, is, to my knowlegde, the only critic to have touched on this (p. 95), though it is probably what many readers feel.

51. As indicated, for example, by 3.27*, where the king soliloquizes a cynical impatience with Śakuntalā's perceived coquetry. Though this is one of those conventional kāvyic verses that emblematizes a typical or universal sentiment, in its immediate dramatic context it shows the king lacking any appreciation of what Śakuntalā has to lose by yielding to him.

52. "Aesthetic and Erotic Entrancement in the *Śakuntalā*"; see earlier notes.

53. The phrase is Sudhir Kakar's; see *The Inner World,* 2nd rev. ed. (Delhi: Oxford, 1981), especially chaps. 3 and 4. Kakar's attention to Indian child-rearing practices and sensitivity to human dilemmas (particularly his treatment of women) make his work far more interesting and complex than other psychoanalytic culture-and-personality studies (e.g., Spratt and Carstairs).

54. It is interesting to see the *Śakuntalā* in this light. Her "bad fate" (alluded to as soon as her name is mentioned in the play, 1.12+) is, in one reading, the ascetic condition from which the hero comes to rescue her. Act 3 invokes the theme of her impending death (through lovesickness), a prospect that sets her friends thinking about how they can engineer an occasion for the two lovers to be alone. We can even see the fight with demons (offstage after acts 2 and 3) as an echo of dragon killing or the like. And, as Northrop Frye suggests for the Andromeda-type myth that he sees informing all such tales (*Anatomy of Criticism* [New York: Atheneum, 1966], chap. 3), the demonic presence is an oedipal substitution for the weakened father (here Kaṇva). The real dragon of this tale, however, is the angry ascetic Durvāsas, who embodies the negative paternal aspect and whom the hero confronts only indirectly in the abortive shouting match with Śarṅgarava and Śāradvata in act 5.

55. That is, the hero becomes the Indian Everyman, inexplicably separated by a veil of ignorance (*mohatamas*) from the radiant nucleus of happiness that represents his true condition.

56. I am referring to Tagore's influential reading of the play as Kālidāsa's indictment of courtly hedonism. The sophisticated sensualist with an arsenal of poetic phrases who takes advantage of a girl's impressionability suffers curse-induced remorse and so arrives at a higher understanding of love. Such a reading, however, altogether ignores the ideality of the encounter in poetic–erotic terms, and it is significant that Tagore never mentions *rasa* in his essay. Nevertheless, it is clear that he has put his finger on something important, though his sentimentalization of Śakuntalā's innocence and the sanctity of Indian motherhood is simplistic. See Rabindranath Tagore, "Sakuntala: Its Inner Meaning," trans. Jadunath Sarkar, in *Sakuntala*, ed. and trans. K. N. Dasgupta and Laurence Binyon (London: Macmillan, 1920), pp. xiii–xxix.

57. In fact, though, it may be that the wife—rarely married for spontaneous love as in poetry—never achieves this position even in fantasy. The magical feminine aura is

retained exclusively by the mother, while the explicitly erotic ideal is lived either fleetingly with courtesans or through poetry or even religion. See Kakar, *Inner World,* chaps. 3 and 4.

58. A former student of mine aptly likened act 4 to Disney's *Bambi*.

59. The king's attempt to recapture the paradisal play world in a painting becomes the play's final symbol of poetry. First there was the actress's song and its thematization in the events of the first three acts. Prominent there was the image of Prajāpati creating Śakuntalā out of his own painting (2.10[9]). Then in the fifth act came Haṃsavatī–Hamsapadikā's song, which stimulated the déjà vu (5.9[2]): art as evocation of a lost world of affection. Finally, in act 6, the attempted reentry of paradise, which proves futile: art as the *rasika*'s appeal for solidarity and pity. Again I refer the reader to my ''Aesthetic and Erotic Entrancement in the *Śakuntalā*'' for a fuller discussion.

60. My ''Dākṣiṇya and *Rasa* in the *Vikramorvaśīya*'' focuses on this issue.

61. The original version of this essay contained another section on the ''Dharmic Father'' and explored further the question of autonomy, so important to notions of *līlā*. The conclusion was that the implicit conflict throughout the play between the worldly *rasika* hero and the ascetic Dharmic Father (cf. the paradox of a garden of love that is simultaneously a penance grove; the ascetic source of the curse; and the angry exchanges of act 5) is decided, in the last act especially, in favor of the latter. This is another indication that the play ideal's pleasure principle is forced to yield to the reality principle (which includes dharmic imperatives). But, more significantly, it indicates that the authorial intelligence of the *rasika* fantasy is not the *rasika* himself. This is an issue I have taken up in regard to Viśākhadatta's *Mudrārākṣasa*, where the ascetic Cāṇakya is an imposing authorial figure: see ''The Divided World of Sanskrit Drama,'' in Peter Baker et al., eds., *The Scope of Words* (New York: Peter Lang, 1991), pp. 229–48.

62. ''*Dākṣiṇya* and *Rasa* in the *Vikramorvaśīya*,'' 303–4.

63. It is essential to see that the *rasa* aesthetic is centered in erotic feeling, as I have argued in the second section. *Kāvya*'s celebration of the Radiant Female and her transformative effects on the *sahṛdaya* is the celebration of *rasa* itself. A neutralist view of *rasa* as extending to all emotions equally simply ignores this thematic focus and therefore the whole subliminal dialectic between *śṛṅgāra* and *karuṇa* that I have traced in the last two section of this paper.

64. In fact, I believe it is the other way around: that the longing for *mokṣa* in the religious sense is derived from the human longing for utopian emotional release.

65. Indian thought, by designating *kāma* as the third *puruṣārtha*, has always recognized that desire is the basis of all pleasure.

6

At the Whim of the Goddess: The *Līlā* of the Goddess in Bengal Śaktism

MALCOLM MCLEAN

I

What fun you have in battle, Śyāmā
(Who is she, this mad Mother, my Mother Kālī?)
The braid of her hair falls loose, like a black snake,
This madwoman my Mother, with streaming hair and sword in hand.
She cuts off the heads of other people's sons
And wears them as a garland round her neck.
The Naked One with matted hair lies prostrate beneath her feet.[1]

Who, indeed, is this Kālī, this madwoman who larks about the battlefield slicing off heads as if it were a game? And who is this poet who can sing of such a strange repellent creature and call her Mother? The poet is Rāmprasād Sen,[2] a Bengali devotee from the eighteenth century who has left a body of devotional songs (*padābalī*) still much loved and much sung by devotees today. The strange Mother is the Goddess, or one aspect of the Goddess as she is worshiped by the Śāktas of Bengal, and her antics in the battle are part of her endless *līlā*.

Bengal is one of the most important areas in India for the worship of the Goddess. Puja time, the time of the autumnal celebration of the Goddess as Durgā (September–October), is the main holiday (here a truly holy day) time, it is the time of almost universal gift giving, and for the three main days of the festival all other life comes virtually to a stop. The streets are blocked by crowds out to visit the temporary shrines where elaborate images of the Goddess have been set up, perhaps to offer their worship with that of the priest, perhaps just to be seen and to enjoy the color and the scents and the music, especially that of the drummers whose arms seem never to be still for three days. Certainly they will come away with some *prasād,* food offered to the Goddess and thus filled with her special grace. Some, mostly the youthful, will join in her *līlā* by dancing with ecstatic abandon in the space immediately in front of her image.

There will certainly be readings of the *Caṇḍī,* that portion of the *Mārkaṇḍeya Purāṇa* known more properly as the *Devī Māhātmya,* which tells of the exploits of the Goddess and extols her as the great Power of the universe. Almost as certainly there will be singing of the songs of Rāmprasād, whose continuing popularity attests to the way he has captured, and summed up in his songs the feelings and aspirations of the people of Bengal. And if orthodox Hindus look somewhat askance at the more heterodox Tantric elements in his work, well, Bengal has often been considered less than properly orthodox, and its Tantric heritage is still strong. Besides, the whole Goddess cult is viewed as rather less than proper by many of the orthodox.

II

Rāmprasād's understanding of the Goddess's *līlā* is clearly shown in a song which begins

All this is the mad Mother's play,
The three worlds are deluded by her *māyā.*
The woman's true nature is hidden by her *līlā*—
She herself is mad, her husband is mad, his two disciples are mad.
Which is her true form and which her disguise, what her true essence, no one at all can say.[3]

Here we find three of the major features of the Goddess's *līlā:* that it deludes all the inhabitants of the three worlds, that it is a kind of game on her part, and that she appears to be quite mad. This is hardly the picture we expect of the divine Mother! And these are themes that are common in Rāmprasād's songs.

When Rāmprasād says that her actions are like a game, the idea he conveys is that the Mother is toying with her creation, she is playful but her game is unpredictable, it is like the game of a child. Yet the consequences of the game can have momentous significance, as one of the most famous of Rāmprasād's songs indicates. Here the game is kite flying:

Mother Śyāmā flies kites
(in the marketplace of the world).
They are mind-kites, floating in the winds of hope, held by the strings of *māyā*.
The frames are made from bones and sinews, covered in exquisite workmanship with her own attributes,
Their strings are coated with the glue of worldliness so their cutting edge is keen.
Of a hundred thousand of them only one or two break free, and you Mother laugh and clap your hands.
Prasād says, They fly away on the southerly wind.
Over the sea of the world to freedom on the other side.[4]

The "game" here concerns the salvation of individuals, and most of them don't make it. Yet the Mother only laughs and claps her hands! The individuals concerned seem to be able to do nothing about this situation, they are held (= deluded) by her *māyā*. Commenting on this song, Rāmakṛṣṇa, another famous devotee of the Goddess, says, "She is full of play. This world is her *līlā*. She is willful[5] and full of joy."[6]

It is this willful aspect of her play, her *līlā*, that is the difficulty. Because of it her actions are entirely unpredictable and take on the frightening nature even of madness. Rāmprasād can even say that she is cruel and heartless:

> Standing naked on Śiva's breast she destroys her enemies,
> O mind, tell me what she's really like, she who kicks her lord in the chest.
> Prasād says, Everyone knows the Mother's *līlā* is cruel and heartless,
> So proceed carefully, O mind . . .[7]

It is when she stands on her husband's prostrate body, or dances wild and naked in the battlefield or cremation ground, that this madness is most apparent. Take as an example the following:

Who is this woman with the wild hair
Who enters the battlefield with such hatred, accompanied by her wanton friends Bhairavi and Yoginī.
She knows no shame as she laughs in delight, and dances on Śiva's breast,
Naked, and drunk with nectar, she becomes absorbed in the terrible fight.
She staggers about, laughing and calling out, Catch me if you can!
Whose wife is she? I don't recognize her, her half-undressed body has bewitched me. . . .[8]

Here she is drunk, shameless, and half-naked, laughing, shouting, apparently totally out of control. In this guise she is almost unrecognizable as the Mother (though Rāmprasād knows who she is). She completely deludes most people. She is a magician, a trickster, hiding behind a show of magic and pretense. Sometimes she adopts the forms of other deities, she becomes Kṛṣṇa and dances in the circle of gopis; in fact, "Śiva, Kṛṣṇa and Kālī, I know they are all one," sings Rāmprasād.[9] They are all forms of the Mother.

But sometimes she is not even a good Mother, as this song demonstrates:

What a vain hope it was, coming into the world.
I was deceived like a bee by a painted lotus!
Mother, you fed me bitter *nīm* saying it was sugar,
Because I wanted sweets I had bitterness in my mouth all day.
Mother, you said you would play with me, but your game has not fulfilled my hope.
Rāmprasād says, In the world's play [*khelā*] what was to be has come to pass,
Now it is evening, take your little child and go home.[10]

This is a very powerful song, with its sharply drawn picture of a mother whiling away the day till evening playing with her infant son. And the message is equally sharp. This mother lies to her own child, she deceives him and leaves him unsatisfied in his play and with a bitter taste in his mouth. Yet his hope in the first instance was misplaced, what has transpired was inevitable, "what was to be has come to pass," he has no right to expect otherwise.

But most striking of all, perhaps, is the unexpected twist in the last line. Here is a mother who has just demonstrated herself to be completely untrustworthy, but the son begs her finally to place him on her hip and take him home. Does he have any other choice? In fact, Rāmprasād does sometimes rail against the unfairness of his Mother's treatment of him,[11] but most often he displays a confidence and trust that seem to fly (like a kite?) in the face of the facts of his situation.

III

Such is the surface meaning conveyed by Rāmprasād. But is there not something more going on here? Devotees don't usually go about criticizing their deities, calling them fickle, cruel, mad, drunk, unpredictable! There must be more to it than this; surely there must be some other deeper meaning.

Let me say first that this is not an idiosyncratic picture of the Goddess. It is not the whole picture Rāmprasād paints, because he also stresses the "good" side of the Goddess, that she is sometimes a mother who cares, that she does save from the sufferings and delusions of the world, and can be trusted to save those who call to her as Mother. But this fact only serves to point up the ambiguities of her nature. For we know that "of a hundred thousand of them only one or two break free," and in spite of Rāmprasād's sometimes confidence, there are times when even such a devotee as he does not know if he is one of them. There still remains the picture of a willful Goddess whose actions are never entirely predictable.

We may note also the Rāmprasād is a true representative of the Śākta tradition. The great nineteenth-century devotee of the Goddess (still enormously popular today), Rāmakṛṣṇa, was very fond of Rāmprasād's songs and stressed just those aspects that I have highlighted here. He was fond of stressing the willfulness of the Mother, her right to do with us and the world whatever she chooses.[12] And Rāmprasād bases his picture squarely on the greatest of all Śākta texts, the *Devī-Māhātmya.*[13] For example, the picture of the Goddess in battle reflects the imagery of the battles in the *Devī-Māhātmya,* to which Rāmprasād also specifically refers, to her slaying of the buffalo demon Mahiṣāsura,[14] her destruction of Śumbha and Niśumbha,[15] and the battle with Caṇḍa and Muṇḍa.[16]

The *Devī-Māhātmya* occupies a pivotal position in the development of the Goddess tradition.[17] It draws together various "goddess" traditions, picturing the many goddesses as but forms of the One and establishes this one as powerful, the creator, preserver, and destroyer, on a par with the great Viṣṇu and Śiva if not in fact greater than them. All later Śākta tradition owes it a debt.[18]

The most important aspects of Rāmprasād's picture are reflected in the *Devī-Māhātmya,* the ambivalent nature of the Goddess, the emphasis on the martial side of her nature as she strides through the battlefields as slayer of demons, and the manifestation of the Goddess as the world itself.

The ambivalent nature of the Goddess is a dominant theme in the hymns the gods sing in her praise after she has saved them from disaster by killing their enemies. She is hailed as Great Illusion and Great Knowledge (*mahāmāyā* and *mahāvidyā*), she is the Great Goddess and the Great Demon (*asurī*), she is modesty and shame (because of her nudity?), she is terrible (martial) and gentle.[19] Her true nature is unknown even to the gods, she destroys whole families, she has gentle forms and terrible ones.[20] She is gentle and harsh, she is an extremely beautiful woman when she appears to Caṇḍa and Muṇḍa to seduce them, but wrathful Kālī when she destroys them, Raktavīja, Śumbha, and Niśumbha.[21] She both bewitches the world and liberates it.[22]

In her martial guise, which she adopts to kill the various demons, she drinks something that makes her drunk and red-eyed.[23] She is black as ink, her eyes are terrifying, her body is emaciated, she has a gaping mouth with a lolling tongue. Into this maw she flings elephants, horses, chariots and their drivers, and grinds them up with her teeth.[24] She howls like one hundred jackals and is accompanied by jackals—an obvious cremation-ground image.[25] She swallows the blood of the demon Raktavīja,[26] and the din she makes is tremendous.[27] The battlefields are littered with dead animals and demons, and run with blood. It is a terrible and terrifying picture.

The battles are cosmic in their effect. The fight with Śumbha explicitly disturbs the whole universe, and earth and sky are only pacified when the battle is over. This is no doubt partly due to the fact that in a unique way the universe is her body. She takes the form of the world at its creation, she is primordial *prakṛti* characterized by the three *guṇas*.[28] She is said to subsist in the form of the world as earth and water, she constitutes all living beings and has the nature of the universe, which she upholds.[29] She supports the world so that when the rains come the vegetation grows out of her own body so that she is known as *śākambharī*.[30]

All this points to the deep meaning symbolized by Rāmprasād in his songs (and the whole Śākta tradition). Who is this Goddess whose *līlā* Rāmprasād is describing? She is a symbol[31] for the world, the cosmos of which we are part. "The Mother's belly is the universe, no one knows its size,"[32] she is "the earth, [she is] water,"[33] she is "archetypal eternal matter" (*prakṛti*),[34] she is "with qualities and without, gross and subtle, the uncaused root cause of all."[35] He also says, "O Mother you are suffering and you are bliss, as it is written in the Caṇḍi."[36] At the microcosmic level human beings are "mind-kites" with "frames made from bones and sinews, covered in exquisite workmanship with her own attributes." The dualities of the Goddess's nature are the dualities of our universe, sometimes threatening and sometimes benign, sometimes inspiring hope and at others despair, sometimes beautiful and sometimes terrifying, sometimes revealing its nature to us and at others totally deluding. We live in a mad, drunken, unpredictable world whose meaning we at times cannot penetrate, and we have no choice; it is the only world there is.

How is the poor devotee to survive, to maintain sanity and equilibrium in such an ambivalent universe? Only by believing, by hoping and trusting that ultimately the benign will triumph over the threatening, symbolized by the assertion that even the terrifying Kālī is the loving "Mother."

But is this not hope flying in the face of the evidence? Yes. But in such an ambivalent universe the devotee has no other option. The predominant response of Rāmprasād in song after song is to fling this faith in the face of a threatening universe, and to get on with living. There is no fatalism in Rāmprasād. At his lowest he can show a quiet acceptance of the inevitable. His faith is the stronger for admitting its doubts; he can remonstrate with the Goddess ("I will not call you Mother anymore / All I get from you is pain and anguish / . . . should a Mother be the enemy of her son?'');[37] he can admit that sometimes the situation seems hopeless, that his power is feeble in face of the Mother's, but still he stubbornly refuses to give up; he persists in believing that she will come through in the end.

Life for Rāmprasād, and for the Śātka devotee, is itself a participation in the Mother's *līlā*. They do not choose to dance; life is a dance that whirls them about like kites on the wind. Those who know this are among the one or two that fly away ''over the sea of the world to freedom on the other side.'' Rāmprasād is confident that because he has special knowledge of the Mother he is among them, and the devotees who sing his songs by doing so identify with this confidence. The wild dance of the Goddess is the dance of death. This is symbolized by its taking place in the battlefield or the cremation ground. Yet the Śākta does in another sense choose to join the dance, by accepting and embracing this fact. Faith is not escapist because it implies this acceptance of the mortality of the world and his or her own mortality. Some Śāktas, no doubt influenced by Tantrism, worship the Mother in cremation grounds.

The future is unknown, except that it is known that the Goddess wields a sword of destruction, which she will inevitably use. This is an essential aspect of her *līlā*. No one knows when that time will be. Yet, almost paradoxically, the moments when Rāmprasād is most confident (and when his humor shines through in his verse) are when he confronts Yama, the messenger of Death. In one song he is speaking to Yama, the god of death:

Prasād says, Get out of here, aren't you afraid?
Look at my Mother with her necklace of heads, today I reckon she'll have yours![38]

And also:

Who is this dark woman who comes to the battle,
Naked, hair disheveled, a sword in her left hand, exultantly slaying demons?
The weight of her feet makes the earth tremble with fear,
And the sight of it makes Śiva fall at her feet on the battleground.
Dvija Rāmprasād says, Why then need I fear?
Yama is easily conquered in life, in death and in battle.[39]

The devotee, then, is enabled through faith to seize the moment and live in joy even with this consciousness of the real nature of life and the world because the thought of death holds no more fear. The god of death is conquered in life, in death, and in the battle that is part of the Mother's *līlā*. Rāmprasād is said to have chosen the time of his own death, placing an image of the Goddess on his head and wading out into the Ganges till he disappeared from sight. As he went he sang a song that ends with these words:

> Prasād says, My mind is made up, gracious Kālī's power is great,
> O Mother, I am finished, I have paid the [priest's] fee.

Knowledge for the Śākta gives freedom, a common Hindu theme. The faith of the devotees enables them to personally transcend the world and all its vicissitudes. This knowledge is insight into the nature of the universe because it is knowledge of the Goddess and her *līlā*. It is ignorance that creates the kind of fear that makes life depressing and a burden. Knowledge allows the devotee to live without this fear.

IV

It is Rāmprasād's humanity and his honesty that are appealing (beside the homeliness of his imagery and the lyric appeal of the music he composed for his songs). For Hindus all worldly existence is unsatisfactory, and individuals are bound to endless cycles of such existence. The myth of the Goddess's *līlā* enables the Śākta to come to terms with such existence, by facing up to its real nature to embrace it in all its ambiguities, and so to transcend it that she or he experiences the *jouissance* (*ānanda*) that is *mokṣa* (release). The Śākta view advanced by Rāmprasād is thus diametrically opposed to that of the West Indian Godfrey in Jean Rhys's novel *Wide Sargasso Sea,* who says, "The devil prince of this world, but this world don't last so long for mortal man."[40] For the Śākta this world does indeed last for very long, for age after age, and rebirth after rebirth. But no devil is prince of this world. This world is the Goddess's *līlā,* in all the ambiguity that that conveys. But it is the Mother nevertheless.

NOTES

1. *koto rong jāno roṇe śyāma,* in Satyanarayan Bhattacharya, *Rāmprasād: jībanī ō racanasamagra* (Calcutta: Granthamela, 1975) (henceforth SNB), #83. All translations are my own. Songs are cited in notes by their first lines.

2. For what we know of the life of Rāmprasād, see my "Tradition and History in Isvaracandra Gupta's Biography of Ramprasad Sen," *South Asia* 9, no. 2 (Dec. 1986): 69–80.

3. *e sob khsepa māyer khelā,* SNB #65.

4. *śyāma mā uṛācche ghuṛi,* SNB #301. The game here is with fighting kites, with glue and sometimes powdered glass on the strings to enable a competitor to cut the string of his opponent's kite, which then falls to the ground.

5. *icchāmoy,* one whose will is law, intent on having one's own way.

6. *śrī śrī rāmakṛṣṇa kathāmṛta,* 1.2.5.1. Ramakṛṣṇa lived from 1836–1886.

7. *se ki sudhu śiber soti,* SNB #315. In the song *"mā āmār khelāno hōlō"* (SNB #251) he calls her a "hard-hearted girl."

8. *bāmā ōke elōkeśe,* SNB #195.

9. *kālī holi mā rasbehāri,* SNB #108.

10. *kebol āsār āśā, bhobe āsā . . . ,* SNB #119.

11. I will not call you Mother any more,
You have given, and are giving me such anguish. . . .
I will not return to my Mother's embrace,
I called to her again and again, is she blind and deaf? . . .
Rāmprasād says, Why does Mother take this line, should a mother be the enemy of her son?
Day and night I wonder what more she will give, than the agony of repeated rebirth.

(*mā mā bole ār ḍākbonā,* SNB #262). He abuses her for turning a deaf ear when he called her name (*jānilām biṣom boro . . . ,* SNB #141), he says her name will forever be stained because of her cruelty to him (*nitānto jābe din . . . ,* SNB #176.

12. See note 4.

13. The *Devī-Māhātmya,* or *Caṇḍī,* as it is also widely known, forms chapters 81–93 of the *Mārkaṇḍeya Purāṇa.*

14. *jāo gō jononī . . . ,* SNB #282.

15. *elo cikūr bhār, e bāmā,* SNB #62; *se ki emni meyer meye,* SNB #314.

16. *āre ei ailo kere ghonoboronī,* SNB #42; *somore kere kālkāminī,* SNB #307. Songs such as *mā boson pōrō,* SNB #259, seem also to refer to incidents in the *Devi-Māhātmya,* and in *śib noy māyer podtole,* SNB #297, he refers to "the words the sage Mārkaṇḍeya has clearly written in the *Caṇḍi.*"

17. See Thomas B. Coburn, *Devī-Māhātmya: The Crystallization of the Goddess Tradition* (Delhi: Motilal Banarsidass, 1984), and J. N. Tiwari, *Goddess Cults in Ancient India; with Special Reference to the First Seven Centuries* A.D. (Delhi: Sundeep Prakashan, 1985).

18. The much later *Devī-Bhagavata Purāṇa* represents a "Sanskritizing" or Brahmanizing process which makes it less popular in Bengal. Rāmprasād, in my opinion, represents a kind of "back to the Caṇḍi" movement, together with a strong Tantric influence. The relationship between the picture of the Goddess in the *Devī-Māhātmya* and that of the *Devī-Bhagavata Purāṇa* is examined in Adrienne Turnbull, "The Transformation of the Goddess in the Devī-Bhagavata Purāṇa," Hons thesis, Otago University, 1987.

19. *Mārkaṇḍeya Purāṇa* LXXXI, 58–64.

20. Ibid., LXXXIV, 6–25.

21. Ibid., LXXXV–XC.

22. Ibid., XCI, 4.
23. Ibid., LXXXIII, 33–35.
24. Ibid., LXXXVII, 5–12.
25. Ibid., LXXXVIII, 22.
26. Ibid., LXXXVIII, 39ff.
27. Ibid., LXXXIX, 17ff.
28. Ibid., LXXXI, 57–59, LXXXIV, 6, LXXXV, 7.
29. Ibid., XCI, 3–6, 31.
30. Ibid., XCI, 43f.
31. By "symbol" I mean a conventionalized sign, a sign which through a particular kind of metaphoric use over time and within a specific cultural setting has acquired the capacity to signify in a conventional way. See R. Barthes, *Elements of Semiology* (New York: Hill & Wang, 1967), p. 38, and U. Eco, *A Theory of Semiotics* (Bloomington: Indiana University Press, 1976), pp. 129ff.
32. *ke jāne go kālī kemon,* SNB #117.
33. *mon gariber ki dōṣ āche,* SNB #217.
34. *mohakāler monōmōhinī sodānondamōyī kālī,* SNB #278.
35. *"soguṇā nirguṇā sthūla sūkṣma mūla hīn mūla"* is a way of stating in precise philosophical terms that she is the whole existence, the phenomenal universe, and the absolute which produces and sustains it; *jononī podpoṇkojoṃ* . . . , SNB #136.
36. *mon goriber ki dōṣ āche,* SNB #217.
37. *mā mā bole ār ḍakbonā,* SNB #262. In *borai koro kise go mā,* SNB #189, he "abuses" her.
38. *ko śomon ki mone kōre,* SNB #81.
39. *kāminī yāmini-boroṇe rone elō ke,* SNB #92.
40. Jean Rhys, *Wide Sargasso Sea* (London: Andre Deutsch, 1986), pp. 18f.

II

RELIGIOUS PLAY IN NORTH AND SOUTH INDIA

7

The Play of Emotion: *Līlākīrtan* in Bengal

DONNA M. WULFF

Vaiṣṇava Bhakti and the Social History of Bengal

In his last writings the social historian Hitesranjan Sanyal has argued that the *bhakti* movement in Bengal between the fourteenth and the seventeenth centuries was in part an expression of a new regional self-consciousness. He contends that the symbols of Vaiṣṇava *bhakti* were appropriated by an emerging Bengali middle class, and that these symbols served at a critical time to enchance this class's self-confidence.[1] Joseph T. O'Connell has argued further that although the Bengali Vaiṣṇava movement did not lead to revolutionary changes in society, it has nevertheless had a significant ameliorating effect on strongly hierarchical institutions in Bengal, especially those of caste and gender.[2] We may thus see the *bhakti* movement as part of a democratizing process taking place within Bengali society. Vaiṣṇava *bhakti* gave Bengalis important new options, freeing them from the overwhelming dominance of Brāhmaṇ teachers and male *gurūs*, from the exclusiveness of the Sanskrit language in ritual and performance, from the more structured classical forms of the royal courts in music, dance, and drama, and from the dominance of north Indian prototypes in architecture, sculpture, and painting.

These liberalizing changes did not take place in the political realm, where Muslim rule persisted, nor to any significant extent in the official Brāhmāṇic regulations governing caste and gender. Rather, they took place largely in an expanding religious community, where there was a noticeable relaxation of the restrictions affecting low-class persons and women. Vaiṣṇava devotion in Bengal has from early on been remarkably inclusive, allowing all who have wished to participate in its worship to do so. Furthermore, certain women as well as certain low-caste men have attained to positions of leadership within the movement.[3]

Paralleling and interacting with these liberating trends, a major religious concept signifying freedom, the concept of *līlā,* came to prominence in Bengali Vaiṣṇava teachings. Put succinctly, *līlā* in this tradition refers to the divine play of Kṛṣṇa with his beloved Rādhā and their close associates, both in the earthly place called Vraja (Braj) and in the cosmic realm in which all their actions go on simultaneously for all eternity.[4] Especially in Bengal it also refers to the divine actions of Caitanya (1485–1533), whose life is conceived on the model of Kṛṣṇa's and who is regarded sometimes as an avatar of Kṛṣṇa, sometimes as the Lord himself, and sometimes as Kṛṣṇa, but incarnated with the fair complexion and the intense feeling of Rādhā so that he might taste the sweetness of her love for him. In each of these usages the term connotes the unfettered and often unconventional nature of the Lord's play.[5]

The period from the fourteenth to the seventeenth century also witnessed the appearance of an array of new or rejuvenated performance forms in which the *līlā* of Kṛṣṇa and Rādhā, and subsequently that of Caitanya as well, were represented dramatically throughout Bengal. During this period the story of Rādhā's and Kṛṣṇa's love gained immense popularity. Songs, stories, and symbols from the Rādhā–Kṛṣṇa cycle were taken up into virtually every regional performance form, including even Muslim forms, such as *fakir gān;* as a sort of cultural common currency they have performed an important integrating function for Bengali society from then until now. I shall argue that they were also a source of liberal images that may well have aided the process of social change.

The two most significant Bengali performance forms to emerge at this time were the regional theater form called *yātrā,* and *līlākīrtan.* The subjects represented in both *yātrā* and *kīrtan* were for a long time exclusively episodes in *kṛṣṇalīlā.* Although episodes from the life of Caitanya have also formed an important part of the repertoire of *yātrā,* in the twentieth century *yātrā* has evolved into a largely political form, with contemporary events, or the lives of figures such as Subhas Chandra Bose or Vladimir Lenin, as its subjects. *Līlākīrtan,* by contrast, has remained a devotional form, adding a whole series of episodes from the life of Caitanya to its earlier repertoire focusing on Kṛṣṇa and Rādhā.

Līlākīrtan in Bengali Vaiṣṇava *Bhakti*

The term *kīrtan* is formed from the Sanskrit root *kīrt,* which means "sing in praise, celebrate." In compound with the term *līlā* it designates the performance form on which this article focuses, as distinguished from the other major stream of Bengali Vaiṣṇava *kīrtan,* called *nāmasaṅkīrtan* or simply *nāmakīrtan,* the singing of the names of Kṛṣṇa, often in conjunction with those of Caitanya. By contrast, *līlākīrtan,* as its name indicates, is the celebration of *līlā.* Unlike *nāmakīrtan,* which may either be performed by a *kīrtan* troupe or sung communally, *līlākīrtan* is always performed for an audience: in it a principal singer, together with a troupe of supporting singers and drummers, renders a story in song, dramatic gesture, and dance.

In what follows I argue that the term *līlā,* especially in its connotations of freedom and spontaneity, aptly characterizes not only the subject matter of *līlākīrtan* but also to an important degree its form. In doing so, however, I am not claiming that *līlākīrtan* has been significantly more spontaneous than other forms of music and drama that were developing at the same time, but rather that it has allowed for greater spontaneity than the classical forms that preceded it. Like other forms of Bengali Vaiṣṇava devotion, it has also allowed women as well as men from a far broader range of caste groups to participate in it, as witnesses and also as performers. The egalitarian spirit that has characterized *kīrtan* performances, as well as other forms of Vaiṣṇava worship, may well have acted as a liberalizing influence on the broader Bengali society.[6]

The term *līlākīrtan* has three synonyms in Bengali, each of which indicates one of its aspects. It is called *pālākīrtan* because each performance represents a single episode—a *pālā*—in the life of Kṛṣṇa or of Caitanya. It is called *padāvalī kīrtan* because the songs of which it is composed are settings of the 15th–18th-century Vaiṣṇava lyrics known collectively as *padāvali,* literally "array of verses [*padas*]." Finally, it is called *rasakīrtan* because it is experienced by its connoisseurs as conducing to the highest aesthetic and spiritual delight (*rasa*).[7] In this article I shall follow the common Bengali practice of calling this form simply *kīrtan.*

If one comes to a study of *kīrtan* with the knowledge that the *Bhāgavata Purāṇa* (ca. 800 C.E.) is the major scriptural text for the Bengali Vaiṣṇava community, one will have several surprises.[8] First, as I have indicated, it is not only the *līlā* of Kṛṣṇa, termed *kṛṣṇalīlā,* but also that of Caitanya, termed *gauralīlā,* that is represented in *kīrtan* performances. Furthermore, Caitanya plays an important role in *kṛṣṇalīlā pālā*s as well as in his own, for a song to him constitutes the *gauracandrikā,* the first portion of every performance of *kṛṣṇalīlā.*[9] Finally, the episodes of *kṛṣṇalīlā* that are commonly performed overlap very little with those narrated in the tenth book of the *Bhāgavata Purāṇa.* What we find in *kīrtan* performances, as in the Vaiṣṇava *padāvalī,* should in fact be called *rādhā-kṛṣṇa-līlā,* for Rādhā's role in these episodes is every bit as important as that of Kṛṣṇa himself.[10] Although we focus in this article on *kṛṣṇalīlā* episodes, much of the broader discussion of spontaneity and structure holds true for *gauralīlā* as well.

If we cannot look to the tenth book of the *Bhāgavata Purāṇa* for the organizing categories for classifying *kīrtan* performances, where can we look? Compilers of anthologies of Vaiṣṇava *padāvalī* and singers of *kīrtan* alike have taken their analytic rubrics from the *Ujjvalanīlamaṇi* of Rupa Gosvami, one of Caitanya's most prominent disciples. In this treatise, Rupa followed the classical writers on aesthetics in classifying the erotic mode into two aspects, love-in-union (*sambhoga śṛṅgāra*) and love-in-separation (*vipralambha śṛṅgāra*).[11] Each of these he further subdivided into four types. For love-in-union, the subdivisions represent grades of intensity; these abstract terms have not become standard names of *kīrtan pālā*s. The divisions of love-in-separation, on the other hand, represent archetypal situations, and three of the four have been used to designate major classes of *pālā*s.[12] These include *pūrvarāga,* literally "first redness," the first dawning of love in Rādhā or in Kṛṣṇa; *māna,* a complex response of Rādhā's to Kṛṣṇa's infidelity, including hurt, jealousy, and anger, but also deep yearning; and finally *pravāsa,* the separation caused by the lover's departure, in this case by Kṛṣṇa's leaving the cowherd village to go to Mathura. The usual name for *pālā*s representing this last situation is thus *māthur.*

In addition to the forms of love-in-separation, certain of the eight states of the heroine enumerated by Rupa have served as major analytic categories. These include *abhisārikā,* Rādhā on her way to a tryst with Kṛṣṇa; *kalahāntaritā,* Rādhā separated from Kṛṣṇa by a quarrel; and *khaṇḍitā,* Rādhā as offended heroine. A fourth category, *proṣitabhartṛkā,* the woman whose husband or lover has departed, coincides with the last form of separation, *pravāsa,* and is thus said to be another designation for *māthur.*

Although the remaining four states of the heroine are enumerated with these four by Rupa and by various anthologists and authorities on *kīrtan,* and although they figure in *pālā*s on various themes, they do not, so far as I am aware, serve as categories for classifying *kīrtan pālā*s. These include *vāsakasajjā,* the heroine who has adorned herself in eager expectation of her lover (this phase figures as the prelude to the bitter disappointment of *khaṇḍitā,* in which Kṛṣṇa has hurt Rādhā by spending the night with a rival); *utkaṇṭhitā,* the heroine tormented by anxiety because her lover is late (this too forms a phase of *khaṇḍitā*); *vipralabdhā,* literally "separated" generically, but said to represent the heroine who has grown discouraged because her lover has not come even after giving her a signal to meet him (this is also a phase of *khaṇḍitā*); and finally *svādhīnabhartṛkā,* the woman who has her lover under her control (an attitude of Rādhā's that figures in certain *pālā*s representing union).

It is clear from these considerations that *kṛṣṇalīlā pālā*s do not correspond precisely with the categories of erotic love enumerated in Rupa's *Ujjvalanīlamaṇi.* Yet this work has clearly had an immense influence on poets, singers, anthologists, and Bengali scholars writing about *kīrtan.* As I worked through portions of it and other theoretical treatises of Rupa for my thesis, one prominent question in my mind was the extent to which these immensely erudite Sanskrit works influenced actual religious life in the Bengali Vaiṣṇava community. I was thus surprised and pleased when I first heard Nanda Kishor Das, a celebrated *kīrtanīyā* who is now in his eighties, quote to an audience of Bengalis the *Ujjvalanīlamaṇi* verse in which Rupa lists the eight types of heroine.[13] Nor is Nanda Kishor the only *kīrtanīyā* that I have heard quote Sanskrit verses of Rupa in performance.[14] Only a small fraction of an audience at a typical *kīrtan* performance would know Sanskrit, yet those who regularly attend such performances soon absorb the categories and terms that apply to *kīrtan.* Most of them would not be able to quote Rupa, but many would understand designations like *kalahāntaritā*[15] and *abhisārikā*[16] in their application to Radha.

In our search for the categories defining the term *līlā*[17] in the compound *kṛṣṇalīlākīrtan,* we have seen that the themes of most *kīrtan* episodes do not come from the tenth chapter of the *Bhāgavata Purāṇa,* and although these episodes correspond with certain categories of Rupa's *Ujjvalanīlamaṇi,* that text also includes a number of categories that have not become themes for *kīrtan pālā*s. In order to compile a list of commonly heard *kṛṣṇalīlā pālā*s, I have therefore consulted the lists given in two Bengali treatises on *kīrtan,* those of Khagendranath Mitra[18] and Harekrishna Mukhopadhyay,[19] both noted authorities, as well as lists of *pālā*s given to me in interviews by several prominent *kīrtanīyā*s in answer to the question "What *pālā*s do you perform?"[20] I have also drawn on my own notes and transcriptions of the roughly four dozen performances that I have recorded. The nineteen *pālā*s I have listed thus give a fairly good idea of the range of the *kṛṣṇalīlā* episodes that have been most commonly performed during the last fifty or sixty years.

Commonly Heard *kṛṣṇalīlākīrtan pālā*s

Goṣṭhā Līlā[21]	Kṛṣṇa and his friends go out to graze the cows.
Uttaragoṣṭhā	Kṛṣṇa and his friends return from grazing the cows.

Dān Līlā	Kṛṣṇa disguises himself as a tax collector and accosts Rādhā and her friends on their way to market.
Naukā Vilās	Kṛṣṇa disguises himself as a boatman and offers to ferry Rādhā and her friends across the River Yamuna.
Subal Milan	Subal dresses Rādhā to look like him so that she can elude her in-laws and go out to meet Kṛṣṇa in broad daylight.
Mahārās	Kṛṣṇa entices the *gopīs* (Rādhā and her friends) to come out to the forest and dance a circle dance with him, and he multiplies himself so that every woman experiences the ecstasy of dancing beside him.
Kuñjabhaṅga	After their blessed night together in the grove, Rādhā and Kṛṣṇa wake up to the painful reality of imminent separation, and all nature grieves with them.
Pūrvarāg	Literally, "first redness," the first dawning of Rādhā's love for Kṛṣṇa or his love for her.
Rūpānurāg	The beauty of Rādhā or Kṛṣṇa and their mutual love.
Abhisār	Rādhā's going out of the village to a tryst with Kṛṣṇa.
Rupābhisār	The beauty of Rādhā combined with Abhisār (above).
Akṣepānurāg	Rādhā's love for Kṛṣṇa and her lamentations at Kṛṣṇa's power over her.
Kalahāntaritā	Rādhā as the heroine who is separated from Kṛṣṇa because of a lover's quarrel.
Khaṇḍitā	Rādhā as the offended heroine who discovers that Kṛṣṇa has spent the night with a rival after promising to come to her.
Mān	Rādhā's state of anger, jealousy, hurt, and deep yearning when she learns of Kṛṣṇa's infidelity.
Mānbhañjan	Kṛṣṇa persuades Rādhā to give up her *mān,* her hurt and anger at his infidelity.
Viraha or Māthur	The portrayal of the cowherd village in the wake of Kṛṣṇa's departure for Mathura.
Holī[22]	The spring festival of colors.
Jhulan	The swing festival in summer.

All these *pālās* center not on actions but on emotions, often a single emotion or complex of emotions of Rādhā or Kṛṣṇa or both. Insofar as the *pālās* have plots, the elements of those plots are largely means of making manifest Rādhā's and Kṛṣṇa's emotional states and the devotion of their close friends and associates toward them. In the persons of these secondary characters, the devotees present at a *kīrtan* performance find proper models for emulation. The performance itself thus provides guidance and practice in the ideal emotions of Vaiṣṇava devotion.[23] As such, it is not merely "performance," in the "entertainment and the arts" sense to which we are accustomed in the modern West, but also, ideally, profound *religious* experience, for performer and devotee alike.

A *kīrtan* performance is a unique blend of structure and spontaneity. In order to understand the major ways in which *kīrtanīyā*s and their troupes convey devotional emotions, we shall consider a typical performance,[24] focusing our attention first on the chief components of its structure and then on the main opportunities that it affords for spontaneity. The freedom of expression evident in *līlākīrtan* may well have contributed to its immense popularity and thus to its ameliorating influence on Bengali society.

A full-length *kīrtan* performance typically lasts between three and four hours. Its performers constitute a *kīrtan* troupe, which consists of one lead singer, called a *kīrtanīyā,* who may be either male or female; several supporting singers, who are always, in my experience, of the same sex as the *kīrtanīyā* and who play small brass hand cymbals; and two or sometimes three male drummers, who play with bare hands on both ends of the slender, barrel-shaped *khol*s. When the performance is to begin, the members of the troupe, usually without the *kīrtanīyā,* walk out onto the performance area with their instruments, ritually touch the earth with their foreheads, and prepare to play a strong opening downbeat. They continue to keep the beat for some time as the drummers control the pace and volume and lead the others to one or perhaps several loud climaxes.

At some point during this instrumental prelude the *kīrtanīyā,* if she or he has not come out with the others, takes a place in the center of the troupe, does obeisance with forehead touching the earth, and assumes for a short time a meditative attitude in order to take on the *bhāva* (the emotional state) appropriate to the *līlā* episode about to be portrayed. She or he then begins the *gauracandrikā,* a song in praise of Caitanya chosen because of its appropriateness to the Rādhā–Kṛṣṇa episode that is to be sung. Like the songs of the *pālā* proper, this song will have as its text a medieval poem embellished and transformed by the additional lines called *ākhar.*[25] It often bears a thematic resemblance to the first song of the main *pālā.*

At the conclusion of the *gauracandrikā,* the *kīrtanīyā* begins the main *pālā,* sometimes announcing its theme and setting the stage in prose (*kathā,* "speaking, telling") before embarking on its first song. The songs of the *gauracandrikā* and the main *pālā* constitute the basic building blocks of the performance. Yet, as we shall see, they also offer important opportunities for spontaneity.

The remainder of the *pālā* follows a similar pattern, alternating between songs and prose portions, the prose including narration, explanation, and exhortation. As in the instrumental prelude, there are multiple points at which the drummers and the main singer lead the others in building to emotional climaxes through increases in tempo and dynamic level. At such points the *kīrtanīyā* often invites the audience to join in, saying ''Hari bol'' (literally, ''say ''Hari,''' i.e., Kṛṣṇa), and at such times the women often spontaneously burst into ululation, making a loud, high-pitched sound that is punctuated rhythmically through the movement of their tongues. As at key points in *pūjā*,[26] a member of the audience may blow a conch shell. Excitement may also be generated by one or more drum solos performed by the lead *khol* player. The final resolution of the plot is also usually a point of climax, and if the audience's emotions have been engaged by the performance, some members may rise and join the performers in singing one or another well-known setting of the names of Kṛṣṇa or Caitanya (*nāmasaṅkīrtan*), and even in dancing and clapping in rhythm, at the performance's conclusion.

In addition to the poetic and musical means of evoking and directing emotion that we have considered, the performers have other powerful means, notably those of dramatic gesture and dance. A skilled *kīrtanīyā* is rarely stationary; she or he makes use of the space in the half circle formed by the other performers and moves out to the edge of the audience in the theatre-in-the-round setting in which *kīrtan* is usually performed, communicating through gesture and characteristic poses as well as through song and speech. One or more of the drummers may also be drawn into the dramatic action at key points, and the drummers may dance with the *kīrtanīyā* as well. These dance movements in time to the music reinforce rhythms perceived aurally, and the result is often a powerful intensification of the emotion being conveyed.

We have surveyed a number of elements that give structure to a *līlākīrtan* performance: the instrumental prelude, the *gauracandrikā* song in praise of Caitanya, and the several songs that delineate subtle phases in the particular episode of Kṛṣṇa's and Rādhā's love that serves as the theme of a given performance. We have noted that each song contains, interspersed among the lines of the original poem, certain additional lines in verse that are called *ākhar*. According to Vaiṣṇava tradition, which I have no reason to doubt, these *ākhar* lines have been improvised in performance by successive generations of *kīrtanīyā*s, but they are now simply learned as part of each song. There are also fixed elements in the spoken portions that weave the songs into a whole; moreover, some of the musical and dramatic elements of the performance, such as the *khol* solo, certain characteristic poses of the *kīrtanīyā,* and the concluding *nāmasaṅkīrtan* with the audience, although not invariable components, are typical enough to play a structuring role.

However, within all this elaborate structure there are innumerable opportunities for spontaneity on the part of performers and audience members alike. Spontaneity is an important aspect of *līlā* as it is usually defined: Kṛṣṇa is said in the *Bhāgavata Purāṇa* to perform all actions spontaneously and effortlessly, like a child playing.[27] A brief look at elements of a *kītan* performance in which spontaneity is especially evident should thus help us identify ways in which *līlākīrtan* exemplifies the major characteristics of *līlā,* especially as *līlā* is understood in Bengali Vaiṣṇavism.

We have noted that the *ākhar* lines probably represent earlier *kīrtanīyā*s' improvisations in the course of past performances; this tradition has come down to the twentieth century most dramatically in the person of the famous *kīrtanīyā* Ramdas Babaji of Barahnagar Path Bari (just north of Calcutta), whose disciples used to take down his spontaneous *ākhar*s during his performances.[28] It is not hard to imagine that such *ākhar* lines, composed extemporaneously for centuries, have conveyed great emotional energy. Ramdas Babaji said that he could create them only in the heightened state achieved in performance,[29] and what he sang in such a state is reported to have had enormous emotional impact. Moreover, even the *ākhar* lines that have become part of *kīrtan* songs are powerful in conveying intense devotional emotions to an audience. It is typically an *ākhar* line that is sung repeatedly by a *kīrtanīyā* in order to build up to an emotional climax through the increase in tempo and dynamic level. Such a climax has the character of a spontaneous expression that channels emotional energy. The *ākhar* lines themselves are often warmly emotional, and they often have musical settings that encourage freer emotional expression than those of the original poems' verses.

A second major arena of spontaneity is found in the narrative and sermonic portions (*kathā*) that serve to link the songs together. Elements of these spoken portions may be found in the notebooks of *kīrtanīyā*s; I would expect, for example, that the verse of Rupa Gosvami enumerating the eight kinds of heroine, which Nanda Kishor Das quotes at the beginning of each *pālā* on Rādhā as one of these eight types, is found in one or more of his notebooks. However, although the narrative portions of *kathā* sections may be partially fixed, the commentarial and hortatory portions are largely spontaneous, so much so, in fact, that they may incorporate an event in the vicinity of the performance area, for example, a distracting noise, into a brief sermon on the highest form of devotion to Kṛṣṇa.

A third realm of spontaneity in the performance is the vigorous rhythmic improvisation of the *khol* solos. Like the *tablā* solos of Hindustani classical music and the *mṛdaṅgam* solos of south India, a *khol* solo by an accomplished drummer is often riveting. Virtually everyone present seems to enjoy this part of a *kīrtan* performance, but for those who appreciate *kīrtan* deeply, and who are especially well acquainted with its musical elements, the rhythmic intricacies of such a solo provide a special fascination.

The *ākhar* lines and their rendering, the spoken portions of the performance, and the *khol* solos are three components of *kīrtan* in which spontaneity is especially evident. However, spontaneous elements are present from the first downbeat of the instrumental prelude of a *kīrtan* performance to the communal singing of Kṛṣṇa's and Rādhā's names at the end. Unlike instrumentalists and singers of Western classical music, the performers sing and play without musical scores of any sort, and they do not have the performance memorized. A performance thus comes into being out of the involvement of the performers with the *līlā* that they are striving together to create,[30] through the specific succession of songs on that *līlā*'s theme chosen by the *kīrtanīyā*. Although each song has a melodic and a rhythmic framework, which are learned, singers and drummers improvise extensively on these basic patterns. The obvious involvement of the performers in the *līlā* inspires the members of the audience to become emotionally involved and to express this involvement by responding to the *kīrtanīyā*'s invitations to shout "Hari bol!" or, in the case of the women, by joining in the ululation that is often heard at an especially intense climax.

In addition to spontaneity, we may look to playful elements in the performance as being particularly illustrative of Vaiṣṇava notions of *līlā* (play, "child's play"). Among these, humor, whether in the plot itself or in the dialogue, plays a major role in most *līlā*s. In one version of *Naukā Vilās*, for example, the *pālā* in which Kṛṣṇa poses as a ferryman in order to meet Rādhā, he bargains with the *gopī*s over the price of passage. The *gopī*s offer him one-sixteenth of one rupee (*ek ānā*). Kṛṣṇa's clever repartee is a pun: *āmi ekā nā* (I'm not alone [i.e., I have Rādhā]). The *gopī*s counter with an offer of two *ānā*s (*du ānā*). Kṛṣṇa responds, "*du monā hayo nā*" ("Don't be of two minds,"); in other words, "Be single-minded in your love for me," a request directed primarily, of course, at Rādhā. The playful haggling continues until the *gopī*s agree to pay Kṛṣṇa sixteen *ānā*s or a full rupee, an amount that signifies fullness and thus promise for eventual union.

Playfulness is found not only in the plot and the dialogue; it is also a characteristic of many portions of the performance especially of lighter *līlā*s. A number of the meters (*tāl*) used in Manoharshahi *kīrtan,* the only one of the original five musical styles to have survived to any great extent to the present day, are performed in a quick tempo (*drut lay*), and there is a certain playfulness in the rhythms found in the songs of such *pālā*s and in their rendering. Dance and dramatic poses may also be humorous: I have seen a male *kīrtanīyā* draw a laugh from his audience by putting the shawl that served as his only prop over his head like the *pallav* of a sari and adopting a look of feminine meekness.[31] Dance postures are also sometimes humorous or at least lighthearted, as, for example, when a *kīrtanīyā* assumed the *tribhaṅga* (triple-bend) pose of Kṛṣṇa and feigns playing the flute. The audience characteristically expresses joy at each of these playful and humorous poses. In some cases, for example, in the punning exchange between the *gopī*s and Kṛṣṇa in *Naukā Vilā*s, such delight clearly comes in part from the experience of being "in the know," being in on something that even some of the characters in the story do not know, something, often, that has religious significance for the Vaiṣṇava community.

We have observed a number of playful and humorous aspects of *kīrtan* performances. It is natural to focus on these in an attempt to understand *kīrtan* as *līlā,* for in them qualities usually associated with *līlā* are especially evident. Yet in so doing we must not forget that some *pālā*s, most importantly *Māthur*—the portrayal of the cowherd village in the wake of Kṛṣṇa's departure for Mathura—are not at all playful, and yet they too are seen as part of Kṛṣṇa's *līlā. Māthur* is performed most often at *śrāddha* ceremonies for the dead; the grief of the bereaved is rearticulated and reexperienced through the grief of the *gopī*s and other inhabitants of Brindavan. Just as Indian classical writers on aesthetics taught that our conception of aesthetic bliss (*rasa*) must be broad enough to include the sorrow of *karuṇā rasa,* so our understanding of *līlā* must likewise encompass the grief of *Māthur.* Yet, as in the classical theory of *rasa,* the experience is not that of the raw human emotion but of a transmutation of that emotion brought about by aesthetic means. Just as one can experience delight at a play portraying the story of Rāma's later years, in which sorrow predominates,[32] so one can experience the inner joy and salvific power of even a tragic *līlā.* Conversely, performances of even the lighter, more playful *pālā*s sustain an intensity of emotional expression that evokes deep feelings from their audiences.

In our attempt to discern the significance of the term *līlā* in the compound *kṛṣṇalīlākīrtan,* we have identified its main structuring principles as well as equally important features of spontaneity and playfulness. In doing so, we have indicated ways in which *kṛṣṇalīlākīrtan* is not merely performance, in the modern Western sense, but also devotion (*bhakti*). By becoming absorbed in the emotions of Rādhā and Kṛṣṇa and their intimate friends and associates, devotees at a *kīrtan* performance are privileged not only to witness but also to participate in the divine *līlā,* which in the Bengali Vaiṣṇava worldview is nothing less than ultimate reality.

Conclusion

As Sanyal has shown, the dramatic spread of Vaiṣṇava *bhakti* beginning in the fourteenth century was part of a larger process of social change taking place in

Bengal.[33] This change was toward greater freedom in several social and cultural spheres; the Bengali Vaiṣṇava concept of *līlā,* with its sense of freedom and spontaneity, may thus have appealed to Bengalis during those centuries in part because of its antinomian elements. The flourishing of the performance tradition of *līlākīrtan* from the late sixteenth century was part of a broad pattern of democratization and regionalization. Its musical forms, although classically derived, are distinctive to Bengal, and the main language used in its performance is Bengali rather than Sanskrit. Moreover, because it evolved as a largely popular form,[34] it has required no court patronage. Finally, women and non-Brāhmaṇs as well as Brāhmaṇs have been able to study and perform it.

We have seen that *līlākīrtan* transmitted and kept alive stories about the divine love affair of Rādhā and Kṛṣṇa and the earthly travails and successes of the ecstatic preacher Caitanya. The first set of stories, in particular, became pervasively known and were continuously reiterated for centuries throughout Bengali society, even in Muslim circles. Until perhaps the middle of the present century no *śrāddha* ceremony for the dead, whether Vaiṣṇava, Śākta, or Śaiva, was considered complete without a *līlākīrtan* performance.[35] Vaiṣṇava symbols and stories thus played a major role in integrating Bengali society, and *līlākīrtan* was a primary vehicle in this process from the sixteenth century onward.

In addition to facilitating societal integration in Bengal, *līlākīrtan* participated in other broad processes of social and religious change that were already under way by the time of Caitanya. It held up images of a playful, iconoclastic deity and a consort whose audacity toward him was a blatant violation of society's norms. Although orthodox Vaiṣṇava teaching has always asserted that the deities are not ethical models for human actions, the repeated dramatization of stories in which venerated deities defy social conventions may well have loosened the hold of the Brāhmāṇic strictures on Bengali society, if only in the realm of the imagination. In particular, the strength of Rādhā and her friends, as they are portrayed in *līlākīrtan,* may have helped inspire women and men alike to work for female literacy and the other reforms on behalf of women that were carried out in Bengal in the nineteenth and early twentieth centuries.[36]

Finally and perhaps most importantly, *līlākīrtan*'s accessibility, which reflects the openness of the Bengali Vaiṣṇava movement generally, has made it an agent of gradual social change. All are welcome to come and participate in a *līlākīrtan* performance, and for its duration all distinctions of caste and gender are transcended. Moreover, *what* is experienced in *līlākīrtan* performances is also rendered accessible to all, not, as is sometimes asserted, by being simplified but by the fact that the devotion is based on profoundly human emotions, which are powerfully represented through performance.[37]

Thus, by helping to integrate Bengali society through the transmission and repeated dramatization of common stories, by holding up images of a playful, iconoclastic male deity and his equally audacious consort, by breaking down distinctions of caste and gender and facilitating the sharing of passionate religious emotions in worship and performance, *līlākīrtan* has made important contributions to the democratization of Bengali society from the sixteenth to the twentieth centuries.

NOTES

Most of the research on which this essay is based was carried out in West Bengal and Brindavan between August 1979 and January 1981 under the auspices of a Senior Fellowship from the American Institute of Indian Studies, a Summer Stipend from the National Endowment for the Humanities, and a Wriston Fellowship from Brown University. I returned to West Bengal briefly during the winter of 1988–89 on a short-term grant, again from the American Institute. I am most grateful for the support of all three institutions.

1. Hitesranjan Sanyal, "Transformation of the Regional *Bhakti* Movement in Bengal," Occasional Paper, Centre for Studies in Social Sciences, Calcutta, 1985, esp. pp. 1, 3, 8–9. A portion of this longer paper was published as "Transformation of the Regional *Bhakti* Movement (Sixteenth and Seventeenth Centuries)," in Joseph T. O'Connell, ed., *Bengal Vaiṣṇavism, Orientalism, Society and the Arts* (East Lansing, Mich.: Asian Studies Center, Michigan State University, 1985), pp. 59–69; see esp. p. 59. By Bengal here is not meant the modern province of West Bengal but a cultural area that is more properly called Greater Bengal, encompassing West Bengal together with Bangladesh and parts of Orissa, Bihar, and Assam.

2. Joseph T. O'Connell, "Social Implications of the Gauḍīya Vaiṣṇava Movement," Ph.D. diss., Harvard University, 1970. See also his "Do Bhakti Movements Change Hindu Social Structures? The Case of Caitanya's Vaiṣṇavas in Bengal," in Bardwell L. Smith, ed., *Religious Movements and Social Identity* (Delhi: Chanakya Publications, 1991), pp. 39–63.

3. For a discussion of caste in the Bengali Vaiṣṇava movement, see O'Connell, "Bhakti Movements," pp. 40–42. On women leaders and teachers in the movement, see D. M. Wulff, "Images and Roles of Women in Bengali Vaiṣṇava *padāvalī kīrtan*," in Yvonne Haddad and Ellison Findly, eds., *Women, Religion and Social Change* (Albany: SUNY Press, 1985), pp. 217–45. On both, see also the two articles of Sanyal cited in note 2.

4. On the concept of *līlā* generally, see Norvin Hein, "*Līlā*," in Mircea Eliade et al., eds., *The Encyclopedia of Religion* (New York: Macmillan, 1987), vol. 8. pp. 550–54. On *līlā* especially in Bengali Vaiṣṇava thought and practice, see my

Drama as a Mode of Religious Realization: The Vidagdhamādhava of Rūpa Gosvāmī (Chico, Calif.: Scholars Press, 1984), esp. pp. 9–10, 45–65; and p. 190 n. 11.

5. Largely because of these antinomian elements, Norvin Hein has proposed that *līlā* was a compensation for a lack of freedom in the political, social, and religious spheres during the period of Muslim rule (Hein, "A Revolution in Krsnaism: The Cult of Gopala," *History of Religions* 25, no. 4 [May 1986]: 296–317). His thesis may fit the situation in north India better than that in Bengal. On Bengal's heterodoxy, see my "Images and Roles," pp. 218–24.

6. See J. T. F. Jordens, "Medieval Hindu Devotionalism," in A. L. Basham, ed., *A Cultural History of India* (Oxford: Clarendon Press, 1975), p. 273.

7. On *rasa* in Bengali Vaiṣṇava thought and practice, see my *Drama as a Mode of Religious Realization,* esp. pp. 25–44. See also David Haberman, *Acting as a Way of Salvation: A Study of Rāgānugā Bhakti Sādhana* (New York: Oxford University Press, 1988, esp. chap. 2–3.

8. Unlike the episodes elaborated in Bengali *kīrtan,* in which Rādhā is celebrated by name, the five chapters in Book X of the *Bhāgavata Purāṇa* that treat Kṛṣṇa's dalliances with the cowherd women speak only of an unnamed favorite and mention no rival. Further, the emphasis in the early chapters of Book X is on Kṛṣṇa's youthful victories over a series of demons. These conquests have been dramatized in *yātrā* performances, but they have not figured prominently in *kīrtan.*

9. On the *gauracandrikā,* see Edward C. Dimock, Jr., "The Place of *Gauracandrikā* in Bengali Vaiṣṇava Lyrics," *Journal of the American Oriental Society* 78 (1958): 153–69.

10. For the meaning of Rādhā for the Bengali Vaiṣṇava community, including those who live in Brindavan, in Uttar Pradesh, see Shrivatsa Goswami, "Rādhā: The Play and Perfection of *Rasa,*" in John Stratton Hawley and Donna Marie Wulff, eds., *The Divine Consort: Rādhā and the Goddesses of India* (Berkeley, Calfi.: Berkeley Religious Studies Series, 1982), pp. 72–88. For a brief survey of her nature and religious significance, see my "Rādhā" in *The Encyclopedia of Religion,* vol. 12, pp. 195–97.

11. Because Rupa wrote in Sanskrit, I use the Sanskrit rather than the Bengali forms here.

12. The fourth is *premavaicittya,* a condition in which the intensity of Rādhā's love leads to a bewilderment that causes her to experience Kṛṣṇa as absent even when he is right in front of her.

13. Rupa Gosvami, *Ujjvalanīlamaṇi* (Bombay: Nirnaya Sagar Press, 1932), pp. 131–40.

14. Another who does so regularly is Ramakrishna Das, a classically trained *kīrtanīyā* younger by about a generation than Nanda Kishor Das.

15. Rādhā separated from Kṛṣṇa by a quarrel.

16. Rādhā on her way to a tryst with Kṛṣṇa.

17. Vaiṣṇava scholars who write about *kīrtan* do not define the term *līlā,* apparently assuming that their readers all know what it means.

18. Khagendranath Mitra, *Kīrtan* (Calcutta: Sri Pulinabihari Sen, B.E. 1352 [ca. 1944]).

19. Harekrishna Mukhopadhyay, *Bāṅgālār Kīrtan O Kīrtanīyā* (Calcutta: Sahitya Samsad, 1971).

20. In January 1989 I conducted a series of interviews of eleven *kīrtanīyās*, several of whom are especially well known. I also interviewed several *kīrtanīyās*, including Nanda Kishor Das, between August 1979 and January 1981.

21. I have not witnessed this or the following *pālā,* but I am told that each includes a secret meeting of Kṛṣṇa and Rādhā.

22. I have not seen this or the following *pālā,* but they are often cited.

23. These findings parallel precisely my judgments of the two full-length Sanskrit dramas of Rupa Gosvami. See my *Drama as a Mode of Religious Realization,* esp. pp. 2–6, 45–98.

24. Typical, that is, in my experience: although I am basing my analysis on a fairly wide set of performances, the roughly four dozen that my research assistant and I recorded, there may be other variants that I have not encountered. I am also thinking primarily of the performances at the upper end of the spectrum, those that I judged to be the most effective.

25. For an analysis of the *ākhar* lines of two *kīrtan* songs and their relation to the lines of the original poems, see my "Internal Interpretation: The *ākhar* Lines in Performances of *padāvalī kīrtan,*" in K. I. Koppedrayer, ed., *Contacts Between Cultures: South Asia,* vol. 2 (Queenston, Ont.: The Edwin Mellen Press, 1992), pp. 317–24.

26. Service to a deity in the form of a hospitality ritual.

27. For example, at *Bhāgavata Purāṇa* X.15.36.

28. I was told of the remarkable feats of Ramdas Babaji by a number of Bengalis, including Dr. Basanti Chaudhury, Department of Music, Rabindra Bharati University, Calcutta, and the late Dr. Bimal Krishna Matilal, Spalding Professor of Eastern Religions and Ethics at the University of Oxford.

29. Bimal Krishna Matilal, personal communication, August 1990.

30. I am reminded of the theological sense of *līlā* set forth by Norvin Hein: "[Līlā] has been the central term in the Hindu elaboration of the idea that God in his creating and governing of the world is moved not by need or necessity but by a free and joyous creativity that is integral to his own nature. He acts in a state of rapt absorption comparable to that of an artist possessed by his creative vision or to that of a child caught up in the delight of a game played for its own sake" ("Līlā," vol. 8, p. 550). I am confident that Bengali Vaiṣṇavas would accept this definition of God's *līlā,* and that they would see a performance of *kīrtan* as an opportunity for performers and audience members alike to become totally involved, for a time, in that *līlā,* which is, for the Caitanya school, ultimate reality.

31. Ramakrishna Das.

32. The example that is usually given is that of Bhavabhuti's *Uttararāmacarita.*

33. See note 1.

34. By calling it popular, I do not mean to take sides in the long-standing debate about whether it is a classical (*mārga*) or a folk (*deśī,* "regional") form. In my judgment it shows influences of both these musical traditions.

35. Tarashish Mukhopadhyay, research scholar, personal communication, 1980.

36. Wulff, "Images and Roles," pp. 217, 228–45.

37. Sanyal, for example, states that Caitanya preached "simple and direct faith among the masses" (Sanyal, "Transformation of the Regional *Bhakti* Movement (Sixteenth and Seventeenth Centuries)," p. 59; cf. his "Transformation of the Regional *Bhakti* Movement in Bengal," p. 3). His view seems to be based on certain notions about what "the masses" are capable of understanding; like such terms as "primitive" and "native," "the masses" needs to be deconstructed.

8

Every Play a Play Within a Play

JOHN STRATTON HAWLEY

The word *līlā*[1] encompasses a huge span of meanings, even within the literature of Kṛṣṇa.[2] My purpose here is to ask: "What is *līlā* in the *rās līlā*s of Brindavan?"

The *rās līlā* is a type of musical drama in which Brahman boys local to the Braj country, of which Brindavan is nowadays the spiritual capital, depict incidents involving Kṛṣṇa, Rādhā, and other participants in the charmed, pastoral world inhabited by these two. For a devotee of Kṛṣṇa, the Braj region, which lies primarily on the right bank of the River Jumna somewhat south of Delhi and north of Agra, is charged with potential meaning, for it is here that Kṛṣṇa is said to have been born in his human manifestation and to have spent his childhood. Within Braj, Brindavan carries a special meaning, for many sectarian communities hold that it was in Brindavan that Kṛṣṇa performed his original *rās līlā* with his cowherd sweethearts (*gopī*s)—not a staged drama this time but an experience of total erotic participation that is usually described as having the character of a dance (*rās*). Troupes of Brahman players based in Braj—*rās maṇḍalī*s—bring this original, perennial *rās līlā* to life every time they perform. They travel throughout the subcontinent with their art, but in Braj—and specifically in Brindavan, where many of them are now based—they are on home turf. Here, especially in festival seasons, pilgrims come to them rather than vice versa, and their audiences, a diverse company, swell to many times their off-season size.

In an earlier work, *At Play with Krishna,* I have translated some of the dramas presented by a single company, that of Svāmīs Śrī Rām and Natthī Lāl, in the summer of 1976. The reader is referred to that book and to the earlier work of Norvin Hein for details about the *rās līlā* as a genre of performance and for a sense of its general ambience.[3] Here my aim is narrower and more specific. Working from a sample of *līlā*s produced in the summers of 1974, 1975, and 1976, I hope to show that it is with justice that the entire genre is called *līlā*. Of course, the word *līlā* has more than one meaning. Bettina Bäumer's essay in this volume points to a dimension in which *līlā*—or its close relative, *krīḍā*—implies a concealment of the divine identity,[4] and there are moments when that sense is exemplified in the Braj *rās līlā*s too. For as we shall see, desception and thievery constitue a major theme in these *līlā*s. A second meaning of *līlā,* "ease"—as in the adverbial formulation *līlayā*—is also apt as a characterization of almost all that transpires in the dramas of Brindavan. In fact, as we shall see, there is often a sense of such ease that nothing really happens. Yet a third core of meanings is even more directly to the fore than either of these: *līlā* as drama, play, fun, mischief, even a certain brand of easy-to-take nonsense. This sense of *līlā* is at the heart of the *rās līlā*s and is implied in the very definition of the genre itself.

Līlānukaraṇ

Formally, the mark that sets the *rās līlā* genre apart from other performance traditions that call themselves *līlā*s is that everything presented in the *rās līlā*s ought rightly to be understood as being a play within a play. What Kṛṣṇa, Rādhā, and the *gopī*s do onstage in modern-day Brindavan is really just an imitation (*anukaraṇ*) of what the *gopī*s did in an archetypal past—*in illo tempore*—and that action is understood as the *Bhāgavata Purāṇa* reports it (10.30.14–23). According to the *Bhāgavata,* when Kṛṣṇa sensed that the women he had drawn into the forest had become too confident of their hold upon him, he disappeared from their midst. Unable to endure his absence, they responded by taking roles so that they could represent to themselves some of the *līlā*s, the principal episodes, or "gestes," that had shaped his life up until that time. What they did became a kind of comprehensive *līlā* in its own right—a selective summation in play of Kṛṣṇa's activities, for the purpose of making them come alive again. So even before the primordial *līlā* of Kṛṣṇa found its culmination as the *gopī*s danced the *rās* and "played" with him a set of limitation *līlā*s (*kṛṣṇalīlānukaraṇa*)[5] had come into existence.

If the great erotic dance that Kṛṣṇa himself initiates—the archetypal *rās līlā*—is the framing play, as the theology of *līlānukaraṇ* suggests it must be, then the *gopī*s' "imitation" in his seeming absence is a play within a play. It is this imitation that is replicated every time the *rās līlā* is performed. Thus each new performance bears a close connection to the "original" imitation, whether one understands it as imitation or continuation. This is symbolized in various ways—by the affirmation that those who perform are not just human beings but *svarūps* ("very forms") of the divinities concerned, by a theology that makes not just Rādhā but all the *gopīs* part of Kṛṣṇa's divine economy, and even by the fact that the stage upon which the *rās līlā* is presented is fashioned in the shape that the original *rās līlā* is thought to have had: a circle. The absent Kṛṣṇa becomes actually present through his dramatic imitation, just as the "real" Kṛṣṇa is himself someone who takes the role of an actor, making his presence felt in this world through the medium of *līlāvataraṇa,* descents in the mode of play.[6] Once the crowns are placed upon the heads of the Brahman boys who take the roles of Kṛṣṇa and Rādhā, these boys are treated by spectators as if they were the divinities themselves.

It is intrinsic to the identity of the *rās līlā* that it is not just representation. These dramas do not merely render reality in the way that a painting or photograph might. Because in their case dramatic representation is a part of the reality that is being portrayed, and because according to the "charter myth" the dramatic imitation of Kṛṣṇa's *līlā* is actually a stage in his *līlā*'s fulfillment, the *rās līlās* of Braj are understood by those who do and see them as more than mere imitation. In somewhat the way that a self requires another to be a self, reality needs imitation to be reality; and that makes imitation more than imitation.

The *Mahārās Līlā*

In the dramas of Brindavan the charter myth of the *rās līlā* is acted out in its fullest form in the *līlā* called the *mahārās līlā* ("The Great Circle Dance"). As now commonly performed in Brindavan, this *līlā* is of relatively recent origin; it was created in the middle years of the present century.[7] Its newness (a fact of which few spectators would be aware, in any case) does not make it any the less popular; it is one of the essential staples in the production of the *rās līlā*. In part because it requires a more elaborate dramatic personae than ordinary *līlās*—there must be enough "Kṛṣṇas" to show how the real Kṛṣṇa multiplied himself around the circle of the *rās* and held the hand of each *gopī*—the *mahārās līlā* draws unusually large crowds whenever it is performed. Another reason for its popularity is that it stands so close to the core of the tradition. In watching the *mahārās līlā,* spectators feel they are seeing "the real thing."

The *rās* portion of any *rās līlā* bears a clear relation to this core, and it is for that reason that no *rās līlā* can be performed unless it begins with the *rās*. The first half of any *rās līlā* presents an "imitation" of how Kṛṣṇa sang and danced with the *gopī*s, Rādhā included; it hints, too, at how he made love with each of them. It is only when this *rās* has been performed that the *līlā* of the day can commence. Such *līlā*s, which vary from day to day, provide scope for the dramatic representation of episodes in Kṛṣṇa's life that the *gopī*s might have imitated in the original *līlānukaraṇ*. The *mahārās līlā* is an example of such a *līlā*, but unlike the others, it is explicitly self-referential. In it the *līlā* of the day is not some more or less randomly chosen vignette from Kṛṣṇa's childhood but the episode of the *rās* itself, so in this one case the schematic, preliminary *rās* can be omitted.[8] Because of its theme and scale the *mahārās līlā* provides scope for laying out the theology of *līlā* with a clarity that is not possible in an ordinary play.

Elsewhere I have translated a performance of the *mahārās līlā* composed by Premānand, a man born in perhaps the last decade of the nineteenth century.[9] Here let me just draw attention to its overall structure, comprising three parts separated from one another by the fall of a curtain.

1. *Preparation.* The drama begins by showing the preparations necessary for the *rās*. The first important act is a battle waged between Kāmdev, the personified force of desire (*kāma*), and Kṛṣṇa. When Kṛṣṇa is victorious, it signifies the defeat of every selfish force associated with love: Kṛṣṇa's *rās* dance will celebrate utterly selfless love instead. Once Kāmdev is vanquished, Kṛṣṇa enlists the help of Yogamāyā, an uncanny magical force that ultimately emerges from Kṛṣṇa himself. Yogamāyā, personified as a woman, explains how she will arrange things in such a way that the dance will be shrouded in secrecy and silence. Moreover, it will occupy a space vast enough to accommodate sixteen thousand *gopī*s and time equivalent to more than four trillion years, yet in a single glade of the Brindavan's forest and a single night in human time. Finally, in this dance Kṛṣṇa will be able to multiply himself so that each girl feels his intimate touch; there will be no jealousy, no sense of loss to pollute each participant's sense of fulfillment.

2. *Testing*. The second part of the play is devoted to showing how Kṛṣṇa tests the *gopī*s' fealty, thus ascertaining their readiness to participate in the *rās* event. Though he has summoned them with his own flute, he taunts them for coming in such haste:

> You're standing there ragged as a pack of yogis:
> What then? Has a lion ravaged the town?[10]

He warns them about the dangers of the jungle—wild beasts and, not the least, himself. They should not think he is just some celibate boy who could never be moved to take advantage of married women. And then there is the matter of marriage: why are they forsaking everything dutiful and holy to be with him?

Are they whores? To each of these taunts the *gopī*s respond by saying that emotion has brought them to where they are, and there is no way back. They plead with Kṛṣṇa not to send them away. In the end he does not: Rādhā appears on the scene, and Kṛṣṇa says he only entered onto this testing as a suberfuge to wait for her arrival. In a sense this is true. Not only does she represent the summation of them all, but theologically she participates in Kṛṣṇa as well; she is the relational force that makes it possible for the *rās* to proceed.

3. *Fulfillment*. That is what happens in the final section of the drama, where speech largely yields to action and song. It is actually Śiva who inaugurates the *rās* dance by agreeing to transform himself into a single *gopī*. This makes a point about the theological status of those who participate, while at the same time underscoring the defeat of one expression of the religious life by another. Asceticism and self-control are supplanted by emotion and self-emptying love. Then as Kṛṣṇa rhapsodizes about this realm of love—Brindavan, he says, is better than heavenly Vaikuṇṭha—the actual *rās* dance proceeds, with much circling, many steps and songs, and the multiplication of Kṛṣṇas around the circle by means of "Kṛṣṇas" recruited from other troupes. In the final moment the audience has a chance to come forward and witness a tableau in which the multiple Kṛṣṇas are arrayed in a single line, a memorable sight.

Most observers undoubtedly feel that the tripartite structure of the *mahārās līlā* is sound. Yet, interestingly, there is a point at which it seems to break down, for the second section, the testing, commences with a remark addressed by Kṛṣṇa to his flute Muralī in which he calls Muralī his "third Yogamāyā."[11] It would have been understandable to hear Kṛṣṇa call Muralī his "second Yogamāyā," for his flute exerts something akin to the magical force that is wielded by Yogamāyā and makes her a principal actor in the first part of the play. But why should Kṛṣṇa call her his "third yogamāyā"?

When I asked Premānand what he had in mind, he replied that he was referring to three forms of *māyā*, the beguiling divine energy that is always represented as a feminine force. The first *māyā* is the primordial one, and this Premānand identified with Rādhā. She is the preexistent principle that makes any differentiation possible within the One, but that also creates the possibility of restoring to the universe an encompassing union with Kṛṣṇa. The second *māyā* is Yogamāyā herself, who cooperates with Kṛṣṇa both in creating this world and in creating the conditions that make the *rās līlā* possible "within" it. Among other things, she abrogates normal time constraints and makes copies of both the *gopī*s and Kṛṣṇa so that the *rās* can go unperceived by those who inhabit reality in its grosser, phenomenal form. Then, finally, there is Muralī, who serves as Kṛṣṇa's agent in beguiling the *gopī*s so that they join in the *rās*. The action of these three *māyā*s may be seen linearly, with Rādhā first and Muralī last, or as a set of concentric circles. Rādhā's realm of activity is cosmic and all-encompassing; Yogamāyā's activity creates and governs the world as we know it; and Muralī exercises her control over its charmed inner circle, Brindavan itself.[12]

Now it can be understood why Kṛṣṇa addressed Muralī as his third *māyā* at the beginning of the second part of the *mahārās līlā*. That part describes Kṛṣṇa's testing of the *gopī*s, and Muralī is his agent in calling them before the bar, as it were. Looking backward, we see that Yogamāyā commands the first section of the *mahārās līlā* in a similar way. She is his main interlocutor there, and the figure that makes it possible for the drama to move to its second stage, the testing.[13] Looking forward, we see that one part remains, and the implication is that the possibility of the *rās*'s fulfillment, which this third part describes, rests upon the *māyā* that is encoded in the universe through the presence of Rādhā herself. Coeval with Kṛṣṇa, she preexists the *mahārās līlā* and creates the conditions that allow it to be consummated. Thus in Premānand's telling (unlike that of the *Bhāgavata,* which does not, after all, mention Rādhā) the testing episode comes to its conclusion with the appearance of Rādhā. It is this, we recall, that Kṛṣṇa says he has been waiting for.[14] (See the following chart.)

Realm:	cosmos	this world	*rās* circle	
Definer of the realm:	Rādhā	Yogamāyā	Muralī	
Mahārās līlā:		preparation	testing	fulfillment

The entire *līlā* that the *gopī*s perform is then to be understood as a product of Kṛṣṇa's own *māyā,* expressed in three feminine forms. This demonstrates in another way the point with which we began—that in its essence the *rās līlā* is self-referential. Furthermore, as the theologians worked it out, it symbolizes and summarizes the way in which our world is to be understood as internal to the divine economy. We human beings, given where we now are, must perceive by means of differentiation and duality, therefore we must name with more than one name—Kṛṣṇa and Rādhā—and see reality as a relation of parts. But we ourselves are part of those parts by virtue of our participation in the *gopī*s, who are themselves expressions of Rādhā, who stands in an indefinable but total relation to Kṛṣṇa.[15]

The "three-*māyā*" scheme also draws attention to the nature of the action that occurs when we see reality from this point of view. It is playful, artful, deceptive. In the second part of the *līlā,* when Kṛṣṇa tests, he deceives: it is a form of *māyā*. He disavows ever having summoned the *gopī*s, claims that he cannot be trusted to help them save thier good names (though unbeknownst to them he has just done so through the actions of Yogamāyā, who makes their absence invisible to their relatives and acquaintances), and attributes to them motives they do not have.[16] And when, through Yogamāyā, Kṛṣṇa prepares the ground for his *rās līlā* in the first part of the play, he does so in a way that also challenges the status of common knowledge. It turns out that the real *gopī*s are the ones who have been attracted to Kṛṣṇa. What their husbands and families see left behind—the gross reality you and I might perceive with ordinary eyes—are mere copies. Owing to the force of *māyā,* variously expressed, it is the play, Kṛṣṇa's *līlā,* that is real. What we know as reality (the *gopī*s we would see if we visited the houses they left as they responded to the call of the flute) is not really "real" at all.

Curiously, Premānand's *mahārās līlā* omits the charter myth of the art form in which he is working. He makes no mention either of Kṛṣṇa's absenting himself from the *gopī*s or of their responding by acting out his various *līlā*s as if he were still present. This is a daring departure from tradition, but when one thinks about it the omission may not be as curious as initially it seems.

First of all, Premānand does provide a verbal anticipation of the moment in which Kṛṣṇa makes himself disappear: in testing them he seems to withdraw his affections. So the element of disappearance is not exactly absent, it just comes in a different form: Kṛṣṇa feigns being inaccessible to the *gopī*s' hearts.[17] The transmutation of this motif from something physically vivid to something entirely emotional, of course, removes the feature in the plot that would call for the "imitation of Kṛṣṇa" on the *gopī*s' part. With Kṛṣṇa there, there is no need for the *gopī*s to act out his *līlā*s. But more may be involved in dictating the absence of the "play within the play" than this. After all, the play that we see before us *is* at least a version of the very play that the *gopī*s produced. In a certain way, therefore, Premānand has eliminated the need for the original *līlānukaraṇ,* the one reported in the great Kṛṣṇa *purāṇa*s, by making the *mahārās* a *līlā* of its own. Perhaps its absence is even calculated to make the audience aware that they themselves are participating in the *līlā* that is being described—and, in another way, not described.

To see things as such would indeed be to accept the reversal of things-as-they-seem that is so close to the heart of the message not only of this *līlā* but of many that are performed in Brindavan. To see things as such would also be to accept the self-referentiality that is demonstrated as the *mahārās līlā* sets out its theology of the *rās līlā*. In the experience of the spectator, it ought not be possible to give thought to another world than that of the *līlā* while the *līlā* is proceeding; one is totally absorbed. And the *līlā*'s own theology makes the claim that this absorption is the nature of reality itself.[18]

Other *Līlās*

This perspective on what *līlā* involves—the undermining of everyday assumptions about life—if fully outlined only in the *mahārās līlā,* but it may not be surprising to find that several of its salient features recur in many of the other *līlā*s that contribute to the repertoire of the *rās līlā* troupes of modern-day Brindavan. Especially prominent are the following motifs: (1) reversal, particularly the sort of role reversal that is represented in cross-dressing between the sexes; (2) deception and thievery, particularly when the impetus is to ask whether these acts of deception and theft are really to be understood as such; and, finally, (3) a mood in which it seems that ultimately nothing really happens at all—this by contrast to the sort of plot that features genuine struggle and conflict, events that lead forward to outcomes that are truly different from what one has when the play begins. In the genre as a whole, these motifs and moods further reinforce the sense that Kṛṣṇa's "dramatic reality" supersedes all others, and they deserve to be examined one by one.

Reversal

One of the commonest themes in the sermons (*pravacan*) delivered by Kṛṣṇa in prose and song between the *rās* and *līlā* portions of the Brindavan *rās līlā*s is that of reversal. Kṛṣṇa often says that his purpose in coming into the world is to play, and the form that this play takes is turning things upside down. He describes himself as a god whose divinity is measured by his eagerness to leave the divine behind. He is a "crazy god" (*bā̃vare ṭhākur*) who prefers the intimate insult of being called a thief to the etiquette with which he would be addressed as the superintendent of an orderly heaven.[19] For him majesty or lordliness (*aiśvarya*), the sentiment that if "God's in his heaven, all's right with the world," is the enemy of play (*līlā*).

Just as it is Kṛṣṇa's desire to reverse his own divine nature as he enters the realm of Braj to play, so it becomes appropriate for the plays of Brindavan to occupy themselves with reversals of their own. The examples one could cite are numerous, but prominent among them are instances of reversal in which clothes are involved. Clothes are the most common symbols of social roles, particularly sexual ones, and sexual roles, because binary by nature, provide an apt language for the motif of reversal as a whole. To doff the appurtenances of one sex and take on those of the other is not merely to change but to reverse.

For any man—and it is well to remember that the architects of the Braj *līlā*s are men—entrance into the realm of the *līlā* itself requires a change of sexual role. The archetype in this regard is Śiva, whose transformation of himself into a *gopī* is the action that introduces the "fulfillment" segment of the *mahārās* *līlā*.[20] For all his majesty—indeed, in part, because of it—Śiva is denied entrance to the sacred circle, the *rās maṇḍal,* until he becomes female. When Kṛṣṇa's buffoonish friend Mansukhā desires to participate in the *rās,* as he does in the *līlā* depicting "The Theft of the Flute," the same transformation is required of him. Much to Mansukhā's displeasure and the audience's amusement, the *gopī*s outfit him with the sixteen marks of female beauty, yet to no avail: Mansukhā has failed to notice that Kṛṣṇa himself is absent from the circle in which he so desperately desires to dance.[21]

Even more frequently, Rādhā and Kṛṣṇa—each theologically a version of the other, but in reverse—adopt one another's dress to gain access to the other's presence. Typically Rādhā takes on the garb of a cowherd to go have a talk with Kṛṣṇa and see if he really loves her, as in the *subal beś* ("Subal's Stratagem") and *gaure gvāl* ("The Fair-Skinned Cowherd") *līlā*s. Kṛṣṇa plays a similar game to sneak beyond the older women who guard Rādhā or to escape Rādhā's own notice if she is too angry with him to receive him under normal circumstances. Well-known examples where this occurs are the *maināvārī* ("The Mynah-Seller"), *candrāvalī* ("Candrāvali"), and *rangrejin* ("The Dyer Woman") *līlā*s, and Norvin Hein's plot summaries of the *rās līlā*s he surveyed in Brindavan from 1949 to 1950 reveal a number of others. The ultimate is the situation in which the audience observes a simultaneous cross-dressing on the part of both Rādhā and Kṛṣṇa, as in the *mundariyācorī* ("The Theft of the Ring") and *rājdān* ("The Gift to the King") *līlā*s. Subsidiary motifs are provided by instances in which Rādhā and Kṛṣṇa hide themselves under the garments of a third character to approach one another, as in the *anurāg līlā* ("The Dawning of Love").

Another set of reversals is provided in *līlā*s where Kṛṣṇa, whose male position ought to rank him higher than Rādhā, grovels at her feet, as in the *naukā* ("The Boatman") and *rādhācaransparś* ("Touching Rādhā's Foot") *līlā*s. These startling reversals in Rādhā's favor accord with the increasingly Rādhā-centered theology of Brindavan and are an unfailing source of delight for audiences who see them. But in thinking about them it is important to remember that however great the exaltation of Rādhā in Brindavan's theology, it would make no sense and would have no force if a prior exaltation of Kṛṣṇa were not assumed. Hence an element of play, *līlā,* is involved when Kṛṣṇa bows at her feet—a play that equalizes.

Similarly, the changing of dress would have little force if the inner status of the person involved were also transformed, since the sense of contrast would be lost. Cross-dressing is piquant and titillating: it is only meaningful if there is an underlying constancy to which it relates as a changed overlay. Hence spectators experience delight not only as a member of one sex puts on the other's garments but also later, when those garments are stripped away. As in other aspects of the *rās līlā*s' plots, then, there is a sense in which nothing really happens. No real transformations are achieved—only temporary exchanges.

Deception and Thievery

Much the same thing is true in regard to another characteristic motif, that of deception and thievery. Here too one typically has displacement without real transformation. In *līlā*s in which Kṛṣṇais cast as the thief—and these are frequent—the dialogue often turns on the question of whether he is really stealing anything at all. This inevitably comes up in both the performance and the interpretation of various versions of the *mākhan corī līlā* ("The Butter Thief"),[22] but it figures even more obviously in the *dān līlā* ("The Gift"). For the "gift" in question is the one demanded by Kṛṣṇa as he stops the *gopī*s on their way to market their milk products in Mathura—seeking to levy a debilitating tax on their milk and curd. The issue is in what measure he is demanding it and in what measure he is merely providing an occasion for them to do what they want to do in any case—give him whatever they have. The question has particular force in relation to milk products, which are symbolic of these women's love for him. Interviews revealed time and again that those who perform and observe these *līlā*s understand this interaction as "play"—not only because of the secret wishes of the *gopī*s so importuned but because, as the supernal deity of all the world, Kṛṣṇa already possesses what he appears to steal away. The action upon which the *līlā* turns, then—Kṛṣṇa's taking a toll, acting the part of a thief—is in a certain sense false from the beginning.

Banter, punning, and deceptions also occupy a prominent place in the plots of the *rās līlā*s, and are appropriate for similar reasons. They are harmless—mere twistings of words in which the speaker hopes to trap his listener in a net of verbal convolutions—and they are ubiquitous. In the *cīrharaṇ līlā* ("The Theft of the Clothes"), just after Kṛṣṇa has snapped up the saris of the bathing *gopī*s and hung them out in the branches of the *kadamb* tree, much time is spent in a dialogue between him and them in which he denies that what they see before them are in fact the *gopī*s' clothes. They are the flowers of the *kadamb,* he says, and in a flight of fancy he claims that the blossoms would be even bigger than they are if there had been no drought. When they dismiss this sort of palaver as useless and insist on getting down to business, he leads them on by demanding that they produce a witness to verify that he has stolen their clothes. Part of the reason they were bathing in the dark of early morning in the first place is that their modesty demands the last cover of night, so of course there will be no witnesses in the normal sense. And on and on it goes.[23]

Other *līlā*s have similarly extended sequences. Whenever Mansukhā is onstage much time is devoted to banter, as one can see in his dialogues both with the *gopī*s and with Kṛṣṇa in the *bansī corī līlā* ("The Theft of the Flute").[24] Rādhā spends an inordinate time punning on the names by which Kṛṣṇa introduces himself in the *anurāg līlā* until he can produce a name for himself that is so individual as to resist punning. The solution is "Butter Thief" (*mākhan cor*). Only when he announces himself according to this inimitable, almost inconceivable, identity does she deign to speak with him directly.[25]

In the *mahārās līlā* Kṛṣṇa himself spends most of the second section of the play testing the *gopī*s with fabrications that he thinks up.[26] For example, he taunts them for their dissheveled appearance, which results from the haste with which they dropped whatever they were doing to respond to the call of his flute. Instead Kṛṣṇa suggests that only an encounter with some demon or crazed animal could have sent them running in this way. As he says so, however, he hints at a concealed motive on their part, for he wonders why it was that only women have flocked to him and not men as well. What have they to say for themselves?

It is significant that the *gopī*s never pass such tests as these in the terms in which they are laid out. Indeed, as we discover at length, there is no way they could have been victorious in their sparring matches with Kṛṣṇa. He is ultimately not concerned with them but with Rādhā, waiting for her to appear. Only that brings his tests, deceptions, and puns to an end.[27] Rādhā is the solution to the *gopī*s, dilemma, but she is external to anything they themselves can provide. Since even collectively they cannot be Rādhā, there is no way they can pass Kṛṣṇa's tests of their character, however much they may claim already to have done so.[28] They cannot succeed in their ordeal by enacting any version of the traditional Indian act of truth or even by sheer strength of endurance. Nothing they say or do is sufficient answer—only Rādhā, a relief that comes from outside. As such the whole endeavor has only the force of a game played for Kṛṣṇa's benefit—a *līlā* to pass the time. It fits well into the framework of his *māyā,* which, it will be recalled, is the means by which Premānand introduces it.[29]

Nothing Happens

This brings us to the third motif that is characteristic of the *rās līlā*s: the sense that in these plays typically "nothing happens." In this regard the *bansī corī līlā* may serve as an example. Its concluding scene pits Kṛṣṇa and Mansukhā, who are trying to recover Kṛṣṇa's flute, against a tribunal of *gopī*s headed by Rādhā. Kṛṣṇa and Mansukhā do not in fact know who has stolen the flute, since it was in Mansukhā's possession at the time it was stolen, and he had fallen into a faint after having been admitted to the rapid swirls of the *gopīs*' ersatz *rās* dance. In the realm of juridical process, it finaly becomes clear that Kṛṣṇa and his friend have not a leg to stand on, despite the sometimes clever arguments that Kṛṣṇa presents. In her role as judge Rādhā hands down this decision.[30]

This would seem an instance where something really does happen. A case has been decided: Kṛṣṇa has no grounds for claiming that his flute has been stolen and ought to be returned. But it is precisely at this point that Rādhā does in fact make a move to return Kṛṣṇa's flute, going beyond the terms in which the argument has been couched—the question of thievery—and moving on to the matter of whose the flute actually is. Even there she stops, however, for her companions restrain her. It is not until the realm of reason and jurisprudence is entirely abandoned that the flute is returned. What makes Rādhā relent is a plea from Kṛṣṇa that he can scarcely be who he is without his flute. Because of this emotional plea she returns the flute, and the status quo with which the drama began is restored.[31]

A Child's World

Not every *līlā* is like this. Some have the "duty" of reporting episodes that were a part of the narrative of Kṛṣṇa's life long before the evolution of the *rās līlā* genre into its present form.[32] At least in the terms that the tradition gives them, many of these episodes are more sober than the sort we have tended to feature here, which are more directly tailored to the *rās līlā* genre, and many are transformed as they fall under its spell. The *yamalārjun uddhār līlā* ("The Rescue of Yamal and Arjun"), for example, focuses much less on the miraculous act by means of which the infant Kṛṣṇa released Yamal and Arjun from the trees they had been cursed to inhabit than on the mischief that caused Kṛṣṇa's foster mother, Yaśodā, to tie him to the mortar by means of which he pulled the trees down. It thus becomes a variant of the "Butter Thief" *līlā,* sharing many of its motifs.[33]

As for the principal statement of the "Butter Thief" *līlā*—what is often called the *mākhan corī līlā* as such—it too transforms the older tradition upon which it is built. In this *līlā* complaints made by the *gopīs* to Yaśodā about her son's behavior are not finally adjudicated by Kṛṣṇa's foster mother. Instead the *līlā* ends, as does its cousin the *maṇikambh līlā* ("The Jeweled Pillar"), with a performance of the famous song attributed to Sūrdās, "I Didn't Eat the Butter, Ma." Its result is that Yaśodā, like Rādhā in the *bansī corī līlā,* simply capitulates to the affection she feels for Kṛṣṇa. In the song Kṛṣṇa presents reasons why he cannot have stolen the butter, trying to show that it is all a frame-up, but these are patently invented. Even so Yaśodā takes him in her arms, and that is that. Justice and logical process are the losers, while feeling and caprice, which are the driving impulses in *līlā,* win.

As if to provide specific data for the sense of self-referentiality that is enunciated in the theology of the *mahārās līlā,* these *līlā*s seem to proceed in defiance of struggle and logic. Struggle may seem to occur, as when the *gopī*s complain to Yaśodā of Kṛṣṇa's butter exploits or confront him as a tax collector, or when Kṛṣṇa does everything he can to recover his flute, but such struggles are rarely resolved in the terms in which they are engaged. There is no real outcome, no logical result. Instead the resolution is apt to come through a bypassing of the conflict at hand, an undermining of it by reference to some more basic reality. The struggles that feature in these plots are mere *līlā*s, gestes, temporary snags in the fabric of reality that seem more like wandering puns or misleading changes of clothes than like challenges able to alter the basic structure of a drama or the characters that appear within it.

As for aspects of Kṛṣṇa's mythology that seem inappropriate to this self-referential vision of what the world-*līlā* is about, they are simply eliminated. This means first and foremost Kṛṣṇa's great battle with King Kans at Mathura, which used to be the event foreshadowed and anticipated in so many other events of Kṛṣṇa's childhood. In the *rās līlā*s of Brindavan the battle with Kans simply does not appear. The closest one comes is the *līlā* describing Kṛṣṇa's departure from the Braj countryside, the *akrūr līlā* (''Akrūr''), but its burden is to convert this happening into a psychological event internal to the pastoral world of Braj. Yaśodā's and the *gopī*s' feelings of loss—and those of Kṛṣṇa and his brother, Balarām, as well—form the real substance of the play.

In recent years one *rās līlā* troupe[34] has begun to experiment with a *līlā* depicting the activities reported in the *Bhagavadgītā,* but this is still very far from the norm, and the drama concerned has little of the feel of a ''real'' *līlā.* The only regularly performed *līlā*s that break beyond the boundaries of Braj and thereby beyond the realm of what the *gopī*s could have known are the *līlā* of Kṛṣṇa's birth, which serves logically to introduce the whole cycle and is appropriate to the festival day (*kṛṣṇajanmāṣṭamī*) in which the *rās līlā* season culminates, and the *sudāmā līlā* (''Sudāmā''). With Sudāmā, too, the Braj connection is clear, for although the *līlā* concerning him takes place during the period when Kṛṣṇa reigns as king of Dvaraka, the reason Sudāmā goes to see Kṛṣṇa at court—penurious Brahman that he is—is that the two were childhood chums and schoolmates.

With precious few exceptions, Kṛṣṇa's childhood and the Braj locale define the realm of the *rās līlā,* and since the sixteenth century, as Norvin Hein has shown,[35] these boundaries have been observed not just in the repertoire performed but in the personnel who do the performing. The actors in these dramas must be children—Brahman boys—and they must be local, too: born and bred in Braj. While the practice of using child actors seems initially to have had nothing to do with the nature of the *rās līlā*—Hein thinks it was borrowed from dramatic practices in the Śākta tradition under conditions favored by Muslim rule—this convention came to have an almost unassailable logic once it was established. It completed the circle of self-referentiality that the theology of the *mahārās līlā* sets forth.

The people who played the sacred children's roles really were children, and their play was not play just in the dramatic sense but in the childish sense as well. What they naturally said and did bespoke a world where play reigns. No spectator to the *rās līlā* can miss the point that these children are not just acting; they are having fun. Theirs is a world where the forces of adult desire—*kām,* which is responsible for the generation of effects in the real world—cannot enter. They are too young for sex (at least sex of the sort that leads to real results, progeny), and that makes them just the right sort of actors for plays that time and again represent their own boundaries as excluding, quite precisely, *kām*. Kāmdev (that is, *kām*) appears with spring (*vasant*) and demands entrance into the enchanted circle of Kṛṣṇa's world, but is either repulsed or dead on arrival. Here again the *mahārās līlā* takes the lead,[36] and we see why at least in the setting of the *rās līlā* (as opposed, say, to the *rām līlā*) these children are in an obvious sense real *svarūp*s. Neither workers (*karm*) nor doers of duty (*dharm*) nor pawns in the hands of desire (*kām*), they can answer to the self-referential expectations that the mythology of the *rās līlā* projects. They do what they do for its own sake, for the fun of it; they are truly at play.

It seems clear that the Kṛṣṇa plays of Braj were not originally "child's play." But once they became that, at a time when influences from Bengal and Orissa were increasingly important and Brindavan was emerging as their vortex, a process seems to have been unleashed whereby these dramas came more and more to be affected by the guiding paradigm of the *rās līlā* itself. In taking that name they pointed with increasing clarity to their own myth of origins, the *kṛṣṇalīlānukaraṇ* or *rāsalīlānukaraṇ*. Episodes from Kṛṣṇa's adult life seem to have fallen away in importance, and even in his childhood world his amorous side received far more emphasis than his heroic actions against the various demons who threatened Braj. Thus despite the somewhat serious, theological mood that sets the *mahārās* apart from most other *līlā*s, it manages to define the circle of actors most relevant to Kṛṣṇa in a way that is echoed throughout the repertoire. The *rās līlā* becomes a genre of drama whose dominantly lighthearted note testifies to the fact that it is doing no work; like the circle of the *rās,* it genuinely points to itself. In it, every play is a play within a play—not only a version or extension of the original *līlānukaraṇ* but a dramatic form whose purpose is ultimately to show that in Kṛṣṇa the world plays too.

NOTES

1. Because the language to which primary reference is made is Hindi, the transliteration of Indic terms in this essay takes the Hindi form as its "default" (e.g., *līlānukaraṇ*). Only in cases where the usage is confined to Sanskrit will the standard system for Sanskrit transliteration be employed (e.g., *līlāvataraṇa*).

2. Especially helpful for observing this variety are Clifford Hospital, "Līlā in the Bhāgavata Purāṇa," *Purāṇa* 21:1 (1980), 4–22; Vasant Yāmadagni, *Rāslīlā tathā Rāsānukaraṇ Vikās* (New Delhi: Sangit Natak Akademi, 1980), p. 44; and Jagdīś Bhāradvāj, *Kṛṣṇa-Kāvya mẽ Līlā-Varṇan* (New Delhi: Nirmalakīrti Prakāśan, 1972).

3. J. S. Hawley, in association with Shrivatsa Goswami, *At Play with Krishna* (Princeton, N.J.: Princeton University Press, 1981); Norvin Hein, *The Miracle Plays of Mathura* (New Haven, Conn." Yale University Press, 1972).

4. Bettina Bäumer, "The Play of the Three Worlds," p. 46 in this volume.

5. This nominal form does not actually occur in the *Bhāgavata,* which has instead the verb *anucakrus* (10.30.14), but one finds closer approximations in the *Harivaṃśa* and the *Viṣṇu Purāṇa,* upon which it builds: *kṛṣṇalīlānukārinyaḥ* (HV 63.26) and *kṛṣṇalīlānukariṇī* (VP 5.13.29). For an expanded inventory of related terms, see Clifford Hospital, "Līlā in Early Vaiṣṇava Thought," p. 25 in this volume. It is noteworthy, as Hospital points out, that the oldest surviving reference to *kṛṣṇalīlā,* that of the *Harivaṃśa,* appears in conjunction with the idea of imitation or performance (*anukaraṇ*).

6. For a discussion of this concept, see Hospital, "Līlā in the Bhāgavata Purāṇa," 7–8.

7. An earlier form, constructed primarily on the basis of passages from the *Rāspañcādhyāyī* of Nandadās, is still in existence but is much simpler than the *mahārās līlā* composed by Premānand, which will form the basis of our discussion here. The earlier form is now performed only by the poorer, smaller *rās līlā* companies of Brindavan. Most people see Premānand's version. For further information, see Hawley, *At Play with Krishna,* p. 167.

8. There is, however, an *āratī* in which the same dramatis personae figure. See Hawley, *At Play with Krishna,* pp. 170–71.

9. Ibid., pp. 167–236. The performance is that of Svāmīs Śrī Rām and Natthī Lāl as observed on August 13, 1976. I regret that the original Braj Bhāṣā version of this or any other performance of the *mahārās līlā* has yet to find its way into print.

10. From a *savaiyā* of Premānand, translated in Hawley, *At Play with Krishna,* p. 199.

11. Hawley, *At Play with Krishna,* p. 194.

12. Premānand, interview, Brindavan, August 29, 1976.

13. Hawley, *At Play with Krishna,* pp. 189–93.

14. Ibid., p. 214.

15. For a condensed statement of this metaphysic, aspects of which were designated *acintyabhedābheda* by Jīv Gosvāmī, see Shrivatsa Goswami, "Rādhā: The Play and Perfection of *Rasa*," in J. S. Hawley and D. M. Wulff, eds., *The Divine Consort* (Boston: Beacon Press, 1986), pp. 74–83.

16. Hawley, *At Play with Krishna*, pp. 199–200.

17. This is also to be found in the *Bhāgavata* (10.29.19–27), which is the only puranic account to attributed the cause of the *gopīs*' *līlānukaraṇ* to Kṛṣṇa's absence. See Hein, *Miracle Plays of Mathura*, pp. 259–61.

18. In the wider world of dramatic theology that developed in and around Brindavan, it is acknowledged that a process of spiritual discipline is required to attain this insight into the nature of reality. See David L. Haberman, *Acting as a Way of Salvation* (New York: Oxford University Press, 1988), pp. 65–114. On the relation between such a process of realization and drama per se, at least as understood by Rūp Gosvāmī, see Donna M. Wulff, *Drama as a Mode of Religious Realization: The Vidagdhamādhava of Rūpa Gosvāmin* (Chico, Calif.: Scholars Press, 1984), pp. 35–44.

19. For example, the *pravacan* of the *mākhan corī līlā* of Svāmī Rāmsvarūp, performed on August 15, 1975. It is interesting that the issue of seeming insanity also comes up in Śaivite discussions of what *līlā* (or *krīḍā*) is all about. See Bäumer, "Three Worlds."

20. Hawley, *At Play with Krishna*, pp. 215–16. A temple to Śiva in Brindavan expressly memorializes this event. The *liṅga* appears in its plain "Śaivite" form in the morning but is dressed in the garb of a woman for evening worship. Śiva is known there as Gopīśvar, or "Lord of the *gopīs*."

21. Hawley, *At Play with Krishna*, pp. 133–35.

22. See Hawley, *Krishna, the Butter Thief* (Princeton, N.J.: Princeton University Press, 1983), pp. 267–68.

23. *Cīr haran līlā* of Svāmī Rāmsvarūp, August 2, 1974.

24. Hawley, *At Play with Krishna*, pp. 121–31.

25. *Anurāg līlā* of Svāmī Rāmsvarūp, August 3, 1974, and August 14, 1975.

26. Hawley, *At Play with Krishna*, pp. 199–214.

27. For example, *vipati* and *vipatti*. See Hawley, *At Play with Krishna*, pp. 205–6.

28. Ibid., p. 212.

29. Ibid., p. 194.

30. Ibid., pp. 148–51.

31. Ibid., p. 153.

32. On the question of the historical background of the *rās līlā* plays, which seem to have attained their present form in Mughal times, see the brilliant final chapter in Hein's *Miracle Plays of Mathura*, pp. 223–71.

33. See Hawley, *Krishna, the Butter Thief*, pp. 248–57.

34. The troupe leader (*rāsdhārī*) is Svāmī Rāmsvarūp, who also allows his company to perform the *rām līlā* in a "*rās līlā*" style, something every other company still shuns.

35. Hein, *Miracle Plays of Mathura*, pp. 230–31, 266–70.

36. Hawley, *At Play with Krishna*, pp. 195–98, 217–18.

9

Who's Who in the *Pāṇḍav Līlā*?

WILLIAM S. SAX

When English speakers ask me what *līlā* means, I tell them it means "play" in two main senses of the English word—playful "fun and games" as well as a dramatic enactment, a "play." Several of the essays in this book have concentrated on theological notions of *līlā* as divine play, as the free, spontaneous, and creative activity of a deity. However, this essay describes the second sort of *līlā,* that is *līlā* as a play, a drama.

Pāṇḍav līlā is a traditional[1] local drama in which *Mahābhārata,* the so-called great epic[2] of India, is represented in recitation, dance, and drama by amateur performers for an audience of fellow villagers and guests. To the best of my knowledge, *pāṇḍav līlā* is found only in Garhwal, in the Himalayan districts of the north Indian state of Uttar Pradesh.[3] It is very prominent there, so much so that one authority has asserted that *Mahābhārata* stories form the "most extensive body of folklore" in the region (Chandola 1977:18; see also Leavitt 1988, 1991).

It is important to remember that *pāṇḍav līlā* is not a text, much less a book, but rather a tradition of performance. Although printed editions of *Mahābhārata* are known of and sometimes (albeit rarely) referred to in performances, *pāṇḍav līlā* is fundamentally oral and dramatic. And because *pāṇḍav līlā* is so popular, most people in Garhwal think of *Mahābhārata* as a performance and not as a book. Ironically, this image of *Mahābhārata* may be closer to its original form than the (by South Asian standards) relatively recent, bibliocentric images with which scholars are most comfortable. As Goldman has pointed out, modern scholarship has turned

> the great and fundamentally oral ancient epics of India into *books*. If we "establish" the text . . . then we have a book we can put on our shelf, hold in our hand, and sit quietly and read, scratching our head in wonder at the bizarre kinds of books the ancient Indians produced and read. . . . The volumes may look gigantic on our office shelves but in fact they were delivered and consumed orally in discrete performance units over a period of time as is indicated in the Ramayana. My suspicion is that when one conceived of a text like the Mahabharata as a whole, if ever one did, it was not so much as a book but as a whole body of literature from which specific characters, incidents, or scenes could be adduced from memory to illuminate questions in social life, etc. (1986:9, 19–20)

Clearly, we are mistaken to continue thinking of *Mahābhārata* as a book, and even more mistaken to think that we could ever "establish" a single, definitive edition of it. The difficulties encountered by those who assembled the Pune edition are legendary, even though that enterprise dealt only with Sanskrit manuscripts,[4] while there are literally hundreds of *Mahābhārata*s in many languages from many historical and cultural milieus—and in any case, *Mahābhārata* was an oral poem long before it was ever a book. Even V. S. Sukthankar, editor of the critical edition, stated that the "essential fact in Mahābhārata criticism [is] that the Mahābhārata is not and never was a fixed rigid text, but is fluctuating epic tradition" (quoted in Coburn 1984:34). So if *Mahābhārata* is not a book, what is it? One might dismiss everything that I have written so far, while simultaneously conforming to current intellectual fashion, by answering that *Mahābhārata* is a "text" with its own history and autonomy, and a wide range of possible "readings." But this too is inadequate because although throughout its long history *Mahābhārata* has always been a text, it has also—as performance, hegemonic discourse, political model, and so on—been much more than that. According to the *Mahābhārata* itself (that is, according to most written versions of it): "*Yadihāsti tadanyatra, yannehāsti na tatkvacit*" (Whatever is here [in the *Mahābhārata*] may be found elsewhere; what is not here cannot be found anywhere else).

Much recent scholarship has concentrated on performance of the South Asian "epics," therby problematizing the easy distinction between oral and written texts.[5] This is a positive development, but what I am suggesting goes further. I think that if we wish accurately and faithfully to capture the reality of what *Mahābhārata* and *Rāmāyaṇa* have been and continue to be in people's lives, we should talk about them as *traditions* that include performative as well as (multiple) textual elements—and much more besides. Ultimately this is a claim about the ontological status of specific texts or kinds of texts, and there is not enough space to pursue such an argument here in detail. Let me simply suggest that when certain texts achieve sufficient historical, political, literary, or religious salience, it becomes more appropriate to think of them as "traditions" than as "texts." Think, for example, of *Romeo and Juliet.* Although Shakespeare did indeed write a play by this name, *Romeo and Juliet* has come to signify very much more than the play. But this is a poor example, one that pales in comparison with the multiple dimensions of *Mahābhārata* and *Rāmāyaṇa* as performances, texts, rituals, and political models for much of Asia. *Mahābhārata* really is a "tradition" with deep and important ramifications, and it is only the prejudices of our own bibliocentric academic culture that lead us casually to assume that it is merely a "text." That is why I write in this essay about "*Mahābhārata*" rather than "the *Mahābhārata.*"

Put another way, I am concerned here with the meaning of *Mahābhārata.* But *Mahābhārata* does not "mean" always or only one thing: it means "epic text" to the scholar, bedtime story to the Indian child, political model to the Indonesian monarch, and a certain kind of performance to the Garhwali villager. Meaning depends on context, and these various contexts are the results of a large and indeterminate number of historical, cultural, and psychological factors. In this essay I shall be concentrating on one factor, the notion of *līlā* as it is borrowed by Garhwalis from the general cultural milieu of South Asia and applied to their own particular interests and concerns.

Pāṇḍav līlā is a "cultural performance" par excellence. Over thirty-five years ago Milton Singer coined this term, noting that his Indian friends "thought of their culture as encapsulated in these discrete performances which they could exhibit to visitors and to themselves" (1955:27). Since then the concept has been invoked over and over again. It has become something of a cliché and, like all clichés, has suffered an impoverishment of meaning.[6] Implicit in Singer's definition is the notion of self-representation, and I propose to explore this notion more fully, to see precisely in what ways Garhwalis think of *pāṇḍav līlā* as representing their own culture. In the next section of the essay I will provide a general introduction to *pāṇḍav līlā,* the circumstances of its performance, and the reasons that Garhwalis give for staging it. Then I will describe the indigenous, explicit model of *pāṇḍav līlā* as a kind of quintessential self-representation. Following that I will provide evidence for what I see as a second interpretive possibility; namely, that *pāṇḍav līlā* represents the Kṣatriyas who perform it not only as the equals of Brāhmaṇs but in some sense as Brāhmaṇs themselves. Finally, I shall suggest that the nature of *pāṇḍav līlā as* a *līlā* facilitates this fluidity of identities.

This all leads to some interesting questions. Are we dealing with Kṣatriyas playing Kṣatriyas, Kṣatriyas playing Brāhmaṇs, Kṣatriyas *becoming* Brāhmaṇs, or something else? In other words, who's who in *pāṇḍav līlā?* Are these various identities "really real" or, as the Garhwalis put it, is this all merely *līlā?*

The *Pāṇḍav Līlā* of Garhwal

There are many different kinds of *pāṇḍav līlā,* or *pāṇḍav nṛtya* (the dance [*nṛtya*] of the Pāṇḍavas), as it is sometimes called. It is performed with considerable variation throughout Garhwal and nowhere else—not even (to the best of my knowledge) in the geographically and culturally contiguous regions of Kumaon and Himachal Pradesh. The people of Garhwal insist that there is one and only one proper time to perform it; however, this "proper time" differs from place to place according to regional custom (*deśācār*). Villagers in the shires (*paṭṭī*)[7] of Lobha and Nagpur conclude their *līlā*s by the month of *mārgaśīrṣ,* and say that there may on no account be a performance during the following, inauspicious month of *pauṣ;* but *pauṣ* is the *only* month when *pāṇḍav līlā* is performed in the shire of Chandpur. Meanwhile, in the shire of Ravain there are *pāṇḍav līlā*s in the months of *māgh* and *śrāvaṇ* as well as *mārgaśīrṣ,* and I am told that in parts of Uttarkashi District they are performed during the hottest month of the year, in *jyeṣṭh*. Performances are astrologically coordinated in order to avoid difficulties. For example, in Jakh village, the local Brāhmaṇ priest Gajendra Prasad Gairola, an accomplished astrologer, calculated an auspicious date for *pāṇḍav līlā* by taking into account the name of the village (the zodiacal sign for the *J* with which *Jakh* begins is *makara* [Capricorn]), the projected date of performance, and the zodiacal signs of the Pāṇḍava brothers Arjuna and Bhīma.

*Pāṇḍav līlā*s come in all shapes and sizes: the first one I ever saw lasted nine days and occurred three years after the previous one in that village; the second lasted thirteen days and occurred after a thirty-five-year hiatus. *Līlā*s may last for as little as three days, or even a single afternoon. These shorter *līlā*s are usually called *pāṇḍav roṇṭ* or *roṇṭ khājā,* terms that refer to the deep-fried bread (*roṇṭ*) and the dry-fried grain (*khājā*) that are offered to dancers and guests during performances. Longer *līlā*s are conventionally and metonymically denoted by the name of the chief episode enacted in them: hence there is the rhinoceros (*gaiṇḍā*) *līlā* performed in Chandpur, the culminating episode of which is the hunting of a rhinoceros in order to obtain its hide for use in King Paṇḍu's funerary rites; the Circular Array (*cakravyūha*), which enacts the capture and death of Arjuna's son Abhimanyu; the Lotus Array (*kamalavyūha*), which enacts another episode from the great *Mahābhārata* battle; and the *śami* tree (*śamivṛkṣ*) *līlā* whose culminating episode is the uprooting and establishing of the tree that protected the Pāṇḍavas' weapons while they were in the court of King Virāṭ. Different shires tend to specialize in one or another of these *līlā*s. But whatever the local emphasis, specialization, or season in which they are performed, all *pāṇḍav līlā*s have this in common—that they are recitative, musical, and dramatic "showings" or "dancings" of *Mahābhārata*.

Shorter performances may last but a single afternoon. These are usually annual affairs, incorporated as subsidiary events in some larger, overarching activity such as the annual worship of a village god or goddess. Along with other village deities, the Pāṇḍavas are invited to attend the festival, dance, and accept offerings. Other deities of an unrefined, inauspicious, and dangerous sort are also likely to attend: after dancing, they are fed uncooked or semi-cooked foods and escorted beyond the village boundaries. But because the Pāṇḍava brothers, along with their mother, Kuntī, and wife, Draupadī, are high, auspicious, and benevolent quasi divinities, they are fed the choicest foods, and individual households seek their blessings. Sometimes the Pāṇḍavas are invited to come to the village for two or three days in a row. In Chandpur this is called *roṇṭ khājā.* Accompanied by a Brāhmaṇ priest, the dancers go from house to house receiving food and cash and dispensing blessings in return.[8] Such short performances do not involve any dramatization of *Mahābhārata* and are not therefore properly called "*līlā*s."

A full-scale *pāṇḍav līlā,* which may last as long as thirteen days and even longer, involves many such exchanges of blessings for offerings, but it also incorporates recitation of the *Mahābhārata* story and dramatization of incidents from it. Local bards pace up and down the square, right hands cupped behind their ears, reciting the story in a highly stylized fashion and sometimes challenging each other to remember particular details. Vibrant group dances by the Pāṇḍavas and their "army" alternate with dramatizations of particular scenes from the story. But all this does not happen at once: *pāṇḍav līlā* is remarkable for the way in which it builds to a climax. During the first few days there are no costumes, weapons, or other props, and often there are few spectators[9] apart from those whose presence is indispensable: the Brāhmaṇ priest and the drummers, members of the untouchable Dās (literally "servant") caste. After a few days the dancers don their costumes: long, flowing white skirts and white turbans for the Pāṇḍava brothers, traditional black homespun woolen garments for the women along with their finest silver jewelry, sometimes a special red costume for Hanumān.[10] Soon after this the weapons are distributed: bows and arrows are given to Arjuna and his son Nāgārjuna (called Babhruvāhana in the Pune edition of *Mahābhārata*), a scythe to Nakula, a discus to Kṛṣṇa, a club to Bhīma, a staff to Yudhiṣṭhira, a writing slate to Sahadeva, a dagger to Draupadī, and other objects to miscellaneous minor characters. These weapons are sometimes distributed by one of the dancers themselves but more often by the guardian deity (usually a fierce goddess) of the village hosting the performance, who is worshiped at the beginning of the *līlā* and distributes weapons through his or her "possessed" oracle. There is always a degree of uncertainty about whether or not the weapons will be successfully distributed, since goddesses are notoriously fickle and quick to anger, and may refuse to give a weapon to a dancer because of alleged moral or ritual failings such as adultery, consumption of meat or liquor, or being in a state of pollution.

Soon the trickle of guests and onlookers becomes a flood. Village homes begin to fill up with friends and relatives; there is a constant buzz of conversation punctuated by the elated cries of old friends reuniting; the morning lineup at the water tap seems endless. Around midday the drums summon everyone to the central dancing square. The Brāhmaṇ priest worships the gods and the Pāṇḍavas, who come and "possess" the dancers taking their parts (see Sax 1991a). Local bards, expert in *Mahābhārata* lore, take turns reciting the story and challenging each other to remember its finer details. Discrete scenes from the story are reenacted in the dancing square. And during the culminating days of the performance, a grand *Mahābhārata* story may be dramatized on a "stage" extending over many square miles, as performers move in procession through the mountains to hunt the rhinoceros, uproot the *śami* tree and carry it home, or do battle with their enemies, the Kauravas.

Pāṇḍav līlā is ritual theater.[11] It is done in order to fulfill a vow to the Pāṇḍavas, or to acquire health, prosperity, and fertility. Various kinds of actions mark *pāṇḍav līlā* as a ritual event. These consist primarily of purification of the site, followed by invocation, feeding, and worship of various divine figures, especially the Pāṇḍavas themselves. There is no rigid distinction between spectators and performers in *pāṇḍav līlā*. This became dramatically clear to me during the first performance I attended, when the drummer began to play the distinctive rhythm of the female character Nārī Ucchaṅga. He had played no more than a few beats when the woman beside me began to tremble and shake uncontrollably. Within a few moments she leaped to her feet and joined the Pāṇḍavas' army in the dancing square. After her part was finished she returned and calmly took her seat again among the onlookers. And this was by no means unusual. Members of the audience are often inspired to join the dancers, and sometimes are compelled to do so because they are possessed by some character in the drama. Bards may cease telling the story and instead join the dancers, and dancers may spontaneously begin to recite. I myself have, in a single night's *līlā,* watched the performance, danced and acted in it, and even recited a small portion of *Mahābhārata.* Avant-garde dramatists and theorists often rail against the "fourth wall" in modern Western theater, but under the starry Himalayan skies during a *pāṇḍav līlā* there are no barriers between those who watch and those who perform.

Garhwalis speak metaphorically of *pāṇḍav līlā* as a *pūjā*. *Pūjā* is the most common form of worship, in which a superior being (usually a deity, more rarely another person) is honored and fed by the worshiper. The Pāṇḍavas are said to be *pūjya,* or worthy of worship, not only because of their great heroism, which is the explicit subject of much of *pāṇḍav līlā,* but also because they are regarded as direct ancestors of the people who stage the *līlā.* And when the Pāṇḍavas are worshiped in *pāṇḍav līlā,* they bless their descendants. Occasional performance of *pāṇḍav līlā* is said to ensure good crops and prosperity, while failure to do so may lead to misfortune. Sometimes villagers vow to perform *pāṇḍav līlā* in return for some particular favor from the Pāṇḍavas. In 1990, for example, much of Chandpur was affected by hoof-and-mouth disease (*khuriyā rog*). I attended *pāṇḍav līlā*s in two villages that year, and in both cases the village council had gone to the local Pāṇḍava shrine, performed a short *pūjā,* and called on the Pāṇḍavas to protect them from the disease, in return for which they vowed[12] that they would perform a *pāṇḍav līlā.* In 1985 the men of Bhatgwali village in Chandpur gave me the following list of reasons for performing *pāṇḍav līlā:* (1) it is a commendable form of worship of their chosen deities (*iṣṭhadevatā*), the Pāṇḍavas; (2) they learn about the *Mahābhārata* story as well as religious and moral matters from performing and observing *pāṇḍav līlā;* (3) *pāṇḍav līlā* literally "closes the circle" of their relations, so that they get an opportunity to visit with genealogically or geographically distant relatives whom they rarely have a chance to meet; and (4) they stage the *līlā* out of self-interest (*svārth*), since a performance is a guarantee of well-being.

The ritualistic aspects of *pāṇḍav līlā,* which seize our attention because they seem so exotic, are simply taken for granted by Garhwalis. They are important in motivating performances, but they do not tell the whole story. Garhwalis call *pāṇḍav līlā* a *kautīk,* that is, a public religious spectacle. *Pāṇḍav līlā* involves singing, dancing, recitation of dramatic stories, possession by the gods, sophisticated drumming, a chance to socialize with friends and relatives, visits by itinerant traders selling special treats and trinkets, an engrossing competition, and much more. These factors combine to make *pāṇḍav līlā* one of the most popular entertainments in Garhwal. In other words, *pāṇḍav līlā* is fun, a play where one may play, freely and spontaneously. And because it is a play, we are entitled to ask how, or if, the players' stage identities are related to their identities offstage. We are entitled to ask, "Who's who in *pāṇḍav līlā*?"

Kṣatriyas Playing Kṣatriyas?

Pāṇḍav līlā is a fundamentally Kṣatriya tradition. In most of the central Himalayas "Kṣatriya" means "Rājput," and this is problematic because different people have different opinions about who is and who is not an authentic Rājput.[13] There seems to have been significant immigration to the central Himalayan region by Rājputs from western India in the late medieval period, largely as a result of pressure from invading Muslim armies. The Paṅwār dynasty of Garhwal and the Chand dynasty of Kumaon were probably both founded by such groups, and prominent local families often claim descent from the dynastic founders' companions. These high-status Rājputs are usually contrasted with the indigenous "*khaśa* Rājputs," presumed to be descended from indigenous, "tribal" ancestors.[14] Elderly Garhwalis can still remember when the appellation *khaśa* was unproblematic and even used self-descriptively, but it has since come to be a term of abuse, and virtually all Kṣatriyas in Garhwal now prefer the term "Rājput." However, they typically insist that one or another neighboring group is *khaśa,* even as they object to the term being applied to themselves. Here I will avoid these issues, simply by assuming that in Garhwal, the term "Kṣatriya" includes any and all local "Rājputs." Garhwali Rājputs comprise roughly 80 percent of the local population and possess a similar proportion of local land and votes, making them the most powerful group in the region.

Garhwali Rājputs regard *pāṇḍav līlā* as their special tradition. It is their most public and self-conscious representation of their own identity. This is so for several reasons. To begin with, they believe that many of the events of the *Mahābhārata* story occurred in Garhwal and the adjoining parts of the north Indian plains. Throughout north India people believe that the Old Fort in Delhi is built on or near the site of the Pāṇḍavas' capital, Indraprastha, and there is still a town called Kurukshetra, located on the Delhi–Chandigarh highway, not far from Saharanpur. The most important religious site in Garhwal, the high-altitude temple of Badrinath, is clearly described in Sanskrit versions of *Mahābhārata* (where it is called *badarikāśrama*), and Garhwalis also believe that the Pāṇḍavas were born in the village of Pandukeshvar between Joshimath and Badrinath. To detail the many ways in which local myth and geography are related to *Mahābhārata* and to the Pāṇḍavas would be the subject of a separate essay; here I will mention only that local cultural and religious forms are everywhere infused with their presence.[15] But for Garhwalis this localization has special importance, since they believe that they are direct lineal descendants of the Pāṇḍavas themselves. Therefore *pāṇḍav līlā* is a form of ancestor worship, and indeed all *pāṇḍav līlā*s include a performance, authentic in every respect, of *śrāddha,* the obligatory Hindu funerary ritual. The *śrāddha* is performed for the benefit of the Pāṇḍavas' father, King Pāṇḍu, by a Brāhmaṇ acting as *purohita* (priest) for Sahadeva, who is regarded as the only biological son of Pāṇḍu (by Mādrī).[16]

There are many other reasons why *pāṇḍav līlā* is fundamentally a Kṣatriya tradition. The main performers, members of the Pāṇḍavas' "army" who usually have ritual duties as well, must be from the village that sponsors the performance, which is nearly always a Rājput village. Bards and pairs of dancers may come from outside to participate, but they too are always Rājputs. I am aware of only one case in which a *pāṇḍav līlā* was sponsored by a predominantly Brāhmaṇ village, and in that case the three Rājput households of the village provided a greatly disproportionate number of bards and dancers. Even so, the event was widely regarded as an aesthetic failure, a sham (*ḍhakosalā*), because Brāhmaṇs are not thought capable of producing an authentic *pāṇḍav līlā*. The participation of Dās and Brāhmaṇs is essential for a proper performance, but their activities are strictly limited to their respective roles as drummers and priests. While it is conceivable that a Brāhmaṇ would play the part of a Kṣatriya or a low-caste person in a *līlā,* it is utterly forbidden for a member of one of the untouchable castes to dance or to recite. Meanwhile, Rājputs are allowed and encouraged to play the parts of non-Kṣatriya characters in the drama. Like *rām līlā, pāṇḍav līlā* involves the temporary incarnation of divine beings in the bodies of actors. Indeed, this presence of the gods upon the stage is one of the defining characteristics of *līlā* as a genre of performance. In *rām līlā* the prepubescent boys who play the parts of Rāma, Sītā, and the others must be Brāhmaṇs "because, when they appear in costume and crown as the very embodiments (*svarūp*s) of the divinities, even Brāhmaṇs will bow down to them and worship them" (Hein 1959:74). By contrast, those who take the parts of the Pāṇḍavas in *pāṇḍav līlā* must be Kṣatriyas, because the Pāṇḍavas themselves were Kṣatriyas.

Another set of reasons why *pāṇḍav līlā* is fundamentally a Kṣatriya tradition has to do with the nature of the representations that are included within it. Chief among these are the weapons (*hathiyār*) with which the major characters dance. In *pāṇḍav līlā* Arjuna and his son Nāgārjuna dance with bows and arrows, Bhīma dances with a club, Nakula with a scythe, Sahadeva with a slate, Yudhiṣṭhira with a staff, Draupadī with a dagger, and Kṛṣṇa with a discus. There are actually two sets of weapons in a full-scale performance. The first set is used by the main dancers while the second set, which belonged to the previous generation of dancers (now mostly deceased), stays on the Pāṇḍavas' altar. At the conclusion of *pāṇḍav līlā* this second set is buried along with th *śami* tree at a pure and holy spot, usually the village water source. Meanwhile, the weapons actually used by the performers are ceremonially placed in a safe place, usually under the eaves of someone's roof, where they will remain until the next performance, which may not occur for another generation. All of this serves to emphasize the continuity of the Rājput community, living and dead, through the transmission of these specially powerful objects.[17]

The weapons are thought of as repositories of power. This is especially true of the iron arrowheads (*bāṇ*) used in the confrontation between Arjuna and

Nāgārjuna, which is the central dance of the *līlā*. These arrowheads, clearly the holiest and most dangerous objects in *pāṇḍav līlā,* must never be allowed to touch the ground: if they do their ''energy may be discharged'' (*śakti chūṭ jānā*), and a person who inadvertently dropped one would be severely punished. Brāhmaṇs may, if they wish, play any part in a *pāṇḍav līlā except* those of the characters who use bows and arrows—that is, Arjuna and Nāgārjuna. ''To shoot an arrow,'' it is said, ''is the *dharma* of the Kṣatriya alone.'' And on the day that the weapons are distributed by the village deity, Arjuna and Nāgārjuna tie strings around their wrists to remind themselves that they, more than any other dancers, must strictly observe certain dietary and other rules; they must remain absolutely pure, lest the power of the weapons be diminished. I noted earlier that village deities do not always or necessarily distribute bows and arrows to those who claim them: this is due in large part to the care with which these powerful objects are handled. I had some experience of this when, during one performance, my assistant, Dabar Singh, encouraged me to join him in performing the main dance, the confrontation between Arjuna and Nāgārjuna. The dance is fairly complicated, and I've always regarded myself as having two left feet; moreover, this most powerful of dances requires one to take up the bow and arrow. Still, I was on the verge of agreement when the villagers said they'd be happy to let us dance—only we'd have to do it as young boys do, with empty shafts, no arrowheads. We politely declined to dance unless we had ''the real thing'' in our hands. In a later performance we danced with bows and arrows, and it was an exhilarating experience.

In its constituted versions *Mahābhārata* is the longest poem in the world; to dramatize all of it would be a hopeless task. Although *pāṇḍav līlā* does seek to represent the whole story from beginning to end, it must of necessity select the episodes it dramatizes from a vast number of possibilities, and the main principle of selection seems to be thematic. The episodes selected for dramatization are those that emphasize the most Kṣatriya-like qualities of the Pāṇḍavas; their martial and royal virtues. Elsewhere (Sax 1991a) I have described two very popular *līlā*s: the hunting of the rhinoceros and the uprooting and erection of the *śami* tree. The first episode emphasizes the Pāṇḍavas' bravery and skill by contrasting them with the cowardice and buffoonery of their reluctant guide, while the second episode can take place only after their victory over the Kauravas and royal accession, of which it is therefore a sign. In all *pāṇḍav līlā*s, Bhīma's club is an object of particular veneration, and he uses it to great effect in defeating a variety of demons who block the Pāṇḍavas' way at various points.

Another *līlā* of great importance is the horse sacrifice (*aśvamedha yajña*). Many people say that it is the greatest story in the *Mahābhārata,* its ''essence'' (*sār*). Commemoration of the horse sacrifice is one of the climactic moments of *pāṇḍav līlā,* and only the people from the sponsoring village are allowed to dance. In Sutol village Arjuna and Yudhiṣṭhira, mounted on artificial horses, were "marked" by local village gods and female dancers. This was called the *rāj-tilak,* that is, the ritual in which the king is confirmed in office by being "marked" by his chief priest.[18] That night's *līlās* also incorporated a large elephant that was made in the jungle and then danced in the square, representing Indra's elephant, a traditional symbol of royal power. Local stories confirm Hiltebeitel's notion that the *aśvamedha* is performed as a kind of expiation (*prāyaścitta*) for the sin of killing relatives, but Garhwalis say that it is also a final confirmation of the Pāṇḍavas as kings, a completion, as it were, of their interrupted royal sacrifice (*rājasūya yajña*). Local stories emphasize the difficulty of capturing the black-eared (*śyāma-karaṇ*) horse[19] and the heroic exploits required of the Pāṇḍavas before they were able to do so. Once again, martial themes appropriate to a Kṣatriya community are the focus of *pāṇḍav līlā.* In fact, the most important episode, one that is performed throughout the region, over and over in every *pāṇḍav līlā,* is the confrontation of Arjuna with his son Nāgārjuna, sometimes called Nāgimalla, better known as Babhruvāhana in the Pune edition of *Mahābhārata.* I hope to make this the subject of a later publication; here it is enough to note that it is precisely Nāgārjuna's bravery, or lack of it, that is at issue. Arjuna has come to Nāgilok (the underworld, *nāga loka*) seeking the black-eared horse. Nāgārjuna knows that Arjuna is his father, so he comes to honor him. But Arjuna is unaware, or has forgotten, that Nāgārjuna is his son, and he chastizes the latter for his hospitality, which he takes to be a sign of cowardice. Here is my translation of a recorded contest between two bards. It takes the form of a riddle wherein each challenges the other (and implicitly the audience) to guess his identity. Note the importance here of being recognized as a "true Kṣatriya."

B: Listen, O listen, my warrior: you are not your father's son. You stayed with another father for twelve months;[20] I think you are also a low-caste bastard! You are not the only son of your mother. Those weaklings Nakula and Sahadeva have a different mother. Your mother bore three sons, and another bastard in her father's house.

A: Listen a while, O warrior, listen: we were not naturally conceived. We are the boon-children of *dharma,* not lechers like you. I had gone to the forest; I was wandering there for twelve years, but your mother didn't leave me alone for a minute. A princely man is never beaten; one of Kṣatriya blood cannot be defeated; (but) you fled to Nāgilok and hid, our of fear of me.

B: Listen, O man, listen: we'll see about your "Kṣatriya blood"! You little bastard! Your mother gave birth to Karṇa in her natal home, and from shame she set him adrift in the river; then she married Pāṇḍu. She lived like an unmarried whore! Hey Rām! She never even slept with your father!

A: Listen, O listen, princely man! Why are you saying such things? Our father married our mother and brought her from King Surasena, who is (also) called King Kuntabhoj.[21] My mother prayed to the sage Durvāsa, who gave her a special *mantra;* that's how we were born. The half of which you've spoken—Nakula and Sahadeva—that half was the boon requested by Mādrī; and the other half were the boon-children of our elder mother [Kuntī]. Hey Rām! Who serves the gods receives such boons, but your mother rubbed Śiva's *liṅga!*[22]

B: Listen, warrior, listen! Today I will show you who's a princely man! I'll tear off your head and throw it all the way to Jayanti [Hastināpura, the capital], and leave your bloody trunk here! Today you will see a true Kṣatriya! Beat the drum and blast the horns![23] Now see if I lie or not!

A: My mother is in far Jayanti, and I'm in Nāgilok. If you cut off my head it will go to my mother's lap! Listen my warrior: such is a princely man, such is a true Kṣatriya. I will return to the mortal world for a year; you stay that year in Nāgilok.

B: You are a Kṣatriya, a true Kṣatriya.[24] You won't be able to reach your mother's lap until my mother comes with her gourd full of ambrosia, bearing the reviving herb, to restore the breath of your life, and you touch your head to my feet—and then you'll take me with you.

A: Listen, O listen, my warrior: your name is Babhruvāhana! I must go to the mortal world. I recognize you as my own, and give you reign over Nāgilok. O princely man, I must go, but you stay here in Nāgilok. I will go to the mortal world.

B: Listen, listen O princely man! A true Kṣatriya will now be seen. Your death is in my hands; I am your son Babhruvāhana; I am even more expert in the science of arms than you.

In this exchange, men's honor as true Kṣatriyas is clearly at issue. And "true Kṣatriyas" are associated not only with martial qualities of valor and bravery but also and by extension with kingship. This is revealed by the epithet *pāvaryā,* which I have translated as "princely man." The term is conventionally applied to a brave warrior, but I suspect that it derives from the Panwar (*paṃvār*) dynasty of Garhwal. Still another metaphoric association with kingship is revealed by the epithet *deś-deś ke nareś*" (kings of many countries), often applied by bards to participants in the *pāṇḍav līlā,* audience as well as performers. In emphasizing their own Kṣatriya virtues the Rājputs who produce *pāṇḍav līlā* are also calling attention to their kingly qualifications; the two are one and the same. It is not simply that the Kṣatriya class was traditionally the one from which kings were selected (or into which victorious kings were placed); more important is the fact that in the modern period, the Rājputs of Garhwal have taken over the royal function. This is a process that has been documented for dominant castes in many parts of South Asia, following the demise of erstwhile Hindu kingdoms in the modern period.

In sum, I have shown that *pāṇḍav līlā* is conceived of as fundamentally a Garhwali Rājput—that is, a Kṣatriya—tradition. This is instantiated in at least five ways. First of all, there is the matter of regional identity. The Pāṇḍavas are believed to have taken birth, traveled extensively, and even to have ended their mortal lives in Garhwal, and local Rājputs consider themselves to be the Pāṇḍavas' direct lineal descendants. Second, indices of royal power, the weapons used in the drama, are passed on from generation to generation, theoretically preserved in an unbroken line within the community. (One recalls that Arjuna first obtained his weapons from his father, Indra.) Third, this community also maintains its corporate integrity by continuing to observe funerary rites for its founding male, King Pāṇḍu. Fourth, the episodes chosen for dramatization, along with certain other aspects of *pāṇḍav līlā,* emphasize qualities like battle, heroism, and rule that are integral to Garhwali Rājputs' self-image as Kṣatriya warriors. They also represent the fruit of these actions, namely, Yudhiṣṭhira's installation as king. Finally, participants in the *līlā* are metaphorically associated with kings.

But that is not all. There is a sense in which *pāṇḍav līlā* in its creative and ludic aspects—that is, *pāṇḍav līlā* considered *as līlā* goes beyond a simple reification of Garhwali society to suggest an alternative social order, not a permanent one but only a temporary and playful representation. This alternative social order is interesting because in it the distinctions between Rājputs and Brāhmaṇs are effaced, Rājputs have the most important qualities of Brāhmaṇs, and as a result they share in the Brāhmaṇs' religious authority.

Brāhmaṇs Playing Brāhmaṇs?

Students of Indian society tend to downplay the envy of lower castes for higher ones, just as we take it for granted that a person's caste identity is unproblematic. But we know that people often regard their caste rank as inequitable, and it seems to me that the whole notion of "caste identity" is problematic.[25] For example, a middle-aged Rājput farmer, a friend of mine, often accuses his Brāhmaṇ neighbors of not being "real" Brāhmaṇs, of only parroting their priestly texts without knowing their meaning while my friend understands the import of Brāhmaṇic language and ritual, and is thus more entitled to the respect given to a Brāhmaṇ than are the Brāhmaṇs themselves. In fact, my friend is somewhat notorious for his habit of challenging Brāhmaṇs in an attempt to demonstrate his greater knowledge of scripture and its meaning. In any case, *pāṇḍav līlā* provides a public forum for demonstrating that Kṣatriyas can be the equal of Brāhmaṇs in matters of knowledge and learning. It clearly asserts that Rājputs are not inferior to Brāhmaṇs.

Displays of bardic knowledge in *pāṇḍav līlā* are usually competitive. One bard will challenge another to recall some part of the *Mahābhārata* story: if the man so challenged is unable to recall the detail, he is considered to be defeated by the challenger. Less often, one bard will "put down" another by interrupting his recitation with a correction, but this is rare because bardic competition is governed by a formal code of politeness. Typically, the challenger begins by showering the preceding bard with praise, and the actual challenge is issued in such a way that it seems to be almost an afterthought.

There is thus a tension between the dramatized episodes that emphasize militant and aggressive action, and recitation that is characterized by a decorous politesse. Though they are public performers, bards are expected to show humility and not to take overt pride in their learning. The most accomplished bard in Chandpur, Bacan Singh Rawat of Toli village, exhibited this combination of knowledge and humility in both his public performances and his private pronouncements. While bardic displays of knowledge are indeed competitive, they are more characteristic of a peaceful debate than a violent battle: in short, bards behave more like Brāhmaṇs than like Kṣatriyas. Through these displays Rājputs are in effect saying that they are as worthy, as learned and controlled, as Brāhmaṇs ought to be (one recalls that the Kṣatriya king Janaka became a Brāhmaṇ after winning a verbal contest). Heesterman (1964) has asserted that along with the Upaniṣadic interiorization of the Vedic ritual, the dominant religious question in Hinduism came to be "Who is the true Brāhmaṇ?" and that it was answered in terms of possession of esoteric knowledge. It is such possession of esoteric knowledge that is tested and displayed in *pāṇḍav līlā*. The very terms of address for bards are ones that are generally reserved for Brāhmaṇs: *śāstrī, vyās, paṇḍit*. Bacan Singh for example, is called *śāstrī-jī* offstage as well as on, despite the fact that he is unlettered. He has in some sense achieved the status, or at least the title, of a Brāhmaṇ. Another bard, Padam Singh Rawat of Sutol village, interspersed his narration of the story with a great deal of edifying material, thus appropriating the preceptive as well as the pedagogical role of the Brāhmaṇ. And he often recited in Sanskrit, a language normally associated with Brāhmaṇs. For these reasons he was proudly referred to by his fellow villagers as "a real *paṇḍit*."

This conflation of Brāhmaṇ and Kṣatriya qualities is not without precedent. The *vrātya*s studied by J. C. Heesterman (1962, 1964) are a mirror image of the Rājput bards of *pāṇḍav līlā*. Whereas the Rājputs become, at least for the duration of the *līlā,* quasi Brāhmaṇs by virtue of their knowledge, the *vrātya*s were a group of knowledgeable priests who became quasi Kṣatriyas by virtue of their participation in violent cattle raids.[26] So long as legitimate violence is associated exclusively with the Kṣatriya and religious preceptorship with the Brāhmaṇ, things are fine. Ambiguities result when the Kṣatriya takes on the role of teacher, or when the Brāhmaṇ engages in aggressive violence. Of course, *Mahābhārata* itself supplies a precedent for the blurring of *varṇa* distinctions. I am not thinking so much of Droṇa, the Brāhmaṇ who became a great soldier and general, but of the five Pāṇḍavas, who unite in their persons the powers of both *brahman* and *kṣatra* (Hiltebeitel 1976:80 n.4, 159; 1988, chap. 8; 1991:50–51). By now it should be obvious that their putative descendants, the bards of *pāṇḍav līlā,* do so as well.

Do the Rājputs of Garhwal truly become Brāhmaṇs during a performance? Who's who in the *pāṇḍav līlā?* Are the performers actually Kṣatriyas, playing the parts of Kṣatriyas? Are they "temporary" Brāhmaṇs, singing the deeds of Kṣatriyas? Or—the most intriguing possibility of all—are they indeed Brāhmaṇs singing the story of that other set of famous Brāhmaṇs, the Pāṇḍavas? The latter possibility is perhaps not so far-fetched as it sounds: Hiltebeitel suggests that the "deepest" indentities of the Pāṇḍavas were revealed during their final year of exile, which they spent disguised as Brāhmaṇs at the court of King Virāṭ (1980:147–48).[27] Just as *pāṇḍav līlā* confirmed Hiltebeitel's intuition of the identity of Draupadī as Kālī (Sax 1991a:289–90), so it also confirms this suggestion regarding the identity of the Pāṇḍavas. Whenever the Pāṇḍavas disguised themselves, it was always as Brāhmaṇs, not only during their year in hiding at the court of King Virāṭ but also, for example, in the city of Ekacakra before killing the demon Baka, or at Draupadī's *svayamvara* where Arjuna assumed the guise of a Brāhmaṇ. Moreover, Arjuna's father, Indra, is said to have won Śrī from Prahlāda while disguised as a Brāhmaṇ (Hiltebeitel 1976:159), and the Pune edition of *Mahābhārata* identifies Draupadī as an incarnation of Śrī, so the pattern is precisely repeated. Perhaps their Brāhmaṇic qualities were more evident because during that year they had consigned their royal power, their *kṣatra,* to the *śami* tree, by hiding their weapons in it. Dhṛtarāṣṭra and Pāṇḍu, sons of the same Brāhmaṇ father, each had Kṣatriya mothers, even as the Brāhmaṇ-like deities Dharma, Vāyu, and the Aśvins fathered Yudhiṣṭhira, Bhīma, Nakula, and Sahadeva[28] on the Kṣatriya women Draupadī and Mādrī. And just as I contend that the bardic "narrators" of *pāṇḍav līlā* are Brāhmaṇs of a sort, so written versions of *Mahābhārata* are narrated by the Brāhmaṇ sages Vyāsa and Vaiśampāyana.

Through their competitive yet polite displays of knowledge, the *pāṇḍav līlā* bards manifest Brāhmaṇic qualities. Are we then justified in regarding them as Brāhmaṇs or crypto-Brāhmaṇs? They themselves do so, for instance, by addressing particularly learned bards as "śāstrī-jī," thereby confirming the opinion of at least some Rājputs that through learning a Rājput can become the "equal" of a Brāhmaṇ. Obviously, such practices raise a more general set of questions: even if we admit that some kind of transfer of qualities between castes takes place within *pāṇḍav līlā,* to what extent is this a "real" transfer, and to what extent is it merely a "playful" transfer, as the term *līlā* would seem to imply? What are the indigenous criteria for such a judgment? What should our extrinsic criteria—if any—be? How might these two sets of criteria compare? In the final two sections of this paper I shall explore some of these issues and suggest a solution that, it is hoped, will satisfy both indigenous and external models.

What's What?

What is needed here is a Hindu theory of play. This is a very large project, but we can get some mileage out of Van Buitenen's suggestion that *līlā* is the opposite of *karma.* Van Buitenen was referring to *līlā* as a theological concept: creation as "mere sport" (*līlā kaivalyam*) for Brahmā, the Creator (*Brahmasūtra* II.1.33). This "sport" is what is called *līlā,* the cosmic play of a Supreme Being who acts with no desire for action's fruits. The desirelessness of *līlā* prompted Van Buitenen's suggestion that it is the opposite of *karman,* since "in creating, sustaining, and resorbing the world God has no cause to effectuate and no end to achieve" (1956:192 n. 83). Because God's cosmogonic *līlā* is not motivated by desire, it generates no *karma.* On the other hand, human creative acts, when motivated by desire, implicate their perpetrators in the *kārmic* chain. In applying Van Buitenen's insight to dramatic *līlā*s, we might therefore infer that one can "play at" being a Brāhmaṇ, a Pāṇḍava, or anyone else, without generating any *kārmic* fruit. Yet as we have seen, fruits *are* believed to be generated by performing *pāṇḍav līlā:* good crops, prosperity, and well-being, "closing the circle" of interpersonal relationships.

A notion of "framing" is called for here.[29] It would be manifestly inappropriate, even dangerous and sinful, for a Rājput to perform the actions of a Brāhmaṇ in daily life. But within a properly framed *līlā,* categories and identities can be juxtaposed, reversed, "played with." And this is precisely what happens during *pāṇḍav līlā,* where Rājputs are normally possessed not only by their own ("Rājput") ancestors but also by Brāhmaṇs and other characters of ambiguous or low caste. Although local Harijans themselves may neither dance nor recite, they are allowed and even encouraged to tease their Rājput patrons, and relations between the two groups are far more relaxed than usual. On the other hand, Rājputs do not scruple to play the parts of Harijan characters, notably Kaliyā Lohār, the low-caste ancestor of all iron-workers who forged the weapons of the Pāṇḍavas; and Rājput performers delight in portraying the Brāhmaṇ sage Nārada as a scatological and obscene buffoon. Another example of the fluidity of identity within the *līlā*'s playful frame is the frequent transformation of men into women: although women dance the parts of female characters in the more remote villages, these parts tend to be played by men in those villages that are closer to the main roads.[30] Such men are thus imbued with the personalities of female characters whose parts they play, thereby making their identities even more fluid and ambiguous.

The atmosphere of *pāṇḍav līlā* is, in short, one of playful abandon, where quotidian identities are abandoned and new ones assumed without fear of the *kārmic* consequences. Such qualities of freedom and spontaneity resonate with other kinds of *līlā*—theological, philosophical, and aesthetic—that are described in this volume. Indeed, freedom and spontaneity seem to be part of the core meaning of *līlā,* however and wherever it is performed. But the freedom is constrained, the spontaneity diluted, by the distribution of power among those who participate in *pāṇḍav līlā.* Rājput men, males in the locally dominant caste, are encouraged to "play with" their identities, becoming now a Brāhmaṇ, now an "untouchable," now a woman. Rājput women, however, do not have so much freedom: they are allowed to play the parts of females from these other castes, but not of males. And the lowest castes are not allowed to "play" in this way at all. Hindu culture is, after all, pervasively concerned with rank, and one would not expect such ludic egalitarianism to last for long. Ultimately, the playful freedom of the *līlā* is circumscribed and limited by the larger "frame" within which it takes place, the "real-world" frame. In the final section of this essay I will argue that for Hindus "reality testing" comes in the form of feasting and transactions.

Who's Who?

Swami Vivekananda once wrote that Hinduism was a religion of the stomach, and there is much truth in that statement. For example, the juxtaposition of identities and the ambivalence regarding who's who in *pāṇḍav līlā* are clarified, and the status quo ante is reasserted, by the feasting and exchange that surround the performance. Not only is *pāṇḍav līlā* an entertainment and a form of worship, it is also an opportunity for village sponsors to display their wealth and power, and to feast their caste mates. As the performance progresses, most village houses fill up with invited guests, friends and relatives to whom unstinting hospitality must be shown. All relatives on both the paternal and maternal sides are invited to the *līlā*. Because of virilocality, this means in practice that "guests" tend to be affines and out-married "village daughters" and their families.[31] During the first few days of the 1985 *pāṇḍav līlā* in Bhatgwali village, my host, Vishnu Singh, fed between thirty-five and one hundred people, twice a day. He calculated that each household spent seven to eight hundred rupees on the *līlā,* including food for its own members and guests, contributions to the collective stores, clothes and sweets for all the *dhiyāṇī*s, and a single rupee given to every guest. Eating guests were almost solely limited to members of the Negī subcaste, since there would be commensal difficulties if Rāwats, Cauhāns, and other Rājputs attended, to say nothing of Brāhmaṇs. The local people took pride in their *līlā,* and confidently asserted that no one was equal to the Negīs in the amount and quality of feasting that they were capable of sponsoring. During the final days of most *pāṇḍav līlā*s, hundreds of guests—uninvited as well as invited—are publicly and collectively feasted by the host village, which hires Brāhmaṇ cooks for the purpose. It is a point of honor among Rājputs to bear the expenses for *pāṇḍav līlā*s and to feast as many friends and relatives as they possibly can. Such feasting and hospitality involve large expenditures of wealth and effort, precisely the sort of maximal (Kṣatriya) transactional strategy predicted by Marriott (1976). It locates *pāṇḍav līlā* in a set of social relationships that foreground the status quo ante of Rājput dominance, a dominance that is partly expressed through such "lordly" actions.

Feasting and hospitality thus frame *pāṇḍav līlā* as a communal activity, a quasi-caste gathering[32] where marriages are negotiated and political alliances formed, and where the honor and prestige of a village are clearly at stake. These are the quotidian activities that frame the event at the broadest level. Within this event, *pāṇḍav līlā* is framed as a ritual by a number of activities, including dietary and other restrictions, the ritual marking of a performance space, the handling of especially powerful weapons, and the summoning of deities who temporarily inhabit the bodies of performers. And the third frame is that of the *līlā* per se, a ludic period in which performers are free to play with their identities, becoming now Brāhmaṇs, now Harijans, now women, but ultimately and once again Rājputs. It is not simply that the transformations are temporary and impermanent because *līlā* is "merely" play; after all, there are levels of both popular and learned discourse according to which all of life is a play. The question to ask in both cases is this: a play in relation to what? In the theological formulations discussed elsewhere in this volume the world is a *līlā* in relation to God, the supreme reality. The ritual and dramatic genre I am discussing here is a *līlā* in relation to daily life, and the kinds of feasting and transactions that frame it also ensure that at the end of the performance the status quo ante of Rājput domination in that daily life is reaffirmed. In this way the context or "frame" of the performance (feasting and display by the locally dominant caste) reiterates the performance's form and content (ancestor worship and the celebration of military themes). In dramatizing the heroism of their kingly ancestors and magnanimously feeding their neighbors, the Rājputs of Garhwal are also pointing to their own fitness to rule. In representing an ideal of Rājput dominance, that dominance is perpetually created anew. In the process of creating and reiterating that political dominance, the Rājputs have also demonstrated their own Brāhmaṇic qualities, managing thereby to call the religious dominance of the Brāhmaṇs into question. And they have done all this in the spirit of *līlā*.

NOTES

I would like to thank the Fulbright-Hays Commission, the National Science Foundation, the American Institute of Indian Studies, and the University of Canterbury for generously funding the research, conducted in 1983–86 and 1990–91, on which this article is based. Thanks also to Alf Hiltebeitel and Toni Huber for their critical remarks on earlier versions. I owe special thanks to the people of Chandpur who took me into their homes and hearts, especially Dabar Singh Rawat, Rajendra Prasad Nautiyal, Devaram Nautiyal, Bhuvan Nautiyal, Gusain Singh Negi, Surendra Singh Negi, Gajendra Prasad Gairola, Shambhu Pal Singh Panwar, and Darshan Singh Bisht.

1. In using the word *tradition* I am thinking not so much of the kind of timeless, ahistorical object beloved of religionists, nor of the "invented traditions" fascinatingly analyzed in Hobsbawm and Ranger (1984), but rather of Hindu *paramparā,* sequences or successions of internally related events.

2. It is unfortunate that Western scholarship on *Mahābhārata* and *Rāmāyaṇa* designates both as "epics" despite the fact that the Indian tradition uses separate terms for each: *kāvya,* or "poetry," for *Rāmāyaṇa* and *itihāsa,* or "history," for *Mahābhārata.* See Sweeney (1991) for a valuable discussion of the pitfalls of carelessly using the term "epic."

3. The origin of *pāṇḍav līlā* is obscure. There is some evidence of bardic traditions associated with royal courts before the eighteenth century (Gaborieau 1977:xvi; Gairola 1977:67–68), but it is unclear what their content might have been. There is ample evidence for ancient (ca. 3rd cen. C.E.) performances in the vicinity of *aśvamedha* sacrifices of the kind that are celebrated in *pāṇḍav līlā* (Ramachandran 1951:3–31), but whether or not such performances are linked to *pāṇḍav līlā* itself can only be a matter of speculation.

4. Dunham asserts that even a census of manuscripts of *Mahābhārata* would be

"doomed to failure because of the intractable complexities of locating, describing and comparing old manuscripts within India and its neighboring countries today" (1991:1).

5. See, for example, Beck 1982; Blackburn 1988; Blackburn and Ramanujan 1989; Blackburn et al. 1989; Brandon 1970; Deshpande 1978; Flueckiger and Sears 1991; Frasca 1990; Gentes 1987; Hein 1959, 1972; Hess 1986; Keeler 1987; Leavitt 1988, 1991; Lutgendorf 1991; Nautiyal 1981; Raghavan 1980; Richman 1991; Roghair 1982; Sax 1990, 1991a; Smith 1980; Ulbricht 1970; and Varadpande 1990.

6. However, there is a large and growing literature on the anthropology of performance. Exemplary studies include Bauman 1977; Bharucha 1983; Chandola 1977; Cowan 1990; Gill 1987; Goffman 1969; Handelman 1990; MacAloon 1981, 1984; Schechner 1982, 1983, 1988; Schechner and Appel 1990; Singer 1955; Spencer 1985; Strong 1973; Tambiah 1985; and Tedlock 1983. See also note 5.

7. The *paṭṭī* is a unit of territory analogous to the *paraganā* of the north Indian plains. Central Himalayan *paṭṭīs* have been reorganized many times; in Garhwal they are generally, though not invariably, associated with the forts from which they take their names (see Traill 1828:178).

8. This custom is locally related to the story of Bhīma's killing of the demon Bakāsur in the kingdom of Naganjīt, a story that is also of great importance in the Draupadī cult *līlās* of Tamil Nadu (see Hiltebeitel 1988, chap. 8).

9. Is is often the case that *pāṇḍav līlā* will not have been performed in a given village for decades, and the young dancers are doing it for the first time. From an aesthetic point of view, therefore, it is perhaps just as well that they have this opportunity to "rehearse" before the audience grows.

10. The famous battle between the half brothers Bhīma and Hanumān, both sons of Vāyu, Lord of the Wind (in the *tīrthayātrāparvan* of the critical edition), has special prominence in *pāṇḍav līlā*.

11. The word I am translating as "ritual" is *devakārya*, or "the work of the gods."

12. The local term for such a promise or vow is *ucyāṇā*.

13. See, for example, Atkinson 1974 [1882]; Berreman 1972 [1963]; Joshi 1990.

14. In an important recent publication, Joshi (1990) has questioned the extent of *khaśa* influence in Garhwal and has suggested that the entire problem may have been "overstressed" by Atkinson and others.

15. This is an example of what Ramanujan (1986:67) has called the "localization" of epic figures in folk traditions.

16. It is said that Sahadeva (or Nakula, according to some) was conceived during King Pandu's fatal intercourse with Madri; cf. Hiltebeitel (1991:29 n. 26), where the Pāṇḍavas' younger sister Cankotari (aka Cankuvati) has the same parentage.

17. Compare the Balinese *sacra* such as hereditary swords, and so forth, which "incorporated the dynasty's power" (Geertz 1980:114–16, cited in Tambiah 1985:327).

18. The term probably derives from a similar ritual performed for the erstwhile kings of Garhwal.

19. My main informant insisted that *śyāmakaraṇ* means "copper-eared" and not "black-eared."

20. The reference is to Arjun's stay with Indra.

21. In the Pune edition, Kunti is the biological daughter of King Śura, adopted by Kuntibhoja.

22. *mādev go ling malyo*. This is an ambiguous, insulting double entendre. It refers not only to the erotic aspects of sexual conception but also to the fact that Nāgārjuna's mother, Vasudantā, had earlier received a boon from Śiva. It also calls to mind the Garhwali custom of rubbing ghee on the *śivaliṅga* at Kedārnāth in order to obtain sons.

23. Literally "let the thirty-six rhythms and the twelve instrument be played!"

24. *khāsā kṣatriya*. This intriguing phrase is a double entendre: it could mean either a Kṣatriya who is a *khaśa* (see pp. 137–38) or a "special" (*khās*) Kṣatriya. Garhwali Rājputs sometimes say that the word *khaśa* actually means *khās* (special).

25. See Moffatt (1979:122–23).

26. According to Heesterman the *vrātyas*, generally seen by scholars as a group of "fallen" Aryans, in fact occupied the interstices of an as-yet-unsolidified *varṇa* system, between Brāhmaṇs and Kṣatriyas. He speculates that endogamy and prescriptive exchange came later, along with the development of the classical sacrifice.

27. In Garhwal, King Virāṭ's realm is identified with the region just north of Lakhā Maṇḍal, itself said to be the location of the attempted assassination of the Pāṇḍavas in the "lac palace."

28. Though see note 14.

29. The classic discussion of "framing" is Goffman (1974).

30. The fact that women do take prominent parts in what seem to be the more "traditional" performances of remote areas contradicts Wadley's assertion that in Indian "religious folk operas and plays . . . the actors portraying a deity are all male . . . the actor must usually be a Brāhmaṇ" (1977:128).

31. In fact, for the *pāṇḍav līlā*, as for all *kautīks*, or "spectacles," in Garhwal, the presence of the out-married daughter (*dhiyāṇī*) is deemed essential (Sax 1991b). She is invited home for the occasion and must be given at least one item of clothing, as well as some money and cooked sweets, before being sent back to her husband's home. Wealthier families will also give her some grain, the standard amount being thirty-two kilograms (one *dauṇ*).

32. Although the core group of performers and guests in *pāṇḍav līlā* belongs to the same caste, members of other castes do participate in *pāṇḍav līlā* as performers and guests. Hence I refer to *pāṇḍav līlā* as a "quasi-caste gathering."

REFERENCES

Atkinson, Edwin T. 1974 [1882]. *Kumaon Hills: Its History, Geography and Anthropology with Reference to Garhwal and Nepal*. Delhi: Cosmo Publications. [First published in Allahabad under the title *The Himalayan Districts of the North Western Provinces of India*.]

Bauman, Richard. 1977. *Verbal Art as Performance*. Prospect Heights, Ill.: Waveland Press.

Beck, Brenda E. F. 1982. *The Three Twins: The Telling of a South Indian Folk Epic.* Bloomington: Indiana University Press.

Berreman, Gerald. 1972 [1963]. *Hindus of the Himalayas.* Berkeley: University of California Press.

Bharucha, Rustom. 1983. *Rehearsals of Revolution: The Political Theater of Bengal.* Honolulu: University of Hawaii Press.

Blackburn, Stuart. 1988. *Singing of Birth and Death: Texts in Performance.* Philadelphia: University of Pennsylvania Press.

Blackburn, Stuart, and A. K. Ramanujan, eds. 1989. *Another Harmony: New Essays in the Folklore of India.* Berkeley: University of California Press.

Blackburn, Stuart, Peter J. Claus, Joyce B. Flueckiger, and Susan S. Wadley, eds. 1989. *Oral Epics in India.* Berkeley: University of California Press.

Brandon, James R. 1970. *On Thrones of Gold: Three Javanese Shadow Plays.* Cambridge, Mass.: Harvard University Press.

Chandola, Anoop. 1977. *Folk Drumming in the Himalayas: A Linguistic Approach to Music.* New York: AMS.

Coburn, Thomas B. 1984. *Devī-Māhātmya: The Crystallization of the Goddess Tradition.* Delhi: Motilal Banarsidass.

Cowan, Jane K. 1990. *Dance and the Body Politic in Northern Greece.* Princeton, N.J.: Princeton University Press.

Derrett, J. Duncan M. 1979. Spirit-Possession and the Gerasene Demoniac. *Man* 14(2): 286–93.

Deshpande, C. R. 1978. *Transmission of the Mahabharata Tradition.* Shimla: Institute of Advanced Study.

Dunham, John. 1991. Manuscripts Used in the Critical Edition of the Mahābhārata: A Survey and Discussion. In *Essays on the Mahābhārata,* ed. Arvind Sharma, pp. 1–18. Leiden: E. J. Brill.

Flueckiger, Joyce Burkhalter, and Laurie J. Sears, eds. 1991. *Boundaries of the Text: Epic Performances in South and Southeast Asia.* Ann Arbor: Center for South and Southeast Asian Studies.

Frasca, Richard A. 1990. *The Theater of the Mahabharata: Terukuttu Performances in South India.* Honolulu: University of Hawaii Press.

Gaborieau, Marc. 1977. Introduction. In *Himalayan Folklore, Kumaon and West Nepal,* ed. E. S. Oakley and Tara Dutt Gairola, pp. xi–xliv. Kathmandu: Ratna Pustak Bhandar. Bibliotheca Himalayica, Series 11, vol. 10; series ed. H. K. Kuloy.

Gairola, Tara Dutt, and E. S. Oakley, eds. 1977 [1935]. *Himalayan Folklore, Kumaon and West Nepal.* Kathmandu: Ratna Pustak Bhandar. Bibliotheca Himalayica, Series 11, vol. 10, series ed. H. K. Kuloy.

Geertz, Clifford. 1980. *Negara: The Theatre State in Nineteenth-Century Bali.* Princeton, N.J.: Princeton University Press.

Gentes, M. G. 1987. Hinduism Through Village Dance Drama: Narrative Image and Ritual Process in South India's Terukkuttu and Yaksagana Ritual Theaters. Ph.D. diss., University of Virginia.

Gill, Sam D. 1987. *Native American Religious Action: A Performance Approach to Religion.* Columbia: University of South Carolina Press.

Goffman, Erving. 1969. *The Presentation of Self in Everyday Life.* London: Allen Lane.

———. 1974. *Frame Analysis: An Essay on the Organization of Experience.* New York: Harper and Row.

Goldman, Robert P. 1986. Structure, Substance, and Function in the Great Sanskrit Epics (1). Paper delivered to the Festival of India Conference on Indian Literatures, The University of Chicago, April 17–20.

Handelman, Don. 1990. *Models and Mirrors: Towards an Anthropology of Public Events.* New York: Cambridge University Press.

Heesterman, J. C. 1962. Vratya and Sacrifice. *Indo-Iranian Journal* 6(1): 1–37.

———. 1964. Brahman, Ritual and Renouncer. *Wiener Zeitschrift fur die Kunde Sud-Und Ostasiens* 8(1): 1–31.

Hein, Norvin. 1959. The Rām Līlā. In *Traditional India: Structure and Change,* ed. Milton Singer, pp. 73–98. Philadelphia: The American Folklore Society.

———. 1972. *The Miracle Plays of Mathura.* New Haven, Conn.: Yale University Press.

Hess, Linda. 1986. Staring at Frames till They Turn into Loops: An Excursion Through Some Worlds of Tulsidas. Paper presented to the Festival of India Conference on Indian Literatures, The University of Chicago, April 17–20.

Hiltebeitel, Alf. 1976. *The Ritual of Battle: Krishna in the Mahabharata.* Ithaca, N.Y.: Cornell University Press.

———. 1980. Siva, the Goddess, and the Disguises of the Pandavas and Draupadī. *History of Religions* 19(1): 47–73.

———. 1988. *The Cult of Draupadi.* Vol. 1, *Mythologies: From Gingee to Kurukṣetra.* Chicago: University of Chicago Press.

———. 1991. *The Cult of Draupadi.* Vol. II, *On Hindu Ritual and the Goddess.* Chicago: University of Chicago Press.

Hobsbawm, Eric, and Terence Ranger, eds. 1984. *The Invention of Tradition.* Cambridge: Cambridge University Press.

Joshi, Maheshwar P. 1990. The Khas in the History of Uttarākhaṇḍ. In *Himalaya: Past and Present,* ed. Maheshwar P. Joshi, Allen C. Fanger, and Charles W. Brown, pp. 193–200.

Keeler, Ward. 1987. *Javanese Shadow Plays, Javanese Selves.* Princeton, N.J.: Princeton University Press.

Leavitt, John. 1988. A Mahabharata Story from the Kumaon Hills. *Himalayan Research Bulletin* 8(2): 1–12.

———. 1991. Himalayan Variations on an Epic Theme. In *Essays on the Mahabharata,* ed. Arvind Sharma, pp. 444–74. Leiden: E. J. Brill.

Lutgendorf, Phillip. 1991. *The Life of a Text.* Berkeley: University of California Press.

MacAloon, John J. 1981. *This Great Symbol: Pierre de Coubertin and the Origins of the Modern Olympic Games.* Chicago: University of Chicago Press.

MacAloon, John J., ed. 1984. *Rite, Drama, Festival, Spectacle: Rehearsals Toward a*

Theory of Cultural Performance. Philadelphia: Institute for the Study of Human Issues.

Marriott, McKim. 1976. Hindu Transactions: Diversity Without Dualism. In *Transaction and Meaning*, ed. Bruce Kapferer, pp. 109–42. Philadelphia: Institute for the Study of Human Issues.

Moffatt, Michael. 1979. *An Untouchable Community in South India*. Princeton, N.J.: Princeton University Press.

Nautiyal, Śivānand. 1981. *Gaḍhwāl ke Loknṛtya Gīt* (Folk Songs and Dances of Garhwal). Prayag: Hindi Sahitya Sammelan.

Raghavan, V., ed. 1980. *The Ramayana Tradition in Asia: Papers Presented at the International Seminar on the Ramayana Tradition in Asia, New Delhi, December 1975*. New Delhi: Sahitya Akademi.

Ramanujan, A. K. 1986. Two Realms of Kannada Folklore. In *Another Harmony: New Essays on the Folklore of India*, ed. Stuart H. Blackburn and A. K. Ramanujan, pp. 41–75. Berkeley: University of California Press.

Ramachandran, T. N. 1951. Asvamedha Site Near Kalsi. *Journal of Oriental Research* 21(1): 3–31.

Richman, Paula. 1991. *Many Ramayanas: The Diversity of a Narrative Tradition in South Asia*. Berkeley: University of California Press.

Roghair, Gene H. 1982. *The Epic of Palnadu: A Study and Translation of Palnati Virula Katha, a Telugu Oral Tradition from Andhra Pradesh, India*. Oxford: Clarendon Press.

Sax, William S. 1990. The Ramnagar Ramlila: Text, Performance, Pilgrimage. *History of Religions* 30(2): 129–53.

———. 1991a. Ritual and Performance in the Pandavalila of Uttarakhand. In *Essays on the Mahabharata*, ed. Arvind Sharma, pp. 274–95. Leiden: E. J. Brill.

———. 1991b. Village Daughter, Village Goddess: Residence, Gender, and Politics in a Himalayan Pilgrimage. *American Ethnologist* 17(3): 491–512.

Schechner, Richard. 1982. *The End of Humanism: Writings on Performance*. New York: Performing Arts Journal Publications.

———. 1983. *Performative Circumstances, from the Avant Garde to Ramlila*. Calcutta: Seagull Books.

———. 1988. *Performance Theory*, revised and expanded. New York: Routledge.

Schechner, Richard, and Willa Appel, eds. 1990. *By Means of Performance: Intercultural Studies of Theatre and Ritual*. New York: Cambridge University Press.

Singer, Milton. 1955. The Cultural Pattern of Indian Civilization: A Preliminary Report of a Methodological Field Study. *Far Eastern Quartely* [later *Journal of Asian Studies*] 15(1): 23–36.

Smith, John D. 1980. Old Indian: The Two Sanskrit Epics. In *Traditions of Heroic and Epic Poetry*. Vol. 1, *The Traditions*, ed. A. T. Hatto. London: Modern Humanities Research Association.

Spencer, Paul. 1985. *Society and the Dance: The Social Anthropology of Process and Performance*. Cambridge: Cambridge University Press.

Strong, Roy. 1973. *Splendour at Court: Renaissance Spectacle and Illusion.* London: Weidenfeld and Nicolson.

Sweeney, Amin. 1991. Literacy and the Epic in the Malay World. In *Boundaries of the Text: Epic Performances in South and Southeast Asia,* ed. Joyce Burkhalter Flueckiger and Laurie J. Sears, pp. 17–29. Ann Arbor, Mich.: Center for South and Southeast Asian Studies. Michigan Papers on South and Southeast Asia, no. 35.

Tambiah, Stanley J. 1985. A Performative Approach to Ritual (the Radcliffe-Brown Lecture for 1979). In Tambiah, *Culture, Thought, and Social Action: An Anthropological Perspective.* Cambridge, Mass.: Harvard University Press.

Tedlock, Dennis. 1983. *The Spoken Word and the Work of Interpretation.* Philadelphia: University of Pennsylvania Press.

Traill, George William. [1828] 1979. *Statistical Sketch of Kumaon.* Asiatic Researches 16. Reprint, Delhi: Cosmo Publications.

Ulbricht, H. 1970. *Wayang Purwa: Shadows of the Past.* Kuala Lumpur, Singapore: Oxford University Press.

Van Buitenen, J. A. B., ed. 1956. *Ramanuja's Vedarthasamgraha.* Pune, India: Deccan College Monograph Series, no. 16.

Varadpande, M. L. 1990. *Mahabharata in Performance.* New Delhi: Clarion.

Wadley, Susan S. 1977. Women and the Hindu Tradition. In *Women in India: Two Perspectives,* ed. Doranne Jacobson and Susan S. Wadley, pp. 113–39. Columbia, Mo.: South Asia Books.

10

Class and Gender Politics in the *Rāmlīlā*

NITA KUMAR

While debating between different titles for this essay, I found myself struggling to keep "Rāmlīlā" out of the name. For me my essay was about serious things: gender categories and their sustenance, political domination and resistance, negotiated constitutions of rationality and decency; not, as might seem from a title "Rāmlīlā," about a traditional performance in dusty spaces repeating a familiar, reactionary myth. The recognition of my dilemma was followed by the realization that there was a polemic I wished to be engaged in, with which I shall begin.

As with most developments in scholarship, we show a rather explicit pattern of following the West in our new regard for culture in history writing.[1] Thompson expressed envy some fifteen years ago regarding the fact that we Indians were liberally surrounded by people's oral traditions, genres, performances, creations, whereas a social historian of England would be overjoyed to discover in his career *one* song that had not been studied before. Given the continued productivity and richness of people's traditional (in the nontechnical sense of from the past) culture all around us, the fact that we have such few historians of work, leisure, family, ritual, everyday life, popular literature, and consciousness can only be attributed to the processes of academic reproduction in institutions self-willingly isolated from surrounding reality. Without a desire to suggest international competition or nationalist signatures to history writing, I would like to express my confidence that *now* that culture and everyday life are coming to be taken seriously by historians in the West, they will progressively come to be seen as important here.

My own work on popular culture[2] was based on an (insufficiently formulated) intuition of an existing—and exciting—gap in Indian History that I wished to fill—the situation of many Ph.D. candidates. As also with so many dissertations, I found, once in the field, that I had bitten off more than I could immediately chew[3] and have not been able to close that chapter of my research yet even while I have taken up other topics subsequently, such as primary education and curricula.

I will first give some arguments in brief for taking culture seriously in history writing, and then overview my particular arguments in this paper regarding the Rāmlīlā.

The central problem for most social sciences, at least the two that I am familiar with, history and anthropology, remains the seeming duality of causation, in structure (social, economic, political) and in human agency. They exist either simultaneously or in closely woven strands of cause–effect relationships. One is produced by the other and in turn conditions the other in one continuous process. This problem is most central to the discipline of history precisely because historians are interested in process and change, although many get away by making a static analysis of some totality in the past.

The problem can also be put as how to come to know structure such as class relations or authority and domination in the process of their structuring, realizing that these relationships are always transmitted through cultural meanings. The inability of much of cultural–symbolic anthropology to sufficiently ground ideologies, philosophies, worldviews, and other constructions of social reality in structural constraints and their social genesis makes historians often bend over backward in paying attention to the social world. That this social world is uttered and constructed by people in ways that can only be called "cultural" may not be debated in principle by most historians but is in practice seldom investigated. They may feel also—as I have found myself feeling in the past—that they are being renegades in looking beyond material structures for agency; and there is always the threat of a return to narrative history.

My simultaneous discovery of feminism as a theoretical perspective gave me important insights in this area. It has to ward off the constantly threatening danger of the categorization "woman," essentialist, determined, universalizable, recoverable, always the object of structures, of patriarchy, of domination, of repression.[4] Agency is elusive, but the political insistence that it must indeed exist gets translated into scholarship (sometimes) that hones methodological tools to overcome invisibility—of documents, data, subjecthood, consciousness itself. This is comparable to the subalternist enterprise where similar methodological questions are being asked, and I think the advance of feminist scholarship in the field is actually due to the essentially political aspect of feminism. To be a feminist means to *believe* in agency; then to be a feminist scholar is to have to produce evidence for agency.

With which I come to my own analysis of the Rāmlīlā. My discussion of it is partly based on earlier work[5] from which I take most of the factual details. But my interpretation of it has been revised in the light of the awareness, among other things, of being marginalized. Like other historians who study popular culture, consciousness, and the practice of everyday life, and use anthropological perspectives in doing so, I find myself on a periphery, because these subjects do not fit into the center, still understood as those phenomena that play significant roles in the "great transformation"—modernization, industrialization, and the emergence of bureaucratic and national states.[6] I do not challenge the importance of these phenomena, but my own interest lies in paying increasingly careful attention to otherness, difference, conflict, to the costs of change, the exclusions, resistances, and invisibility of historical losers.

So I find in concepts and practices like the *līlā* and the Rāmlīlā a way of recreating the experiences of the excluded; in a perspective that does not underestimate "great" transformations or reject material constraints, but which does see the notion of "totality"[7]—of cultural unity and continuity, of a unilinear development of history—break down. I find that in this so-called overarching "*līlā*" concept of the Hindus, women are excluded both grossly and subtly, at the level of its application in everyday life and less explicitly at the level of performance. Similarly, by studying its history I find that the meanings of religious experience, service to the Lord, *darśan,* and all the associated meanings of the Rāmlīlā are not separable from the history of the production and dissemination of these concepts. The Rāmlīlā is not a residue of the past or a fundamental part of folk culture. It is a live genre that has been the field for control and domination, expressing social relations, defining the self and others, decency, and progress. It is not "traditional," but has been constructed to seem so. It is not "folk," but is historically becoming so. It is not even "religious," having been equally a "social" or "political" event until recently. It raises the question, who has the power to bestow meanings? Which other powers does it accompany?

The Rāmlīlā has been studied by scholars of religion, civilization, and culture. The "*līlā*" concept has been studied mainly by Indologists.[8] In my paper, I first suggest an alternative view of the *līlā*. Then, in the first part, I look at the gendered nature of (*a*) the concept of *līlā, līlā* seen as Banārasī lifestyle, and (*b*) the performance of *līlā*. In the second part, I look at its history to present the class conflicts that have characterized it. In summing up, I throw up some questions it raises about the nature of change, not all of which are answered here.

The concept of *līlā* is an extraordinary one. It presents some of the most creative, subtle, original, insightful paired oppositions in Hindu thought, putting the concept of dialectic itself to shame: the idea of abandon but also control, playfulness but total application, freedom achieved through discipline, amusement coexisting with purposefulness, superhuman bliss and joy within the earthly mundane, divine presence evoked by human craft, ecstasy that breaks the bound of the self while celebrating the human senses. It is the same concept as revealed in meditation and asceticism, in Hindu cosmogony and *bhakti,* in the images and values drawn upon by Hindus in both aesthetics and the sciences. Examples are limitless: the *rāga*s of classical music, the forms of Śiva, present-day Hindu saints such as Deoraha Bābā and Ānandmayī Mā, the image of the elephant drunk with pleasure in the rains, and at my local level, the Banārasī immersed in pan mastication and all-night celebratory chaos as he participates in the appearance of his gods on his home-ground. . . .

The pervasiveness of the *līlā* concept in Hindu life is so marked that one may well analyze it as being at least the one constant of Hindu life, since like Ramanujan's notion of context-dependence[9] it permits that very flux and change, moving and varying with sociological complexities and historical exigencies, that more rigid concepts cannot handle.

But what if *līlā* is also a discourse, a set of rules with which statements can be made both about what is true and what is false? What if, like other discourses, it is also necessarily located in power, power that works not through the better recognized forms of repression or domination, but through the sheer creation of knowledge, specially the knowledge of what is right? What if its rules, like those of any discourse, while producing what count as truthful and meaningful statements, consistently marginalize and trivialize others? And, most of all, in doing so, its statements still pose as natural and essential, rather than being part of a necessary heterogeneity and differentiation?

The best reason for considering it a discourse is that *līlā* has in fact come to be seen, by intellectuals both within and without the society, as a Thing out there, to be comprehended, defined, discovered in texts and performances, taken in all seriousness as Philosophy. In doing this, scholars have swallowed the whole discourse *potlā-potlī* (bag and baggage, that is) and consider it natural, without history, without subjects, without contestation and without the play of power. The most marked characteristic of a discourse is its naturalness. What sounds, in present scholarship, more natural in Hinduism than the concept of *līlā?* Who would construct it, who would contest it, whence could there arise conflict within it? This proclivity of scholars is part of the largely essentialist enterprise of academia in general[10] where so much respect is given to authority and authenticity in general that the lived-in world, with its undersides of suppressed meanings and disunited fragments, and even rather powerful tensions, is ignored. That there is continuous construction of everything in society, including all texts and belief systems, is a lesson to which usually only lip service is paid. The nature of academic specialization is such, moreover, that a scholar of a certain kind of texts—whether inscribed or oral—remains basically confined to that and the methodological project of looking deliberately for contradiction, heterogeneity, and alterity, whether within or outside the texts, becomes difficult.

This is of course not an original discovery of mine and the point has frequently been made in recent years.[11] There are projects that seek to apply the postmodernist stance of searching for seams, openness, difference, and contradiction, even if they do not always do so consciously.[12] I have arrived at my present approach from battling for many years with data from Banaras on both lifestyle in general and its Rāmlīlās, especially one episode called the Cutting off the Nose, in particular. Looking at both these areas, I tend to see *līlā,* in both concept and practice—and obviously not coincidentally both, since they are part of the same discursive formation—as highly contested ground, in which conflict and violence have been endemic, victories unstable and temporary, and discursive displacements notable. Two striking areas of conflict are in gender relations and class relations.

Beware of the Ladies' Men

Banaras is called by male informants *puruṣoṃ kā śahar* (a city of men). They speak boastfully of a past when no woman was ever seen on the streets, and women stayed well within their bounds. Change has come, in popular view, from the immigration of "refugees" like Punjabis, Sindhis, and heterogeneous elements, whose womenfolk cannot be kept in check. They dispense with head covering, even wear short hair, work outside, transact business on the streets, and are certainly visible. Their influence has spread like a cancer and the old purity of Banaras is no more. Whereas there is little to support this view of women's invisibility in the past—it might rather reflect a male inability to *see* women when they are, publicly, producers, consumers, and distributors, as they have always been in Banaras, and to tend to see them as symbols instead—the image is a powerful one. It is one of the parts of a larger construction regarding balance, order, and virtue in society which are all variously summoned up to buttress more particular actions.

Banaras residents sport what I have called elsewhere an ideology of leisure and recreation[13] which fully exemplifies the male nature of the city. That is, the people of Banaras feel defined by their activities and lifestyle, and each of these is exclusively male or male-centered. Clearly articulated ideals are at work here: *mauj, mastī, akharpan, phakkaṛpan*—carefreeness, abandon, eccentricity, joie de vivre—all of which are male. It is necessary to understand these in some depth, as well as the place of *līlā* in them.

The Banaras resident (*banārasī,* a term with cultural connotations of being true to the spirit of Banaras, a term that necessarily stands only for males) describes his pleasures as the following: working out in *ākhāṛa*s (indigenous gymnasiums), going for outdoor trips outside the city for bathing and drugs, making and listening to music, celebrating festivals with public worship and processions, and simply wandering around the city. None of these activities include women: women do not visit *ākhāṛā*s, they do not go on outdoor trips, they do not participate in weekly or fortnightly singing, they do not participate in processions or organize public pujas, and they certainly do not wander around, drinking tea on outdoor benches or eating by the wayside. This exclusion from the city's prime fun activities is still a minor point, because of course women must have an alternate, rich and complex, world of activities of their own. But it has no name, no coherence, no public articulation, no swagger (but of course a body language), and no sanction in Tradition. What is far more significant than women's total exclusion from the "Banaras" world of leisure and pleasure is their exclusion from the discourse of *banārasīpan* (Banaras-ness, what it means to be a Banārasī), a far-reaching discourse of power and control.

The notion of *banārasīpan* is similar to that of *līlā;* in saying this I am but stirring the Banaras cultural pot with an analytical ladle to bring up some of the conceptual sediments sticking unobtrusively to the bottom. Here is the notion, the ideology or discourse of *banārasīpan* or *līlā:* life is play, modeled on the example of the Lord, in this case Śiva, the patron deity of the city. Not only did Śiva found the city and locate it on his trident, thus becoming a Banārasī once and for all, his whole personality—supreme dancer, unpredictable eccentric, potent but controlled, terribly creative and horribly destructive, gentle to the point of bovinity and femininity, raw, uncouth, beastlike, beyond all mundane cares and trivial pursuits—is precisely what forms the self-image of the Banārasī. The *līlā* of the Lord is the definition of life for his devotee. The Banārasī, therfore, is always engaged in a kind of spinning of *līlā:* a supreme craftsman, but jealous above all of his freedom, the freedom to abandon all work and simply wander, dream, sport in water, become intoxicated and perhaps destructive. Mud, garbage, refuse, shit, in proper beastly, jungle fashion, are objects regarded with bemused tolerance, indeed ritualization and pleasure, as they are explicitly by some *saṃnyāsī*s (those at the last stage of asceticism). Defecation, as I have analyzed at length elsewhere,[14] is particularly a multivocal ritual for the people of Banaras, and not a bodily function only, but an aspect of the highest philosophy of life—one that sees, as it were, the divine among the dung—that can treat everyday cares with absolute indifference and engage in play instead, the goal being noninvolvement.

Like all discourse, this *līlā* discourse assumes its opposite, what is suppressed in order to give it the tight feeling of unity and consistency that it has. Behind the abandon and noninvolvement in cares is the shadowy female figure squatting in the shades of house walls, blowing at embers to make the bread rise, worried for the time when the city trotter will return to eat and sleep. There is no trace of play, sport, freedom, or divinity—in short, of *līlā*—in domesticity, and none of domesticity (witness Śiva's example again) in the play and sport that comprises *līlā*.[15] The overall conceptual system, the discourse, of *līlā,* is invoked by Banaras men to validate a lifestyle through summoning up symbols, subconcepts, Histories, and models, and confirm the discourse as totally natural and given, indeed as the only one possible. What is left out are the positions of others, and all the meanings and possibilities of meanings that are treated by the discourse as irrelevant, but are addressed regularly by others. *Līlā* is a highly gendered discourse, and as such, "a primary way of signifying relationships of power . . . a primary field within which or by means of which power is articulated."[16]

It may be that for all my (deliberately mild, controlled) stirring of concepts with my analytical ladle, the taste of the pudding is not quite right for my readers. Let me just reiterate how I line up my analytical categories to allow me to equate the concept of the *līlā* with Banārasī men wandering around and chewing their mouths red with *pān*.

First, by listening to the representations themselves. The appearance, intersection, incarnation of the divine on this earth is translated by banārasīs as the ability to philosophize about and pull oneself free of nagging everyday cares, including the fear of death. *Mokṣa* is a powerful metaphor in Banaras that refers not merely to release *after* death, but in everyday practice, under different names, to release from worry about purposes and achievements. As with the lord at his *līlā,* this means intense involvement with *chosen* aspects of living, those that signal freedom, beauty, sensuality, and oneness with nature. So short of actually saying, "Oh, the concept of *līlā:* we actually apply it in our everyday lives. That's what we call Banārasīpan," male informants in Banaras would make all the representations necessary for us to draw the analogy. But if pressed, they would ponder the stench and filth surrounding them and pontificate, "God is everywhere, in every stone and mudpile in the city, and continues to create [*racanā*] his *līlā*. So must we be part of the garbage but *above* it."

A second device is to look for what the representations exclude and suppress. The *līlā* discourse directly and indirectly constructs male and female identity in Banaras by making naturalistic statements about the one and suppressing the other, while suggesting it continuously as the residual. Female saints (Ānandmayī Mā, Beṭījī Mahārāj) and courtesans aside, this residual category is the opposite of the free, the acting agent with moods, personalities, preferences; the playful personage who chooses to recede or to get involved. Playfulness is *not* the prerogative of women, as is not lack of worry, carefreeness, abandon, and mouths dripping uncontrollably with *pān*. In what the discourse excludes as well as what it states, banārasīpan shows itself to be a subset of *līlā*. For both, local power relations make possible these kinds of discourses, and these discourses, as Foucault puts it, are used to support power relations.[17]

So, in both its statements and their necessary exclusions, the discourse of *līlā* / banārasīpan bases itself on the two rules: one, that a celebration of the pleasures of this world, with the recognition that everything is god, leads to a carefree, sportlike involvement with it which is a reflection of god's own sporting with and in his creation, ergo, an expression of the highest wisdom of life, *līlā* itself. And, two, that women are not part of this vision of the good life as subject participants. They are simply not spoken of, excluded the most effectively by total silence, accompanied by the manipulation of symbols that are incontestably male.

The Rāmlīlā is the staged theater extending over many evenings based on the *Rāmacaritamānas* of Tulasīdās, familiar to everyone who knows north India. There are dozens of Rāmlīlās in Banaras, each to a ward, *muhallā,* or group of *muhallā*s (ward and *muhallā* being administrative divisions, with eight wards in the city, and approximately 50–100 *muhallā*s in each). Each has an elected, mostly registered, body that collects funds, and appoints the amateurs and professionals who will stage the play. Almost all Rāmlīlās have histories—stories of beginnings and sometimes ends, and often resurrections—that are written about or known publicly, and all are expected to *have* histories, that is, to display the same dynamic quality that people experience in every other aspect of their lives. I chose to study the Rāmlīlā of Chaitganj, a neighborhood in Banaras, and one episode of that Rāmlīlā called *nākkaṭayyā,* or Cutting off the Nose, for reasons that will become clear, but I fully believe that any of the other local neighborhood Rāmlīlās of the city merits a similar analysis.

The plot of the evening consists of Rāvaṇa's sister, Śūrpaṇakhā, trying to tempt the two virtuous brothers, Rāma, and then Lakṣmaṇa, to "wrongdoing," whereupon an outraged Lakṣmaṇa slices off her nose to humiliate her for her conduct. The enraged demoness goes to her brothers to complain and they take out an army in procession. After hours of the procession winding its way through the lanes of Chaitganj, the rest of the evening's theater is enacted.

Sīta is taken in by Rāvaṇa disguised as a deer and foolishly begs her husband to trap the beautiful creature for her. Rāvaṇa then tricks her into thinking that Rāma has gotten injured and is crying for help. The lady now forces her brother-in-law to follow Rāma. Lakṣmaṇa is reluctant to leave her unprotected, but cannot disobey, so draws a *lakṣmaṇ rekhā* (line of Lakṣmaṇa), a protective line around her and their cottage that would spit fire on anyone who tried to cross it. Rāvaṇa arrives, disguised as a mendicant. (The vainglorious, thoughtless) Sītā steps out of the magic line to give him alms and is promptly abducted. Rāma and Lakṣmaṇa then fight to rescue the lady, as her brothers have readied themselves for battle to avenge Śūrpaṇakhā.

This rather bare plot, familiar from the Tulasīdās *Rāmacaritamānas,* consists of the story of two women who transgress the bounds set on them by men, rather explicitly as a line in Sītā's case, implicitly as an expectation of moral conduct in Śūrpaṇakhā's case, and how their trespassing leads them to fates worse than death, not to speak of overall warfare, wastage of resources, destruction of men, and a turning upside down of society.

A Society with Classes

So the *nākkaṭayyā* episode is permeated through and through with statements about asymmetrical gender relations. The plot of the vindictiveness of the ladies' relatives just outlined, however, is really the barest core of the Chaitganj *nākkaṭayyā.* The heart of the event lies in a *julūs,* a procession, which finds its excuse, as it were, in the march of the demon army. When the *nākkaṭayyā* is spoken of, it is the procession that is referred to and merits a brief description.

Chaitganj, a market area (*ganj*) of some antiquity (founded by Chait Singh?) has a wide central avenue which is cleaned up and prepared elaborately for the evening by residents through public donations. Each shop is decorated, the street lined by stalls of eatables, toys, and crafts. Gates are put up by local merchants advertising their products, and the rows of lights and countless loudspeakers that characterize every Banaras public event are at their maximum. Policemen are posted every few yards; it is clear that this is no ordinary *līlā* where prerehearsed sobriety prevails; it is an overwhelming, gigantic affair that is potentially combustible.

The procession starts after midnight and is led by a hermaphrodite and a prostitute, suitably liminal and demonic, dancing and leering at the spectators. Then follow in quick succession bands of musicians, troupes of dancers, performers of traditional tricks of sword and pole wielding, magicians, fire breathers, animal trainers and their pets. The third and main part of the procession consists of some one hundred floats (*lāgās* and *vimānas*) that depict four kinds of situations: (*a*) gods put together in combinations of elaborate balancing feats, such as Śiva holding up a globe merely with his trident, on which rotate other deities, or Hanumān with Rāma, Lakṣmaṇa, and Sītā on each shoulder and tail, respectively; (*b*) a mime of a secular nature, such as in 1986 the assassination of Indira Gandhi; (*c*) little children dressed up as royalty frozen into statues on intricate metal thrones; (*d*) feats of mechanical motion (cycles, spheres, tubes, and girders), or electrical craft, powered by deafening electric generators.

The main street of Chaitganj is alive with activity well before the procession starts: lights, music, noise, shopping, wandering around. As the parade takes over the space, some few yards get cleared before it, and spectators line up on either side, and swamp back into the space as the parade passes on. There is a curious mixture of performance—hired and designed shows and art—and people's event, since there *are* no formal boundaries. How does all this constitute the *līlā?* The *nākkaṭayyā* can best be understood as falling squarely within the repertoire of Banaras public events, displaying those qualities which make for appreciation in Banaras, which we must understand in order to see how it has been an object of contention. The power of the event lies clearly in the popular mind in the following features:

(*a*) Its size: attendance in it is reputed to be over 100,000, making it a *lākhī* (*lākh* = 100,000) *melā,* one of the three largest *melās* in the city. Size in everything, and for public events in calculation of the numbers attending, is a cultural preoccupation in Banaras, making it always more expensive and troublesome an occasion for the hosts or organizers, its rationality lying, in Bourdieu's term, in its display of symbolic capital.[18]

(*b*) It goes on all night, which is also indicative of bigness, all public events in Banaras striving to extend their hours through the night into the early hours.

(*c*) The parade is a double winner, in itself as procession, and second, as display of craft and glitter. A procession is a highly charged political event, the clearest display of one's powers, leaders, and symbols, and indeed is used for agitations and political rallies the most frequently. Processions at festivals make the same statement about the solidarity and strength of the constituency of the particular god being displayed; they are also charged occasions where the boundaries between audience and performers, stage space and real space, melt away. Muharram and Gurū Nānak Jayanti, the immersion parades of Durgā and Viśwakarma, are all political and symbolic statements, as well as occasions of community gatherings.[19] In 1911, for those who could not witness the *darbār* in Delhi, parades were organized with officers taken out in state. In Banaras it was "the procession of the Collector sahab":

> Publicity posters and announcements had already been taken care of a day before, so there was a good crowd on the roads. The *julūs* to accompany the carriage started getting ready on the campus of Queen's College in the afternoon itself. At the head was the Superintendent of Police, mounted, behind which were pole bearers, five cavalry, four cannons, and the band and platoon of Mahārāj Banaras, then on a decorated elephant the pictures of Mahārāj George V and Mahārānī Mary, behind which was a police regiment, then the Collector Sahab on a fancy elephant, followed by the elephant of Mahārāj Jañgam, and about twenty elephants of the *rāīs* (aristocracy). After that came the incomparable musicians of Mahārāj Bhiñga, soldiers of Mahārāj Banaras, lines of camels, the cavalry of Mahārāj Banaras and scores of phaeton carriages of the *rāīs.*[20]

The description continues with details of the route taken, the gates and tents, the flower decorations at shops and homes on the wayside, and the pleasure of the crowds. The obvious satisfaction in such reports and all oral ones on the subject of processions in general, and of course the significations created, make me evaluate the role of processions in Banaras public life very highly. The *nākkaṭayyā* has the additional attraction of being a display of craft and circus feats, which exerts a kind of magnetism, as with Muharram *tāziyā*s and Durgā images, making it imperative for people to attend, to compare this year's show with last year's and this *muhallā*'s display with the other's.

(*d*) The *nākkaṭayyā* includes certain characteristics that people in Banaras believe to be central to any popular activity, among which is supposed sanction in tradition, and a deep moral structure in which good triumphs over evil (picturesquely described as the *ākhirī nicoṛ*, the final wringing). The Rāmlīlā fulfills this condition in two ways, one through storytelling as in a mythological film, and the other through *darśan,* giving a chance to view one's favorite gods in highly amplified settings, as at the annual celebrations at temples and shrines.

(*e*) Compulsory to the popularity of public events in Banaras is also the presence of, or a past or imagined existence of *bāharī ālaṅg*, the 'outer side'. This is open space, uncrowded, free, cool, receptive, one's own. Banaras residents behave like the citizens of a metropolis in seeking escape to open spaces, but a look at the ward of Chaitganj makes this problematic. Not only is it tightly packed and close to the center, the fair itself attracts so many thousands that it is one of the most bustling, overpacked events, which needs constant police and volunteer supervision to prevent the heightened feelings and sheer crowd mentality from erupting into anarchy. Yet, when questioned why they like this Rāmlīlā, people maintain that they feel free and in the open, wandering here and there with friends, stopping to taste this, enjoy that. . . . In my analysis, it is never *people* that crowd people in popular thinking, but only buildings that do. If the space is an open one, under the sky, regardless of the numbers in attendance, it is felt to be open. Gigantic fairs and gatherings, such as the Kumbh Melās, with *millions* attending, are not uncommon in India, but never spoken of critically or complainingly by their constituents.

(*f*) Competitiveness is rife in Banaras cultural life and equally part of Rāmlīlās like the *nākkaṭayyā*. Floats and performers, animal trainers and fire swallowers are awarded prizes, shops fronts and decorated spaces compete to dazzle, and the most explicit competition is between the different *ākhāṛā*s, or clubs of sword and pole wielding. All the awards are broadcast in the printed Rāmlīlā program, in banners and signboards, and over loudspeakers. At the next level the whole affair is competing, although its primary position is long established, with all the *nākkaṭayyā*s of all the other neighborhoods in Banaras, and some features such as metal thrones or artisans' stalls are regarded as better at the Kashipura (the metalworkers' locality) and Khojwa (the woodworkers' neighborhood) *nākkaṭayyā*s, respectively. This brings us to the next feature, the commercial aspects of the fair, because prizes are voluntarily given, and their announcement provides an avenue for publicity for the person or business assuming the role of patron.

(*g*) People spend at the Rāmlīlā, on food, trinkets, local crafts, and childrens' attractions. This economic activity is what is basically meant by *melā,* or fair, so that a righteous critic might claim that the *melā* is nowadays taking over from religion altogether. Chaitganj is an important business area, and its traders and shopkeepers donate heavily toward its Rāmlīlā; its size and attractiveness and attendant reputation clearly constituting symbolic capital for them. Chaitganj is not famous for anything as much as for its *nākkaṭāyyā,* and it is the capitalists of the ward who have the most to spend and the most to gain from the popularity of the fair. An interesting fact is that the date for the *nākkaṭayyā* is fixed for *karavā cauth* (Pitcher Fourth), an important woman's fast that every wife keeps for her husband. Why *karavā cauth*? It is a date that no woman will forget, and by extension her whole family. Although the consumption is chiefly by males on food, and by families on children's overpriced balloons and titbits, women are supposedly the most religious section of the population and can be trusted not to forget significant dates. The bringing together of unconnected dates such as *karavā cauth* and *nākkaṭayyā* is a kind of sleight of hand by which the significance of the fast is made to extend into the fair, making both publicity and persuasion for the public unnecessary.

(*h*) Finally, we come to the conflict and difference. In my analysis so far, the *nākkaṭayyā* exemplifies Banaras popular culture to the full by standing for the pleasures of bigness, artistry, competition, *melā, julūs, darśan,* and *bāharī ālaṅg*. All agree to that, whether they participate in the event or not, as for example police officers when in a neutral mood, for whom the evening is otherwise an oversize law and order problem only. But for *nākkaṭayyā*-goers these are all positive characteristics, whereas for critics they are all subsumed under the characterization of the *nākkaṭayyā* as *aślīl, asabhya,* uncivilized. The *nākkaṭayyā* highlights splits in Banaras society that are evidenced by other popular activities as well, not quiet and unmarked divisions, but active tensions and conflicts that have worked themselves out variously over the nineteenth century. The history of popular entertainments in Banaras shows them to have been simultaneously accorded respect as *dhārmik,* that is, religious or righteous, sanctioned in tradition, and condemned as *aślīl,* that is, crude or obscene. The most outstanding examples are the *sṛṅgārs*, or annual celebrations at temples where it was customary for courtesans to perform and for the audience to enjoy their virtuosity and lack of virtue to the full. The popular festival of Diwālī, likewise, was berated for its gambling, and Holī because of its obscene processions, drinking and drugs, and most of all *gālīs*, structured and rehearsed obscenities directed at members of the public, often printed and illustrated.[21]

The Chaitganj Rāmlīlā was started in 1888 in a similar way to most of the others in Banaras, through a coordination of efforts of a merchant devotee (Mohan Sahu, a tobacco merchant, in this case) and a popular *sādhū* (Bābā Fateh Rām). The *nākkaṭayyā* as a specially significant episode of the Rāmlīlā series is first mentioned in local newspapers as a procession of floats in 1905. In a few years, it is never simply mentioned, it is described annually in great detail, and takes on the nature of a problem.

The *nākkaṭayyā* was both more literal and metaphoric at that time. It took the business of being a demon army more literally in that the floats consisted of depictions of evil, of all that was considered worst among social practices: problems such as drunkenness, wife-beating, infidelity, bigamy, prostitution, and gambling—not in a spirit of preaching or direct criticism, but rather with that special fascination with horror which enables one to savor what is unsavory and forbidden from touch as a rule, and made available on one special occasion. The *nākkaṭayyā* was akin to carnival and charivaris in that it reversed social structure for an evening, making available to the senses in artistic, rehearsed ways what was condemnable and forbidden the rest of the year. It was never quite carnival in that there was no overall license to overthrow structure; all the floats and mimes were planned and permitted, and the demon army was finally a group of performers, albeit close to spectators given the nature of public processions. An article called "Swāṅg [mime] in the Rāmlīlā" in the *Bhārat Jīwan* describes the event:

> There used to be a rather good Rāmlīlā in Kāśī in many places, but now they are all gone . . . [mention of a few that are finished]. The Kāśīrāj's Līlā in Rām-

> nagar continues, of course, but it is not like it used to be; it gets completed somehow. In other places in Kāśī, Rāmlīlā is that only in name. The *nākkaṭayyā* is now a *swāṅg*. The cutting of Śūrpaṇakhā's nose, Khardūṣaṇ's collecting their army to attack Rāma—these are unimportant; all that counts are the mimes. The whole form of the *līlā* is changed. Floats are decorated showing males and females of low castes at their work [examples of gardeners, traders, etc.], of a bride and groom at their wedding, and so on. It's not enough that men and women are shown in intimacy, people dressed up as washermen and washer-women and other low castes, create a real disturbance. Abusive actions and immoral behaviour [are] shown and vulgar words spoken. What is this trend of showing the faulty *līlā* of the world behind the facade of God's *līlā?*[22]

There was a perceptible trend to criticism from the beginning, but we also know, through oral history and the local journalism of the period, that the patronage for the *nākkaṭayyā* in the early twentieth century was not restricted to any particular class of people. Gender, yes; as a part of the Banārasī lifestyle, *nākkaṭayyā* was the domain of men in their love of freedom and sport, excellence in craft and performance, and *akharpan* (eccentricity) in general. But the wealthy and the educated, the thoughtful and the cultured (*rāīs, buddhijīvī, cintāśīl, sabhya*) all gave money toward, and often took out their own floats annually in, the *nākkaṭayyā*. Such participation was part of the overall sharing between classes of notions of the good life, of *mauj, mastī,* and *śauk,* the love of something for its own sake. *Śauk* is not a term usually used in a religious context, and refers to habits such as *pān* chewing, tea drinking, smoking, indulging in music and entertainments that verge on the unbridled. A lecherous old man, for example, may be described as *śaukīn*. In Banaras, given its lack of division between the sensuous and the righteous, so may a regular Rāmlīlā-goer be described, with a different set of accompanying gestures. Wealth and aristocracy in Banaras have been exemplified by *śauk,* the taste, means, and consequently preference for patronage of singers and dancers, good food and compatible company, boating on the river and racing on horse carriages. This is the *banārasīpan* shared at all levels by the men of Banaras, albeit with varying means, elaborated in the local press, in essays by the literati, as well as the reports of informants.[23]

Beginning from the 1920s and gathering momentum in the 1930s, the critical assessment of the *nākkaṭayyā* took on severe and strident tones. The nationalist movement took on a hegemonic role, as it did almost everywhere in urban India, and a new discourse was constructed. This struggled chiefly with definitions of the self: how shall we be in private *and* what shall we display of ourselves in public? Sometimes the imagined comparison was with Christianity, and despair expressed at a situation where Hinduism was being displayed in the worst possible light to other faiths: "Not to Muslims, because they actually are in this and co-operate to take it further. We particularly mean padres. Padres come from across the seven seas to bring light to Indians, and Indians who in actuality are the light givers, prove by such activities that they in fact live in pitch darkness.''[24] But most often it was concern with creating a suitable national identity which could do justice to the *authentic* in Hinduism, in the history of the country, and the philosophy of the people. For that a purging, a reform, a casting out of vice was necessary, and a containment of proclivities that were labeled injurious. The descriptions of the terrible scenes witnessed at the *nākkaṭayyā* became more distanced:

> Milksellers, flowersellers, trinket sellers . . . were these presented earlier at *nākkaṭayyā* as mimes? Is there any other Rāmāyaṇa where we can see them? Then why do these *swāṅgs* come out and why are they permitted? Or even if we allow them to be shown supposing there's no harm in that, what has to be questioned is their explicitly immoral behaviour, their extremely lurid talk, and their veritable shower of abuses. Even worse, when they reach a place with a big crowd of women, they say such crude, obscene things that it seems that shame has gone behind a *pardā,* for neither the mimics nor the audience feels any shame.[25]

The danger was voiced of the government taking steps to stop such a procession. With the growth of the nationalist movement came explicit suggestions for reform:

> Such shameful scenes should be completely stopped. The organisers of the Rāmlīlā can stop them in one day. If educated young men would make groups and plead with the makers of floats, these corrupt scenes could be done away with. . . . Scenes to arouse people should be shown on such occasions. Supposing you are oppressed by taxes and you want to arouse the public, you can make an image of a fat, prosperous man asking an emaciated one for tax, and alongside have three or four young boys walking and chorusing, ''Down with taxes!'' . . . Men, women, children, and the aged will understand the problem in one day. Or take out giant posters of the leaders of the nation, and recite their lives and characters in brief or distribute them as printed pamphlets. . . .[26]

What is significant is that in this passion for reform, critics, intellectuals, and nationalist leaders yet did not speak of a separation, of themselves as apart and aloof from society, and of the rest of the population as the object to be worked on. A consensus was always assumed, and practices in general had to be reformed. Certain practices had already been targeted by reform movements, and the locus of agitation was the caste or the subcaste through caste meetings and associations: practices such as drinking, gambling, bigamy, and child marriage. The new development that may be marked in Banaras from the 1920s onward (and surely in other places as well, if looked for) is reform at the popular cultural level, such as of the patronage of courtesans.[27] After some years of this kind of struggle for reform arose a consciousness of separation: Banaras cultural life came to be divided into the crude and the reformed, gradually to coincide with the lower and the upper classes, the illiterate and the educated, the old-fashioned and rural versus the modern and progressive. This was reflected in a linguistic separation of "we" and "they":

> We want to assure the officers that Bhagwān Rāma's *līlā* has no relationship with this barbarism and vulgarity. . . . In our opinion it is time that the law took over and removed this abuse. If that is not done then those who do not wish to participate in such unseemly exhibition will be forced to do *satyāgraha.*[28]

The *nākkaṭayyā* went through three phases: first, as an ideological statement on Hindu society, that presented its values both directly (as the Rāmlīlā story) and as reversal (the themes of the floats in the demon army). Together with depiction was a powerful element of activism at this stage: the *nākkaṭayyā* was actually performing a function, interfering in perceived problems in society to cure them through a certain kind of statement making. And this ideology, the activism, and the methods adopted to execute both were consensually held and valued by all classes of Banaras society.

In its second phase, a nationalist discourse spells out the nature of virtue, the self, and the community. The method—a festival procession—may still be retained (that itself is never criticized by our male subjects, only its content) and the reform is necessary for the *whole* of society, not merely some classes or castes, but the discourse is not amenable to debate. It assumes rightness, naturalness, and representativeness, and has no spaces where those who believe in bigamy, for example, or the naturalness of drink and drugs, may make their statements. It is a hegemonic, controlling, unilaterally acting discourse, and to the extent that the nationalist movement was a middle-class phenomenon in general, it started off as a class-based discourse.

The first stage may be called that of a naive (unself-conscious) and unchallenged caste structure, and a Hinduism that is not imagined or *supposed* to be homogeneous and unified, with legitimacy accorded to local practices, and an active participation in the problems of everyday living assumed on the part of the people of a neighborhood. The second stage contests the heterogeneity, the openness, and the dynamism, in culture, structure, and ideology. *One* definition of Hinduism is offered, based on a vision of progress, and no conflict in interpretation is accorded respect. *One* definition of the self is advanced, based on a vision of citizenship and nationhood, and no complexity is countenanced. To these extents, without explicating any difference, the nationalist discourse indulges in violence throughout, not "us" against "them," but an indifference and ignoring of who the "them" might constitute.

At both stages the discursive formations are gendered ones. They are created by men, for men, and assume only men to be conscious agents. Women are acted upon, in the earlier discourse, as objects of malpractices: wife-beating, bigamy, and early marriage, and also the main sufferers from the practices of drunkenness and prostitution. In the latter discourse, they are the victims to be raised up, through the overall raising of society's morals, through education, promotion of nationalism, secularism, and a refined Hinduism.

The third stage followed after a brief and uneasy victory for the nationalist movement. The *nākkaṭayyā* was "purified" of its obscenities, and simultaneously rid of its function of ritual reversal, of the ritual depiction of social features otherwise considered taboo. It did for many years actually include nationalist floats, but from the 1950s onward there has been no urge toward that either. No social problems or concerns are visible in the procession today, as they were in either of the earlier phases. All social (and also economic, political, and all other) issues are today totally the domain of the government through its various agencies—the new multiarmed deity, one is tempted to say.

What is the function of the Rāmlīlā, then? It is firmly lodged in the repertoire of activities that constitute the world of Banaras popular culture. That it continues to be popular is a very significant comment on the resilience of popular cultural forms in the face of seemingly powerful competition from movies, Amitabh Bachchan, and orchestra music (as westernized music is called in Banaras); not to mention the ever alert arms of the administration and the police nervous about disorder and particularly on religious celebrations. This is a matter that merits some thought, because the circus and iconic content of the *nākkaṭayyā* makes one realize that it does not successfully compete in any objective sense with either movies or the circus. At either, easily available in Banaras as in all towns, specially the former on video, one may either see far better performances of acrobatic feats, or displays of electronic wizardry, or representation of the gods. The much lamented demise of precapitalist culture when people made artifacts with their own hands, put on performances themselves, and audiences actually interacted with the stage, rather than the capitalist method of professional production of culture, thick-skinnedly marketed, and mindlessly consumed—this demise seems to be greatly exaggerated. Banaras is not a preindustrial city. Yet its public events are all produced by people themselves and presented to live, interacting audiences.

But, respect this continuity as we may, we should labor to uncover those aspects in which the Rāmlīlā is nothing like what it was, precisely because it is those that are opaque at first sight. The issue of *dharma* may be taken up first lest it be felt that the forest is being obstructed by the trees. To have the story continue as a plot is remarkable in that given the brunt of nationalist fervor, and Gandhi's manipulation of symbols like *rāmrājya,* there were ample opportunities for adjustment in and appropriation of the messages of the Rāma story over the last one hundred years, yet no adjustment or appropriation has taken place. This, I would argue, is because it is the charter for another discourse, that of gender, a totally silent, unaggressively presented, peacefully incorporated discourse. No men, "traditional" or "modern," have targeted the Rāma story as an issue.

What of the religious content of the procession? If it was heterogeneous and open in the first phase, and rigid and centralized in the second (or sought to be), what kind of religiosity are we witnessing in the hundred-odd floats of the *nākkaṭayyā* today? Just as temples and shrines proliferate, so do images and icons, but just as the former are no longer cultural centers, so are the gods not active agents with powers to interfere in social life. Those powers have been completely appropriated by administrative and police agencies, and there are, at best, two rival loci of power, the government and the divine, with the former in the ascendant. This is not a trifling change, because in my analysis, the power of religion and of *līlā* lay in that it was not a separate or constricted domain, but because it referred to lifestyle, social structure, and the whole business of life in general. Gods were not someone you worshiped at certain times, but another level of being in a continuous chain from yours whose model you followed, whose stories you alluded to, whose *līlā* was an example for your own *līlā*. This being all true for males and part of their discourse, belief system, culture, and ideology. Presently, gods are perhaps boon granters, and their *darśan* is valued for wish fulfillment and as tradition (*paramparā*). That they can be seriously emulated in lifestyle or considered role models, or imagined to have any interaction with social life today is a matter of skepticism. This is obviously a much larger issue than I am capable of addressing here, and I would invite students of Hinduism and its cultural expressions to look for the evidences of function change in sign systems—discursive displacements, to use the apt phraseology of Spivak[29]—to make for a better-documented case one way or the other. To a large extent this is a class issue. Poor and illiterate people in their traditional occupations are still in a sense two phases "behind," in the language of this analysis; those who consider themselves modern and are in different productive relations, assess reality differently.

So, the Rāmlīlā continues, different in social structure—it is now the property of the lower classes; and in function—it does not enact ritual reversal, or indeed comment on social life directly at all, acceding leadership to the police and administration. The discourse that constitutes the *līlā* was, and continues to be, gendered. Our historical analysis, however, does not allow us to leave it with an image of two homogeneous units, males and females. The particular statements the Rāmlīlā made for men's space, freedom, and selfhood have been greatly constricted over the last eighty-odd years from challenges from other discourses, such as those directed at progress, control, the nation, and work ethic; so that now the *līlā,* both as concept and performance, is male dominated but distinctly lower class. How the processes of differentiation and control worked themselves out within *women's* spaces over this same period is yet to be understood.

NOTES

1. A landmark that comes to mind is the Seminar on New History, Delhi, 1988.

2. Nita Kumar, *The Artisans of Banaras: Popular Culture and Identity, 1880–1986* (Princeton, N.J.: Princeton University Press, 1988.)

3. Nita Kumar, *Friends, Brothers, and Informants: Fieldwork Memoirs of Banaras* (Berkeley: University of California Press, 1992).

4. Among other good statements, see Jane Flax, *Thinking Fragments: Psychoanalysis, Feminism, and Postmodernism in the Contemporary West* (Berkeley: University of California Press, 1990); Julie Stephens, ''Feminist Fictions'' in R. Guha, ed., *Subaltern Studies VI* (Delhi: Oxford University Press, 1989); Chandra Mohanty, ''Under Western Eyes: Feminist Scholarship and Colonial Discourses,'' *Feminist Review,* no. 30 (Autumn 1988), pp. 61–88.

5. See Kumar, *The Artisans,* chap. 7.

6. The case for, or rather against, such marginalization is well made by Hans Medick, '''Missionaries in the Row Boat?' Ethnological Ways of Knowing as a Challenge to Social History,'' *Comparative Studies in Society and History* 29, no. 1 (1987), pp. 76–98. For the dualism inherent in most perspectives, see also Pierre Bourdieu, ''Social Space and Symbolic Power,'' *Sociological Theory* 7, no. 1 (Spring 1989), pp. 14–17; but it is a problem that much social science writing takes up.

7. The term used by Tambiah, with whose understanding of history I cannot but disagree, in Stanley Tambiah, ''At the Confluence of Anthropology, History, and Indology,'' *Contributions to Indian Sociology* 21, no. 1 (1987), p. 190.

8. I participated in ''The Concept of Lila in South Asia,'' an international confer-

ence sponsored by the Center for the Study of World Religions, Harvard University, April 1989, where I heard a particularly rich collection of papers. I thank all the participants for their discussion and comments, most of all the organizer, William Sax.

9. A. K. Ramanujan, "Is There an Indian Way of Thinking?" in McKim Marriott, ed., *India Through Hindu Categories* (Delhi: Sage Publications, 1990). Ramanujan, of course, calls it "Indian" rather than "Hindu," an unfortunate, if typical, oversight.

10. See Dominick LaCapra, *History and Criticism* (Ithaca, N.Y.: Cornell University Press, 1985); and idem, *Soundings in Critical Theory* (Ithaca, N.Y.: Cornell University Press, 1989).

11. Flax, *Thinking Fragments;* Joan Wallach Scott, *Gender and the Politics of History* (New York, Columbia University Press, 1988).

12. For a friendly review of some such projects, see Gayatri Spivak, "Subaltern Studies: Deconstructing Historiography," in R. Guha, ed., *Subaltern Studies IV* (Delhi: Oxford University Press, 1985).

13. Kumar, *The Artisans.*

14. Nita Kumar, "Open Space and Free Time: Pleasure for the People of Banaras," *Contributions to Indian Sociology* 20 no. 1 (1986), pp. 41–60.

15. I am speaking here not of the domesticity analyzed by Madan from primarily textual sources, where he opposes it to renunciation and equates it with the pleasures of the flesh. Since his analysis excludes women, as do the texts and informants he uses for data, his notions of domesticity do not correspond with mine, where I maintain that women are the "domesticated," and Man the Householder as I find him in Banaras has forged an approach to incorporate both pleasure and noninvolvement in it; T. N. Madan, *Non-Renunciation: Themes and Interpretations of Hindu Culture* (Delhi: Oxford University Press, 1987).

16. Scott, *Gender and the Politics of History,* pp. 44–45.

17. Michel Foucault, *The History of Sexuality* (New York: Vintage Books, 1978), p. 98.

18. Pierre Bourdieu, *Outline of a Theory of Practice* (New York, Cambridge University Press, 1977).

19. See, for example, the report "The Procession of Sri Annapurnaji," *Bhārat Jīwan,* 23 December 1912, p. 9.

20. *Bhārat Jīwan,* 11 December 1911, p. 10.

21. For a larger discussion of this, see Kumar, *The Artisans,* chaps. 6 and 7.

22. *Bhārat Jīwan,* 23 October 1905.

23. There are at least a dozen periodicals important for the 1880–1950 period, the most articulate and widest circulated being *Āj* and *Bhārat Jīwan:* among many articles by local authors are Bharatendu Harishchandra's in Shivprasad Misra, ed., *Bharatendu Granthāvalī,* vol. 1 (Vārāṇasī: Nāgarī Pracāriṇī Sobhā, 1970); Mukundlal Sarraf's collection in *Gauravmayī Kāśī* (Vārāṇasī, n.d.); and most of the articles in *Dainik Jāgaraṇ Vārāṇasī Praveśāṅk* (Vārāṇasī, 1981).

24. *Bhārat Jīwan,* 28 October 1907.

25. Ibid.

26. *Āj,* 17 October 1920.

27. See Kumar, *The Artisans,* chap. 6; for comparable processes Amrit Srinivasan, ''Reform or Conformity? Temple 'Prostitution' and the Community in Madras Presidency,'' in Bina Agrawal, ed., *Structures of Patriarchy* (London: Zed Books, 1988).

28. *Āj,* 10 October 1938.

29. Spivak, ''Subaltern Studies.''

11

The Realm of Play and the Sacred Stage

VASUDHA NARAYANAN

Līlā seems to have been popularly understood in at least three different ways by Vaiṣṇava Hindus. The creation of the universe is the sport of Viṣṇu; his descent into the world, especially in leading the idyllic life of Vṛndāvana, is seen as divine play; and finally the extravagant ritual dramas of northern India in which episodes from the epics are enacted are known as *līlā*. In this essay I shall portray a Śrīvaiṣṇava understanding of "*līlā*" by initially discussing the occurrence of the word in that community's literature,[1] and later, by describing their Festival of Recitation. The multiple meanings of the concept of *līlā* seen in the writings of the Śrīvaiṣṇava *ācārya*s are conveyed by this ritual, which may well be one of the earliest surviving enactments that fit in the performative *līlā* genre. Though the Śrīvaiṣṇava community uses the word "*līlā*" only in discussions for theological concepts and *not* for its enactment rituals, we shall see that the ritual dimension is connected with its theology, on the one hand, and bears similarity to the north Indian performances of *Kṛṣṇa-* and *Rāmlīlā*s, on the other. However, it must be emphasized that the Festival of Recitation, as well as the theological discussions in Śrīvaiṣṇava literature, reflect a Vaiṣṇava concept of *līlā* rather than an exclusively "Kṛṣṇa" or "Rāma" form of it.[2]

Līlā in the Writings of the Early Śrīvaiṣṇava *Ācārya*s

Rāmānuja uses *līlā* principally in the context of creation. The context is instructive; his favorite phrase, "he whose sport [*līlā*] is the creation, maintenance and destruction of the worlds,'' occurs usually in a set place in a frequently occurring litany. This litany includes all of Rāmānuja's favorite themes in a particular order (the order in his introduction to the *Gītā Bhāṣya* and in the *Śaraṇāgati Gadya,* for instance, is almost identical). It starts with the Lord's purity and opposition to all that is filthy, and continues with lists of his auspicious qualities. Then come the qualities pertaining to his divine form, his association with Śrī and other goddesses, the list of servants who serve him faultlessly in heaven, his lordship over the realm of enjoyment (*vaikuṇṭha*), and finally, the creation, maintenance, and destruction of the worlds which is his ''play.'' The context of mentioning creation as sport—more often than not—is when Rāmānuja speaks of the glory and splendor of the Lord and rejoices in it. While we frequently interpret ''play'' as the ease with which the Lord creates, I am inclined to say that the notion of *celebration* is prominent in the writings of Rāmānuja. *Līlā* is a display of the Lord's wealth and dominion, and a joyful expression of his power and abundance. In this context the sport of creation is perhaps more analogous to custom-designing and crafting a sports car than to playing with a bat and a ball.

The word *krīḍa* (''play'') is also used by Rāmānuja's disciple Kūrattāḻvāṉ when he speaks of the Lord's creation:

> Glancing at Śrī's face, heeding her every wish,
> Hari creates, destroys, and protects [the worlds];
> He gives heaven and hell, and the highest state.
> United with her in his pleasure, he creates all;
> for without [Śrī] this play [*krīḍa*] [of creation]
> brings him no joy—
>   May that Śrī bring us happiness.
>
> *Śrī Stava,* 1

Viṣṇu's wishes conform to Śrī's; without her happiness there is no enjoyment of his play. The celebration and display of glory are fun only when shared with his beloved consort, Śrī.

Kūrattāḻvāṉ's son Bhaṭṭar says that creation makes manifest the Lord's hidden splendor:

> O Lord who fulfills desires!
> Like a peacock shaking loose its brilliant feathers
>   and holding them high in front of a hen,
> by your wish you spread out the expanse of souls and matter
>   that are [hidden] and one with your body
>   during the time of dissolution,
> and playfully [*krīḍa*] [display your glory]
>   before the eyes of Śrī.
>
> *Śrī Raṅgarāja Stava,* pt. 2, 44

Like the ease with which the peacock displays his plumage, the Lord shakes loose creation from matter so subtle that it seems to be one with him. This cosmos is a manifestation of the Lord's glory and splendor, and he playfully displays it in front of Śrī. There is, of course, an underlying erotic note in this verse; the peacock usually dances in full glory to attract the hen. Creation, then, is part of *love play* between Viṣṇu and Śrī in Śrīvaiṣṇava literature; *līlā* is seen in the creation of the worlds as well as the realm of *śṛṅgāra* between Śrī and the Lord. Creation is the expression not only of the Lord's magnificence but also of his enduring passion for Śrī. In the temple rituals of Srirangam, says Parāśara Bhaṭṭar, Viṣṇu and Śrī *play* with flowers, adorning themselves with fresh blossoms,[3] celebrating the vibrancy of spring and the creation of life. Śrī *playfully* uses the crook of the Lord's arm as her pillow,[4] and the marks of her braid are imprinted (along with the marks made by his bow Sārṅga) on his arm. The *ācārya*s rejoice in the *līlā* of the Lord's love for Śrī—and for other devotees.

This usage of the word *līlā* in the context of romantic love is seen in yet another place in Śrīvaiṣṇava literature. The story is from a thirteenth-century hagiography, *The Splendor of Succession of Teachers* (*Guruparamparāpra-bhāvam*). Rāmānuja apparently was searching for the "festival image" (*utsava mūrti*) of Viṣṇu, who was enshrined in Tirunārāyaṇapuram (Melkote) when he "fell asleep; the Lord Tirunārāyaṇa graciously came to his dream and said, 'My festival [form] is called Rāmapriya and is now in Delhi; [in that form I] am *delighting in play* [with the princess] in the house of the Turkish king. . . .' "[5] The Tamil words "*līlai koṇṭāṭi*" have been translated as "delighting in play." *Koṇṭāṭutal* is "to celebrate or rejoice" in—as in celebrating a festival or *utsava*. With the word *līlā* it takes on erotic overtones, and the phrase is usually taken to mean "consorting with," as in fact that episode makes clear in subsequent paragraphs.

To summarize, in Śrīvaiṣṇava literature, *līlā* is a celebration of the Lord's magnificence made manifest through creation; it is also a celebration of the intimate and passionate love that he has for Śrī and for his devotees. Thus, the multiple meanings of *līlā* as the sport of creation and love play are not mutually incompatible.

The word *līlā,* however, is striking by its absence in the *ācārya*s' discussions of the Lord's *avatāra* form. Rāmānuja does briefly mention it when referring to the Lord's incarnation as "the younger brother of Indra" and as Rāma,[6] but there is no expansion of this line of thought in his later writings or in the writings of other *ācārya*s. In one sense the Śrīvaiṣṇava community accepts that the Lord's descents are part of his *līlā,* because the *Viṣṇu Purāṇa* says so, but there is no further endorsement of this issue. However, the word *krīḍa* is used to describe the ironic humor of the Lord acting inferior to other gods or to the human beings whom he created.[7] The fun of an *avatāra* is only celebrated in the apparent paradox of the supreme Lord acting in a lowly fashion.

The reason for not using "*līlā*" in the context of an *avatāra* may lie in the emphasis that Śrīvaiṣṇava *ācārya*s place on the doctrine of the Lord's desire to save the earth and his devotees. Norvin Hein has pointed out the tension between the conception of God's playful activity and the older picture presented in the *Bhagavadgītā* of God acting to assist devotees and maintain righteousness.[8] It is fair to say that the devotional literature of the Śrīvaiṣṇava community emphasizes not only the overwhelming compassion through which Viṣṇu is born as equal to his devotees and destroys their enemies, but also his desire to be physically close to his devotees. Thus this literature keeps alive the tension between the Lord's perfection and lack of desire, on the one hand, and his spontaneous overwhelming love for his devotee, on the other. Listen to the following verse of Kurattāḻvāṉ, which brings together the notions of creation as play and the Lord's desire to embrace his devotees and destroy their enemies:

> O Lord who fulfills desires!
> There is nothing that you need
> nothing that you stand gain [by birth],
> for the creation, maintenance, and destruction
> of these worlds come by your play [*vilāsitam*].
>
> Even so, [having every wish fulfilled]
>   to embrace your devotees
>   and annihilate their enemies
> you descend into clans
>   of the divine ones and human beings.
>
> *Śrī Varadarāja Stava,* 64

The creation of the universe is easy—it is like play for the Lord. But the killing of those who harm his devotees seems to be work—the Śrīvaiṣṇava community, starting with the twelfth-century theologian Nañjīyar, has insisted that the Lord cannot tolerate any offense done to his devotee. To show his concern, he is born as lowly as the created beings and destroys their enemies rather than simply kill them by his will.[9] The *avatāra* provides the opportunity to embrace his devotees and be close to them. The divine *need* to embrace the devotee and the desire to be dependent on them are concepts seen only in the intensely devotional paeans of praise written by the *ācārya*s—literature very different in texture from the measured tones of Rāmānuja's major theological writings. Kūrattāḻvāṉ makes this clear:

O Lord who grants all desires!
The Vedas say you are independent;
but we think of you
    who depend on your loved ones
as a dependent being . . .
Varadarāja Stave, 20

Although ontologically speaking the Lord is independent and has every wish fulfilled (*avāpta samasta kāman*), emotionally he is dependent on the devotee. He intensely craves to be with his bhakta, and this need detracts from the principle of *līlā* as a playful exercise of the Lord's perfect existence. The Lord's embracing of his devotees, however, is a celebration of love, as we saw in the story of Rāmānuja, the festival image of Viṣṇu, and the Muslim princess. This theme of celebration is continued in discussions of the *rās* dance; the word associated with the *rās* is not *līlā* but *utsava,* a jubilee of celebration, a festival, a joyous occasion.[10] This celebration of the Lord's splendor and glory, along with his close relation to his devotees, is seen in *utsavas* of the *rās* and other wonderful deeds in the past and in ritual temple celebrations in the present. The Festival of Recitation (*adhyayana utsava*) in the "sacred stage" (*śrī-raṅgam*) is such a celebration of the Lord's glory as made manifest in the words that he himself spoke (as the Śrīvaiṣṇava community believes) through his devotee Nammāḻvār.

The Festival of Recitation

The *Tiruvāymoḻi,* a Tamil poem of 1,102 verses, was composed by Nammāḻvār, a poet–saint (*āḻvār*) who lived around the ninth century C.E. *Tiru* is the Tamil word used to denote the Sanskrit *śrī:* that which is auspicious, that which is sacred.[11] The word *vāy* means "mouth," and *moḻi* is "words" or "language." *Tiruvāymoḻi,* therefore, is "sacred word of mouth" or "words of sacred mouth." The first translation emphasizes the sacrality of the words, and the second focuses on the sacred nature of the one who utters the words. Perhaps the closest we can get in translating the word is "sacred speech" or "sacred utterance." The word *vāy,* or mouth, highlights the *spoken* or uttered aspect of the hymn.

In the eleventh century C.E. the Śrīvaiṣṇava community introduced the poem into the temple and home liturgies and began to comment on it—initially orally and through the performing arts, and then later in writing. Selections from the *Tiruvāymoḻi* are recited daily at Śrīvaiṣṇava homes and temples. The poem is one of the few works I know of that is recited in its entirety during both auspicious and inauspicious rituals: thus it is recited at funeral services, ancestral rites, birthdays of saints, sixtieth-birthday celebrations for males, and rituals connected with pregnancy, and during the investiture of the sacred thread for young boys and several temple rituals.[12] A full recitation with verbal and performative commentaries is also held during the *adhyayana utsava,* the annual Festival of Recitation. These ritual contexts comment upon the *Tiruvāymoḻi* and inform us about the poem and the community—perhaps more so than even a verbal commentary. Through the elaboration of the commentarial tradition (oral–written–interpretive) on the *Tiruvāymoḻi,* the Śrīvaiṣṇava community affirmed some distinctive positions that defined its identity. These positions included (1) the attribution of equal importance to the Sanskrit and Tamil *Veda*s (2) holding the *Tiruvāymoḻi* to be a text that gave salvific knowledge (*mokṣa*), (3) the consideration of Nammāḻvār, a saint believed to have been born in the "fourth class" (*veḷḷāḷḷa śūdra*) as the paradigmatic devotee and the mediator between human beings and God, and (4) the belief that the sacred places where Viṣṇu resided—especially Śrīraṅgam—are like heaven (Tamil: *tiru-nāṭu*) on earth. In the process of elucidating the *Tiruvāymoḻi* through oral, written, and performative comments, the Śrīvaiṣṇava community promulgated the idea that the earthly arena where the sacred poem was chanted or enacted could be transformed into heaven. The rituals were perceived to both articulate the awakening of salvific knowledge in a human being and re-create on earth the passionate devotional experience that was perceived to be available to the liberated soul in heaven.

Nāthamuni, the first Śrīvaiṣṇava teacher (*ācārya*), who lived in the tenth century C.E., is said to have recovered the Tamil poems of Nammāḻvār and eleven other poet–saints (*āḻvār*s) from obscurity and divided them into passages that could be set to music and verses that could be chanted. The Śrīvaiṣṇava community understood this to be an act that emphasized the equivalency of the poems to the Sanskrit *Veda*s; *The Splendor* says that just as the legendary sage, Śrī Veda Vyāsa, divided up the Sanskrit *Vedas* according to the forms of chants involved,[13] Nāthamuni set the Tamil poems to divine music and divided them into *icai* (music) and *iyal* (chant). Nāthamuni is said to have transmitted the proper singing and interpretation of the *Tiruvāymoḻi* to his two nephews, and *The Splendor* specifically mentions that another disciple called Uyyakoṇṭār was given the task of disseminating the *Tiruvāymoḻi* and the other works of the *āḻvār*s.[14] There is epigraphical evidence that the *Tiruvāymoḻi* was chanted in temples at least from 1023 C.E.,[15] and *The Splendor* tells us that Nāthamuni introduced the *Tiruvāymoḻi* and other Tamil hymns into home and temple liturgies and initiated an annual Festival of Recitation which lasted twenty-one days. The whole festival is one of rejoicing and splendor, celebrating the quest of Nammāḻvār—and every devotee—for union with the Lord.

The Festival of Recitation takes place in the month of *mārkaḻi* (December 15–January 14) in all Śrīvaiṣṇava temples—or at least as many as can afford it. Over twenty-one days, the 4,000 verses composed by the *āḻvār*s are chanted. During the first ten mornings the first 2,000 verses of the *āḻvār*s are recited and explained with oral and performative commentaries. This is followed by ten nights during which the focus is on the 1,102 verses of the *Tiruvāymoḻi*. (The *Tiruvāymoḻi* is usually counted as the fourth thousand in the corpus of hymns composed by the *āḻvār*s.) On the twenty-first day there is a fast-paced recitation of 1,000 verses of the *iyaṛpā* section (the third thousand) of the Tamil hymns. The program for twenty-one days, starting with the new moon, includes: (1) the recitation of poems; (2) processions of the festival image through the streets; (3) the dressing up of the festival image in various costumes;[16] (4) enactment of particular episodes from the *āḻvār* poetry or the epics by special actors called *aṛaiyar*s in Sriraṅgam, Srivilliputtur, and Alvar Tirunagari;[17] and (5) enactment of particular verses from the *āḻvār* poetry. On each day the processional image of the Lord used for celebrations (*utsava mūrti*) is dressed up in special costumes and Viṣṇu is worshiped in his other manifestations.

It seems fairly obvious that the *Tiruvāymoḻi* gets the most time in the festivities (about one thousand verses over ten days, while the other three thousand are compressed into eleven days). According to one traditional source the whole festival was started by Tirumaṅkai Āḻvār just to declare that the poem was a *Veda.*[18] The crowds pay special attention to attires of the Lord, and a special favorite with the pilgrims is the Lord dressed as Mohinī: "Truly," they say, "tonight, the Lord is more beautiful than the Goddess [Śrī] herself." It is also possible that this festival may reflect one of the earliest instances of ritual enactment of episodes from the epics in a temple context. (As early as the fourth-century Tamil epic, *Cilappatikāram,* the *rās līlā* was enacted by young girls, but that was not in a temple context.) It must be emphasized that the word *līlā* is never used for the temple performances; they are part of the *utsava,* or celebration, just as the *rās* dance of Kṛṣṇa is an *utsava.* The enactment of particular verses of Nammāḻvār, or myths that are alluded to in the *Tiruvāymoḻi,* is called *aṛaiyar cēvai,* that is, "service [*cēvai;* Sanskrit: *seva*] by the *aṛaiyar.*"[19] The recitation and enactment of the verses are considered by devotees as a service to God and the community. While *līlā* in the Śrīvaiṣṇava context is God's celebration of his own glory, *seva* or *cēvai* is the human celebration of God's dominion.

The recitation of the *Tiruvāymoḻi* begins formally on the *ekādaśi* day, that is, the eleventh day after the new moon of *mārkaḻi.* In Sriraṅgam, preparations for this ritual are actually started a full month in advance, in the Tamil month of *kārtikai* (November 15–December 14). During this month a "divine proclamation" (words spoken by one of the temple priests) is issued to the temple scribe—who is also the accountant[20]—and he is asked to write an invitation that is issued to Nammāḻvār. This invitation is tied to the head of the "chief of the temple servants" and in earlier days was sent to Nammāḻvār's birthplace, Alvar Tirunagari. The poet (in his image form) was formally invited to come to Srirangam and witness the performance of the *Tiruvāymoḻi.*[21] According to traditional Śrīvaiṣṇava accounts, the image of Nammāḻvār was brought to Srirangam from Alvar Tirunagari for this festival until the time of Rāmānuja. Apparently, bad weather prevented it one year, and after that time the local Nammāḻvār image in the Srirangam temple has been used for the festivities.

On this eleventh day in the bright half of the moon in *mārkaḻi,* the heaviest crowds of the year are expected at the Srirangam temple and most other Śrīvaiṣṇava temples. In recent years there has been extensive television coverage of these moments, when the Lord passes through the "gates of heaven." This is the only day of the year when the northern doors of the Srirangam temple, known as the "gates of heaven" (*vaikuṇṭha vācal* or *paramapada vācal*) are opened, just prior to the recitation of the *Tiruvāymoḻi.* These doors are kept closed for the rest of the year and are kept open *only on the ten days of Tiruvāymoḻi recitation and interpretation;* during these ten days heaven is contiguous with earth.

In Srirangam, for the ten nights of the festival, the processional image of Viṣṇu is brought through the "gates of heaven," taken to the temple tank, and then brought to the "hall of a thousand pillars."[22] In the Parthasarathi temple at Triplicane, Madras, the Lord and Nammāḻvār are taken in a procession around the temple, with Nammāḻvār going in front. The image of Nammāḻvār faces the Lord, and the priests carrying the palanquin on which Nammāḻvār is borne go in front of the Lord, but it seems as though Nammāḻvār is walking backward. The Lord, it is said, loves Nammāḻvār so much that even during the procession he cannot bear not to see his devotee's face. The street processions with the deity and Nammāḻvār occur before the recitation of the poem. The priests in the Triplicane temple usually chant a Sanskrit poem called *Upadeśa Ratnamālai,* written by Maṇavāḷa Māmuṉi in the fourteenth century C.E. The *Tiruvāymoḻi* is never chanted outside the temple limits, because it is the Veda, it is sacred, and has to be recited with proper attention. In the Triplicane temple, after the procession, the two images are brought into the temple and kept in a large hall, which, unlike Srirangam, does not have a thousand pillars.

In Srirangam the festival image of the Lord is called "the handsome bridegroom" (*aḻakiya maṇavāḷan*). He is brought for every one of the ten nights through the gateway to heaven and, passing the *candra puṣkariṇi* (lotus-lake of the moon), enters the hall with a thousand pillars. This hall is decorated for the festival with leaves, flowers, and, in recent years, neon lights. In the Śrīvaiṣṇava's perception there is no doubt that this hall represents heaven (minus the neon and tube lights). The *Kauśītaki Brāhmaṇa* says that the supreme realm has a thousand pillars (*sahasra sthūṇa*), and these verses are quoted or paraphrased by Śrīvaiṣṇava teachers.[23] This large hall has no side walls but is supported by the pillars. The "handsome bridegroom" is kept under "the great sacred canopy of gems" (*tirumāmaṇi maṇṭapa*), which is also said to be like the one in heaven.[24] Images of the twelve *āḻvār*s and some important *ācārya*s are seated at the sides, and the audience is seated behind them on three sides of the hall. Here, for the next ten nights, the audience will be treated to an exhaustive interpretation of the *Tiruvāymoḻi*.

While the Festival of Recitation is conducted in many Śrīvaiṣṇava temples, the *araiyar cēvai* (the service [rendered by] the *araiyar*) takes place only in three places. The principal performers of this *araiyar cēvai* at Srirangam, Srivilliputtur (the birthplace of Āṇṭāḷ, the only female *āḻvār*), and Alvar Tirunagari[25] belong to families that have been associated with the temples for several centuries. Only male members [26] of these Brahman families have the authority to perform the interpretation of the *Tiruvāymoḻi;* they trace their art to the time of Nāthamuni in the tenth century C.E. and their rights back to the eleventh century. They are called *araiyar*—a Tamil word with multiple meanings.[27] The word is generally taken to mean "king," and the *araiyar* is said to be the monarch of the *āḻvār* verses; indeed, for the duration of the performance he assumes the roles of the *āḻvār,* as well as the roles assumed *by* the *āḻvār*. A chorus of Śrīvaiṣṇavas chant at the side. The *araiyar cēvai* may only take place in front of the Lord (the processional or "festival" image) and nowhere else.[28] The Lord listens to his own poem, for, according to tradition, he himself uttered the words through the saint Nammāḻvār. Nammāḻvār made that bold claim himself in *Tiruvāymoḻi* 7.9.1,[29] but here, during the Festival of Recitation, the authors (the deity and the saint) see the poem recited and performed. As Norman Cutler says: "God and devotee are respectively both author and audience. The two are bound together in a closed circuit that is activated by the Tamil hymns."[30]

Traditionally, recitations of the *Tiruvāymoḻi* begin with the chanting of laudatory verses (*tanian*) composed between the eleventh and thirteenth centuries C.E. The verses celebrate the *āḻvār* and the poem, but in this performance the laudatory verses are omitted. It is said that the *araiyar is* the *āḻvār,* and reciting verses praising himself would be immodest.

The performance begins with the reading of the introduction to *Tiruvāymoḻi* commentary (the *Thirty-Six Thousand paṭi*)[31] written by Vaṭakku Tiruvīti Piḷḷai in the thirteenth century. This is followed by the *araiyar cēvai,* which is typically divided into five parts: praise and celebration, singing the song, interpretation through mime and dance, recital of an anonymous commentary (one that is still in palm-leaf manuscript and has not been published) composed by an earlier *araiyar,*[32] and a final set of verses praising the Lord.[33]

The first verse of the *Tiruvāymoḻi* is interpreted through dance on the first evening. Two *araiyar*s (usually father and son) sing together, while only one *araiyar* does the dance. The *araiyar* dances, using facial interpretation (*abhinaya*), footwork, and gestures to make his point. Phrases are repeated, with a single line sometimes repeated and elaborated several times, in a manner akin to modern south Indian Carnatic music performances. The *araiyar* conveys the depth of the *āḻvār*'s emotion or the philosophical import of the verse by going back to a phrase and expressing it in different ways, and it is here that we begin to understand what the community means when it calls the poem "a text that is to be experienced" (*anubhava grantha*). The classical commentaries sometimes alluded to the many interpretations of a line given by the teachers; here the performer achieves a similar effect by dancing out the same line several times.[34] The performance is sometimes called "visual poem" (*dṛṣṭi kāvyam*).[35] While *The Splendor* and the commentaries on the *Tiruvāymoḻi* refer to several incidents from which we gather that many—if not all—verses of the *Tiruvāymoḻi* were thus interpreted, now only 10 out of the 1,102 songs are given the "full-service" interpretation[36] with song, dance, and prose comment, and they are fairly representative of the many themes of the *Tiruvāymoḻi*.

After the dance and mime, the commentary for that individual verse is recited from memory. There is a prompter at hand with the palm-leaf manuscript to remind the reciter if he were to miss a word or so. The origin and date of this commentary are not known; it is simply called *tampirān-pati,* or "the commentary [*paṭi*] written by the *araiyar* [*tampirān*]." The commentary is recited with emotion and expression; this is not just an intellectual interpretation of the poem. Notice that this commentary is memorized and chanted; this is *not* like other oral commentaries, where the written ones served as inspiration for the orator, who then had the freedom to improvise within certain parameters, using standard jargon. Here the *araiyar* keeps to the text on hand.

What is interesting is that while the dancing and the singing can be seen by all, the commentary alone is read softly with a screen drawn across the stage; this is considered to be "sacred" and is to be made available only to a small Śrīvaiṣṇava audience close at hand. It is remarkable that there is a sudden concern that the *Tiruvāymoḻi* is to be interpreted *orally* only to a worthy audience, one that is fit to hear it with faith, and not to the hoi polloi. The explanation I have heard, and which seems to be fairly common,[37] is that since this deals with sacred matters (*bhagavad viṣayam*) it ought to be communicated only by a master to student, orally, and not broadcast to a general audience. This aspect of the ritual seems to be a preservation of a time when the elucidation of the *Tiruvāymoḻi* was jealously guarded and carefully transmitted only to those who had a desire to learn. The interesting feature is that the performative aspect of the commentary is considered to be available for all, but the sacred meaning that is articulated through words is reserved only for the faithful.[38] By safeguarding the commentary, the community affirms the importance of the text as one that leads one to salvation. While the *Tiruvāymoḻi* is sometimes portrayed as an accessible text (as contrasted with the Sanskrit works, which are inaccessible), in actual practice the "accessibility" is only for Śrīvaiṣṇavas, although, it must be admitted, for Śrīvaiṣṇavas of every stripe, without consideration of caste or sex. After the *aṛaiyar cēvai,* the chorus of Śrīvaiṣava devotees resumes the recitation for the day. The *aṛaiyars* join in toward the end and conclude the services for the day.

While the depiction of the various emotions is carefully rehearsed and very little improvisation takes place today, there is evidence to show that eight hundred years ago there was a considerable amount of audience participation. Members of the audience would suggest alternate ways of interpreting a verse, and apparently, at least in all the cases reported, the *aṛaiyar* accepted the suggestions with good grace.[39]

Every evening for the duration of the *Tiruvāymoḻi* recitation there is an enactment of the Lord showering his grace on Nammāḻvār.[40] Nammāḻvār's head is made to bow deep and touch the feet of the Lord. This ritual is called *tirumuṭi cēvai,* literally "service with one's head," but generally is taken to mean "display of grace by the Lord placing his feet on the sacred head."[41] Thus, throughout the days of recitation of the *Tiruvāymoḻi,* the liberation of Nammāḻvār through the Lord's grace is stressed. On the seventh night the image of Nammāḻvār is dressed as a woman, pining for her beloved. In *Tiruvāymoḻi* 7.2.1–11 Nammāḻvār (in the guise of a girl) speaks of his longing for the Lord at Srirangam, and these verses are recited on the seventh night. The Lord is carried and held in the priest's hand for a while; meanwhile the *aṛaiyars* stand in front of Nammāḻvār and chant the eleven verses.

The final emancipation of Nammāḻvār is enacted on the tenth and last day of the recitation (during the *cāṛṛumuṛai*[42] ritual) when the last twenty verses are recited. In *Tiruvāymoḻi* 10.9.1–11 Nammāḻvār speaks of his ascent to heaven and being greeted by the servants of the Lord. On this day Nammāḻvār's image is not dressed in the usual silk clothes and gold ornaments. Rather, he comes attired in simple white garments, a tulasi garland, and twelve *nāmam* (the Śrīvaiṣṇava sectarian marks) painted on his body. The Lord is brought from the innermost shrine (*garbha gṛha*) into the thousand-pillar hall and is offered large amounts of food that is later distributed; Nammāḻvār is brought in with umbrella, fans, and other royal honors.

The ceremony begins as usual with the temple priest speaking for the Lord and issuing commandments to all the *āḻvār*s and the early *ācārya*s to be present and to be seated; then the chanting of *Tiruvāymoḻi* 10.1 begins. The salvation drama begins when the *araiyar*s come to *Tiruvāymoḻi* 10.9, which speaks of the final ascent to heaven. This is recited twice for emphasis. In the Pārthasārathi Perumāḷ temple (Triplicane) the image of Nammāḻvār is carried carefully by the temple priests (*arcaka*), who slowly circumambulate the deity. Two priests lead the way, carrying flaming torchlights. They are followed by *arcaka*s carrying Nammāḻvār. These *arcaka*s have scarves tied around their mouths so their earthly breath does not touch Nammāḻvār. Nammāḻvār is accompanied by priests; one fans him and one carries an umbrella behind him. The gait of the priests is slow and deliberate, and the circumambulation finishes with the end of these ten verses (recited twice for emphasis) describing Nammāḻvār's ascent to heaven. At the end of these ten verses Nammāḻvār is made to bow before the Lord and curtains are drawn, hiding the Lord and the saint from the audience. The priests cover Nammāḻvār with tulasi leaves, which are sacred to Viṣṇu; five minutes later, as the curtains are drawn apart, the priest waves a radiant flame (*dīpa ārati*) and the audience can only see a mound of tulasi leaves, which covers the image of the saint. The covering of Nammāḻvār with leaves indicates his liberation.

The last ten verses are now recited, and the audience joins in with the chorus and the *araiyar*s. The chanting of the last verse of the *Tiruvāymoḻi* is followed with the very first verse of the whole poem, thus coming full circle. The reason for this is in the format of the poem itself; it is composed in the form of an *antāti* ("end-beginning"), with the last word of the first verse being the first words of the next one and so on. Thus, the last words of the last verse are also the first words of the first verse of the *Tiruvāymoḻi*. The linking together of the verses is clear when one recites or hears the poem and the last verse leads one back to the first verse, forming a garland of words for the Lord.

A representative of the Śrīvaiṣṇasva community then goes up and asks the Lord for Nammāḻvār and recites verses from the *Śaraṇāgati Gadya,* a prayer written by Rāmānuja. The Lord's reply—words spoken through a priest—thunders forth: "We give him back to you." The request and its affirmation are repeated three times, at which point the saint and the deity are covered with a curtain again. The tulasi leaves are removed, and Nammāḻvār is returned to humanity as the audience and the *araiyar*s recite the poem composed by Maturakavi Āḻvār, the disciple of Nammāḻvār. Śrīvaiṣṇavas believe that the Lord took up Nammāḻvār with his earthly body into heaven, but Nammāḻvār returns to be the teacher of human beings.[43] While achieving salvation he remains as an indispensable link between human beings and the Lord. Liberated from mortal life, he is yet one with the living people, drawing them to the feet of the Lord, where he abides. Through his presence and by the sacred words that he spoke—words that are considered divine yet spoken in a human voice (*tiru vāy moḻi*)—he binds the devotee to the Lord and becomes the person in whom the divine and the human realms intersect.

Maturakavi Āḻvār is considered the first disciple of Nammāḻvār. While Maturakavi was the only person in hagiographic accounts to learn from Nammāḻvār, in a wider sense the poet is considered to be a teacher of *all* Śrīvaiṣṇavas, reconciling them with God. He is a teacher and a mediator, ending the separation between the human being and the Lord. By becoming the master for Maturakavi Āḻvār, he becomes the spiritual teacher of Nāthamuni and the rest of the Śrīvaiṣṇava community. Thus, the ritual of Nammāḻvār's emancipation ends not with his being at the side of the Lord but with his return to humanity. This particular role of Nammāḻvār's mediation is brought out rather explicitly in a ritual that takes place the day before his own salvation.

On the last day of the ten nights of chanting the *Tiruvāymoḻi* an elaborate drama is enacted by the *aṛaiyar*s in Alvar Tirunagari, the birthplace of Nammāḻvar. This performance is not directly connected with any *Tiruvāymoḻi* verse but is said to portray Nammāḻvār's role as mediator and teacher. The ritual is called *praṇaya ḳalaham* and depicts a lovers' quarrel between Viṣṇu and his consort, Śrī.[44] The festival image of the Lord is taken out during the day, presumably for a day out without his wife watching over his shoulder. When the Lord comes in later that evening, he finds the doors of temple locked. He then comes in through an alternate entrance, a side door near Rāmānuja's shrine. Śrī is waiting here and confronts him, wanting to know where he has been all day, and a quarrel ensues. The *aṛaiyar*s vocally assume the roles of Śrī and Viṣṇu, stand by the images, and communicate the messages of the deities to each other. Viṣṇu says that he was out hunting all day and has now brought flowers (*pārijata*) for his wife. Incensed, Śrī asks him leave, saying that she is not falling for *that* line again. The *aṛaiyar*s sing and act out three verses (two of Tirumaṅkai Ālvār and one of Nammāḻvār's [6.2.1]) in which the poets show their anger against the Lord. Subsequently, Nammāḻvār enters the scene. Śrī is persuaded to give up her anger at the Lord *because of Nammāḻvār;* the divine pair are reconciled and exchange garlands.

This rather curious ritual is difficult to interpret in a consistent way but presents several possibilities. The classical Śrīvaiṣṇava position is reported briefly by S. Venkataraman: "Thus Nammāḻvār establishes his role as a teacher."[45] According to this traditional view, Śrī's grace and mediation are necessary for a human being's salvation, and Nammāḻvār teaches us that divine justice is not divorced from divine grace but that the two are inseparable. Another way of interpreting this ritual is to see Śrī as representing a human soul; the mask worn by Śrī is that of a classical heroine who is bereft of her lover. Śrī—and the human soul—are reconciled to the Lord by Nammāḻvār.[46] It is this multivalency of symbols that makes the drama rich in meaning.

The *aṛaiyar* expresses the *āḻvār*'s emotions through mime and dance, but in some significant rituals like the granting of salvation to Nammāḻvār it is Nammāḻvār's image, and not the *aṛaiyar,* that plays the role of the poet. It is important to note that both the *aṛaiyar* and Nammāḻvār's image share the main role in the course of the ten nights of recitation. The actors are the *aṛaiyar*s, and the images of the *āḻvār,* the Lord, and Śrī. The *aṛaiyar*s and Nammāḻvār assume roles; the *aṛaiyar*s act out the parts of Nammāḻvār and the characters that Nammāḻvār assumes in his poems. Nammāḻvār speaks as a lovesick girl, the girl's mother, or friend, and the *aṛaiyar* enacts all these roles, conveying the depth of the *āḻvār*'s love for "her" beloved. While chanting the poems of Tirumankai Āḻvār, the *aṛaiyar* also assumes the role of a gypsy fortune-teller who looks for omens to tell the "girl" that the Lord will come to be with her soon. However, at crucial moments—as in the granting of liberation to Nammāḻvār—it is his image (*arcā*) that is used. This prominence given to the *arcā* is a distinctive characteristic of Śrīvaisnava worship and ritual; the Lord is fully and completely present in the *avatāra* seen in the temple (*arcāvatāra*). The divine presence is in both the *mūla vigraha* (the immovable primary image in the innermost shrine of the temple) and the festival image, the *utsava mūrti.*[47] At any time of the year the Lord is said to be present in the Śrīvaiṣṇava temple; he is fully and completely there as he is in heaven, and the temple precincts are a piece of heaven on earth. While all Śrīvaiṣṇava temples are "transhuman" in this way, the temple at Srirangam is considered "*the* Temple" and is called *bhūloka vaikuṇṭham* (heaven on earth).

The Sacred Arena

Śrīvaiṣṇava theologians use the words *nitya-vibhūti* to describe heaven where the Lord dwells permanently and *līlā-vibhūti* to speak of the created realm. Rāmānuja uses the terms *bhoga upakarṇa* and *līlā upakarṇa* (instrument of enjoyment and instrument of play, respectively) to speak of heaven and earth. While both heaven and earth are enjoyed by the Lord, the difference seems to be in the nature of their permanence. Both are real, but while heaven is continuous and eternal, "the instruments of his cosmic play, though real, being cognizable through valid means of cognition, are subject to change and therefore not abiding.''[48] While the Śrīvaiṣṇava temples are part of heaven, it is during the rituals that this notion is explicitly emphasized.

Srirangam is an island in the middle of the river Kaveri near the city of Tirucchirapalli, and the temple here seems to have been compared to heaven more often than any other by the Śrīvaiṣṇava teachers. Parāśara Bhaṭṭar claimed that the river Kaveri was like Virajā, which surrounds heaven, and by bathing in it one's sins were destroyed. The supreme land of Viṣṇu's, he said, is on earth, and we may point to Srirangam and say, ''Lo, it is here!''[49]

It is in this sacred land that the festival takes place: then, the gates between heaven and earth are opened and all of humanity, by crossing the threshold, may hear the sacred words, gain salvific knowledge, and get liberation. The whole festival promotes the idea that the *Tiruvāymoḻi* is a text that grants salvific knowledge and has the ability to transform earth into heaven. By focusing on the salvation that is assured for Nammāḻvār, it promises salvation to all human beings who listen to him. The *araiyar* acts as Nammāḻvār, portraying his emotions vividly, making the meaning accessible through song and dance. Like a good actor, his task is to include the audience in the emotional drama, involve them in the poet's quest for salvation. By assuming the identity of these characters, the *araiyar* incorporates the audience into the cosmic drama of liberation. The audience participates in this pilgrimage, identifying with the *araiyar* and, through him, with Nammāḻvār—and conveys meanings and emotions that are perhaps not possible through an oral discourse. A story in the *Thirty-Six Thousand paṭi* commentary makes this point. Nañjīyar (early twelfth century) is quoted as saying that though he has studied the *Tiruvāymoḻi* three times under Tirunaṛaiyur Aṛaiyar, he learned more about the poem when he saw his teacher so moved by a verse that he wept while trying to interpret it.[50] What is even more interesting is that the reference here is to the *araiyar*'s *real* emotion and not to mime or skillful acting on his part. Perhaps the distinction between total participation and acting is lost in some cases—in a Geertzian sense, the actor becomes Rangda, the actor becomes the character he plays.[51] The intensity of emotion that is available through identification seems to be the ideal that the Śrīvaiṣṇava *araiyar* strives for. The audience is drawn into the emotion of the *āḻvār* and journeys with him through his moments of despair and celebration. It is in this participation that revelation is experienced by the devotee in the city that is, in fact, called the ''sacred stage'' (*Śrī-raṅga*). Here there is an ultimate role reversal: through their enjoyment of and participation in Nammāḻvār's poem, the *araiyar* and the Śrīvaiṣṇava community become the actors and ''the Lord of the stage'' (*Raṅga-nātha,* the name of Viṣṇu in Srirangam) becomes the audience, enjoying the community's enjoyment of the poem which he spoke through Nammāḻvār. Revelation is not frozen in myth with the Lord speaking through Nammāḻvār; for the Śrīvaiṣṇava, it appears to be ongoing, occurring whenever there is an inclusive participation of the devotee in the unfolding of the poem. Along with the reiteration of the *Tiruvāymoḻi* as a salvific text, perhaps it is this notion of ongoing revelation that is the dominant message that comes through in the ritual commentary on the poem.

The recitation and interpretation of the *Tiruvāymoḻi* locate the deity and the devotee within the paradigmatic pilgrimage of Nammāḻār's search for union with the Lord and the perceived fulfillment of his desire. The verbal and ritual commentaries *create* those significant moments in the life of the community when the devotee participates in the poet's quest for the Lord and celebrates the assured nature of the Lord's grace, which is seen through his revelation of the sacred word. By the revelation of the divine word through a human poet, the divine mercy of the Lord is understood as being extended to all human beings. By chanting that divine word every day, and by acting it out annually in the Festival of Recitation, the devotee participates in the Lord's granting of salvation to the poet and, in fact, to the entire community of Śrīvaiṣṇava devotees.

The recitation and dramatic interpretation bind the devotee to other worshipers who participate in the liturgy and also link him to the chain of earlier religious teachers who rejoiced in chanting the holy word. They create an extended family of Śrīvaiṣṇava devotees, stretching vertically through a line of past *ācārya*s and horizontally in the present, encircling all participating worshipers.

Through the recitation of the text and the exposition through ritual commentary, heaven is invoked on earth. The recitation of the holy word in the divine presence of the deity, in the temple, or at the home shrine, is itself an occasion to rejoice in. This is not considered a pale imitation of future happiness; for the Śrīvaiṣṇava it is one way of experiencing heaven on earth.[52] While the text of the verses (TVM 10.9, 10.10) indicates that Nammāḻvār *ascends* to heaven in his physical body (verses that are acted so vividly in the *araiyar cēvai*), the opposite, in fact, seems true for the Śrīvaiṣṇava devotee. For the devotee, heaven *descends* to earth, and Srirangam becomes the arena to experience the sacred presence of the divine. The visual perception of the Lord is as important as hearing the sacred word; they both translate as partaking in divine grace. The Lord is said to actually be present in the words of Nammāḻvār; we may find him, says Parāśara Bhaṭṭar, on the banyan leaf (during dissolution), in the *Vedas,* close to the breast of Śrī, and *in the words of Nammāḻvār.*[53]

During the Festival of Recitation, it is eary to understand why Srirangam is hailed as "heaven on earth" (*bhūloka vaikuṇṭham*) by pilgrims. According to the Śrīvaiṣṇavas the revelation of the holy word in the *Veda*—Sanskrit or Tamil—seems homologous to the manifestation of the deity in the temple. The

Lord in his true form is said to be imperceptible to human eyes; but because he loves human beings, he is said to manifest himself on earth and make himself visually perceptible here. Parāśara Bhaṭṭar put it this way:

> [We] hail the Lord of Srirangam
> as he who has no beginning.
> Like the revealed words [he appeared on his own];
> and the stain of human beings does not touch them [or him].
> They fulfill all desires, but their intent
> is to bestow liberation [*sāyujyam*].
> They remove all doubts.
> The Lord of Srirangam is our refuge.
>
> *Śrī Raṅgarāja Stava,* pt. 1, 44

This comparison between the Lord, who is said to have manifested himself in image-form, and the *Veda*s, which are "revealed," synchronizes with the classical Hindu notions of sound and music: there is ethereal sound, which cannot be perceived by human beings but nevertheless forms the basis of the entire perceptible universe. In contrast to this imperceptible form is the *ahata nāda,* the "struck note," which, unlike its eternal prototype, resonates and is made audible to ordinary mortals.[54] We may say that according to the Śrīvaiṣṇava, just as the imperceptible God makes himself accessible (in sacred places) by manifesting himself in a *visible* manner to human eyes (sometimes seeming to be the very embodiment of *śṛṅgāra rasa*),[55] he, out of his mercy, reveals the sacred word and makes it *audible* to human beings. For the Śrīvaiṣṇava, divine presence in visual form and in sound simultaneously creates the experience of salvation—on earth, as it will be in heaven.

Līlā, then, is manifested and perceived at the intersection of the divine and the earthly realms. Inasmuch as there is such an intersection in the entire cosmos, because the Lord pervades all that he creates, all of creation is *līlā.* The cosmos is a celebration of the Lord's glory and therefore an expression of his *līlā.* In the thought of north Indian theologians the Lord's *līlā* is perceptible at those points of time when the Lord descends to earth and is here. In his *avatāra*s his actions are inscrutable and mysterious to human beings and therefore seem to follow a different drumbeat, or at least a different melody from the magic flute, and Vallabha, Caitanya, and others celebrate these descents of the Lord. But the Śrīvaiṣṇava community rejoices in the ascent—or the transformation—of the earthly realm into the divine realm. With the gates of heaven being open for the ten days of chanting, the sacred land of enjoyment is contiguous, spatially and temporally, with the land of play.

NOTES

Research for this essay was done with financial assistance from the National Endowment for the Humanities (summer stipend, 1987) and a grant from the Division of Sponsored Research, University of Florida (1988). I am also grateful to Mr. and Mrs. V. R. Rajagopalan, Neelangarai, Madras, for facilitating my visits to various temples in 1987 and 1988. Sri R. Raghunathan very kindly provided video recordings of rituals of the *aṟaiyar cēvai* and important information during visits to Srirangam. Parts of this chapter have appeared in my book *The Vernacular Veda: Revelation, Recitation, and Ritual* (Columbia: University of South Carolina Press, 1994).

1. I shall primarily refer to the Sanskrit works of the early *ācārya*s, especially to those of Rāmānuja and his disciples, Kūrattāḻvāṉ and Parāśara Bhaṭṭar. Parāśara Bhaṭṭar was the son of Kūrattāḻvāṉ, Rāmānuja's scribe and close associate.

2. The poetry of the Tamil poet–saits is *Vaiṣṇava* in texture and cannot be exclusively called "Kṛṣṇa-devotion" as Friedhelm Hardy does. For my arguents on this subject, see my essay "Hindu Devotional Literature: The Tamil Connection."

3. *Śrī Raṅgarāja Stava,* pt. 1, 39.

4. Ibid., v. 108.

5. Piṉpaḻakiya Perumāḷ Jīyar, *Āṟayirappaṭi Guruparamparāprabhāvam* (henceforth referred to as *The Splendor*), p. 233; emphasis added. The word "Turkish" (*tulukka*) is a generic Tamil word for all Muslims.

6. Rāmānuja, *Vedārtha-Saṅgraha,* trans. S. S. Raghavachar, par. 149.

7. This is particularly seen in Kūrattāḻvāṉ's *Atimānuṣa Stava,* v. 11. Here the poet speaks in wonder of Viṣṇu bowing to Śiva and calls it his *krīḍa*.

> You saved [Śiva] from a heinous sin;
> when the holy water from your foot
> touched his head, he was purified.
> And you bowed before Śiva
> and sought a boon from him—
> all this is your sport,
>   what marvel is this?
>
> *Atimānuṣa Stava* 11

Annangaracariyar, a twentieth-century Śrīvaiṣṇava scholar, interprets *krīda* as Viṣṇu's *līlā* (*Atimānuṣa Stava,* p. 11). The poet continues, in the next verse, to say that this playfulness (*krīḍa vidhā*) is part of the wonder (*māyā*) of the Lord, bewitching people.

8. Hein, "Līlā," in *The Encyclopedia of Religion,* ed. Mircea Eliade et al., vol. 8, p. 551. New York: Macmillan.

9. These sentiments are clearly stated by Annangaracariyar in his comment on this verse. He quotes Nañjīyar and the fourteenth-century theologian Maṇavāḷa Māmuṉi in support of his interpretations. *Varadarāja Stava,* v. 64, pp. 66–67.

10. The word *rasotsava* is used by Kūrattāḻvāṉ in *Atimānuṣa Stava,* v. 47. He discusses the *rās* dance in verses 45–52.

11. Some Indologists have trouble translating *śrī* or *tiru* as "sacred." Śrī is the name

of Lakṣmī, the consort of Viṣṇu, and is also used as a name for any Hindu goddess. In its most general meaning it denotes "auspiciousness," that which increases the well-being of people, either in this earthly life or in the state of liberation. It is a very important word in Hindu life; letters, books, and all important documents begin with the word *śrī.* It is also used as a prefix to names of people; *śrī* (Tamil *tiru*) is used for men and *śrīmati* (*tirumati*) for women. While the word does not always mean "sacred" (as opposed to the profane), there are many cases where it clearly means something more than what is earthly, and its meaning approximates the English "sacred," as, for example, when used as a prefix to works that are considered to be part of the "scriptural" canon. Thus, the name of almost every work in the *Nālāyira Divya Prabandham* (*The Sacred Collect*) either begins with or includes the word *tiru.* These names were given many centuries after their composition by people who clearly deemed these works to be holy. I have therefore translated *tiru* as sacred when it seems warranted.

12. Details of the ritual context were kindly provided to me by Sri Ashtagothram Nallan Chakravarthy Parthsarathy Iyengar, Triplicane, Madras. I had the opportunity to hear the *Tiruvāymoḻi* durning funeral rites and ancestral ceremonies in 1965 and 1983. I have made recordings of the entire *Tiruvāymoḻi* with two different scholars: Sri Parthasarathy Iyengar (honorary secretary, Sri Parthasarathi Koil Veda Adhyapaka Goshti, 1987) and Sri T. Saranathan (Sri Venkateswara Temple, Pittsburgh 1988). Recitation of selected portions of the *Tiruvāymoḻi* by Sri Manavala Iyengar were recorded in 1980. I was able to witness and hear the recitation of members of Sri Nammalvar Sanniti (Bangalore) during their *Brahmotsava* in 1983 and 1985 but could not record them during the ritual celebrations. Further information was obtained during visits to Sri Parthasarathi temple (Triplicane, Madras) during the Festival of Recitation (1989) and the Srirangam temple in 1987 and 1990. Details on the *araiyar cēvai,* lines of transmission, methods of study, and interpretation were provided by, in addition to the scholars mentioned earlier, Sri Vankatacharlu (Pittsburgh) and Sri Krishnamacharlu (Los Angeles). Videotapes of the *araiyar cēvai,* the Vaikuṇṭha Ēkādaśi celebrations, and other rituals were generously made available by Sri K. S. Veeraraghavan, Neelangarai, Madras.

13. The division was into *udātta* and *anudātta. Udātta* is "high, elevated; acutely accented," and *anudātta* is "not elevated or raised, accentless [in chanting]." Meanings taken from Apte's *Student's Sanskrit-English Dictionary.*

14. *The Splendor,* pp. 122, 124. The *Kōil Oḻugu* (p. 34) states that Nāthamuni established classes in which the *Tiruvāymoḻi* was taught.

15. See K. V. Raman, "Divyaprabandha Recital in Vaiṣhṇava Temples," p. 36.

16. The costumes for the first ten days of the festival at the Pārthasārathi Temple in Triplicane are (1) Vēṅkaṭa Krishnan (for the main deity), (2) Vēṇu-gōpālaṉ, (3) Kāḷiṅga Mardanam, (4) Kōtaṇḍa Rāma, (5) Kaṇṇaṉ (Krishna), (6) Paramapada Nāthan, (7) Bakāsura Vada, (8) Paṭṭābhi Rāmaṉ, (9) Rādha Krishnan, and (10) Nācciyār Tirukkōlam, that is, sacred dress as a woman or Mohini.

17. The *araiyars* reside only in these three temples today. On the fourth day they act out the killing of Kaṁsa; on the seventh day, the incarnation as Vāmana; on the ninth day, a gypsy telling the fortune of the *āḻvār;* on the tenth day, the killing of Rāvaṇa.

During the seventh night of the *Tiruvāymoḻi* recitation, the slaying of Hiraṇya is acted out; on the eighth night, an incident from the life of Tirumaṅkai Āḻvār; and on the tenth night, the granting of salvation to Nammāḻvār.

18. The *Kōil Oḻugu,* or the *Chronicles of the* [*Srirangam*] *Temple,* a document that was compiled over several centuries and that sometimes tried to "fill in the gaps" for previous times when entries were not made, tells us how the *Tiruvāymoḻi* came to be held high in esteem as a *Veda.* According to this work, Tirumankai Āḻvār, one of the twelve *āḻvārs*, petitioned the Lord at Srirangam to have the *Tiruvāymoḻi* chanted in that temple and to give it equal status as a *Veda.* The Lord had been pleased with Tirumaṅkai āḻvār and apparently acceded to the request. In commemoration of this, the *Tiruvāymoḻi* is chanted once a year in the Festival of Recitation (*adhyayana utsava*), and it is significant that the Sanskrit word *adhyayana* (literally "learning, study, especially the *Veda*s"), which is traditionally reserved only for the study and chanting of the *Veda*s, should be used in this context. Apparently, this custom was abandoned and later revived by the *ācārya* Nāthamuni. *Kōil Oḻugu,* trans. Hari Rao, pp. 9–10, 33–35.

19. The word *araiyar* is usually taken to mean "king." See note 25 for further details.

20. The scribe had evidently moved a long way from his original lowly position, which Frits Staal and Cheever Mackenzie Brown have spoken about. For an excellent summary of Staal's position and other arguments detailing the Hindu bias against writing, see Brown's article "Purāṇa as Scripture: From Sound to Image of the Holy Word in the Hindu Tradition." The temple accountant in Srirangam was originally a Veḷḷāḷḷa, the caste that Nammāḻvār is said to have been born in. Although Veḷḷāḷḷas were considered Sudras by the Brahmans, they occupied a fairly high status in the Tamil country.

21. The actual divine invitation is announced by a priest. The words are supposedly spoken by the Lord himself:

> Every month of *kārtikai,* on the sacred day [when the star] *kārtikai* [is near the moon] . . . I am seated on the Cēra-Pāṇḍyan throne under the pearl canopy of Sundara Pāṇḍyan . . . in the sacred tower of the Handsome Bridegroom [a name of the festival image of Viṣṇu in Srirangam] and listen to the words of Kaliyaṉ (Tirumaṅkai Āḻvār). Then, the chief of the temple servants, the followers of Rāmānuja [and other Vaiṣṇavas] come near me and petition that I should honor my Śaṭhakōpaṉ (Nammāḻvār) as I have done before. I am sending the shawl that I have worn, perfumes and flowers to Nammāḻvār through the chief servant.
>
> *Write* that I have done this. *Read* this [aloud]. Read it again.

22. According to one interpretation at least, this journey of Viṣṇu to the "hall of a thousand pillars" is said to be symbolic. Lord Raṅganātha is said to represent the *mumukṣu,* or the aspirant for salvation, and the details of his passage to the hall (which is heaven) is considered to have allegorical meaning. It is also seen as an acting out of some lines from *Tiruvāymoḻi* 10.9, which speaks of Nammāḻvār's ascent to heaven. I

have here summarized the interpretation offered by Sri Uttamanampi S. Narasimmayyankar in *Vaikuṇṭa Ēkātaci Utsava Vaipavam,* pp. 17–19:

Ritual	*Meaning*
doors closed when the Lord leaves *garbha gṛha*	sense organs shut and controlled
bearers of palanquin glide like serpent	movement of *kuṇḍalīni*
Lord goes through main doorway	life passes through the hole on crown of head
Lord greeted by non-Brahman devotees (*cāttāta*)	soul greeted by Śrīvaiṣṇavas
Lord is greeted with water	soul is honored by celestials greeting it with water
Lord orders a gateway to be opened	"Viṣṇukrānti" is opened in the *suṣumna* (an artery in the human body)
Lord stands in front of "door to heaven," facing north and orders it to be opened	"Rudrakrānti" breaks
Lord reaches a well	soul reaches river Virajā
Lord discards a shawl and wears new garland	soul assumes new body
Lord wears clothes with gems	soul is radiant in glory
servants of the Lord lead the way	radiant residents of heaven lead the way
women servants wave lamps/jars	women devotees making offerings near the Sacred Canopy of Gems
images of *āḻvārs* brought near Lord	soul renders continuous service with other devotees to the Lord

23. The *Kauśītaki Brāḥmaṇa* verse is referred to, for instance, by Vedānta Deśika (13th cen.) in *Śrīmad Rahasya Traya Sāram* (Chap. 1, p. 18) and by Parāśara Bhaṭṭar (12th cen.) in his *Śrī Raṅgarāja Stava,* v. 38.

The Srirangam hall is called *āyirakkāl maṇṭapam,* or the "hall of a thousand pillars," but apparently the count comes to a few short of a thousand. So, just for this festival, an extra thirty-three temporary pillars are added to be sure that this hall resembles as closely as possible its prototype in heaven.

24. Uttamanampi S. Narasimmayyankar Svami, *Vaikuṇṭa Ēkātaci Utsava Vaipavam,* p. 15.

25. It is only in these places that we have a full-fledged *aṛaiyar cévai* performance. In Melkote, near Mysore, there is a tradition of *aṛaiyar* music, but the tradition of

dance came to an end a long time ago. This art, like many others, has been reduced over the years, and today the dances for a few verses are remembered and others have been lost.

26. When a man has no male offspring he usually adopts a boy from the family circle and teaches him the art. Women were generally not allowed to perform in the *araiyar* tradition. The *araiyar* performances have to be done on certain days of the year, and it is possible that one reason for excluding women had to do with the pollution associated with their menstruation and childbirth days. At these times women were not allowed into the temples. There was a distinct possibility, therefore, that they would not be allowed to participate on key festival days. Another possible reason may have been the connection of the performing arts with the *devadāsi* ("temple-dancing") tradition, and women of high-class families would have been prevented from learning anything that was associated with suspected prostitution.

There is a revival of the *araiyar* tradition among women dancers today, in the context of classical *bhārata nāṭyam*. Usha Narayanan, a well-known exponent of this araiyar art, frequently performs in this style on national television. The *araiyar* art was performed *only* in front of the deity (the processional image) in the Śrīvaiṣṇava temples, and for the first time since its inception, the dances are now performed in secular settings.

27. See Parthasarathi, "Evolution of Rituals in Viṣṇu Temple," p. 399 n. 3(c); and S. Venkataraman, *Araiyar Cēvai,* p. 1–2.

28. While discussing music Donna Wulff says: "Indeed, it is ultimately for God and not for an earthly audience that the devotee plays or sings." Wulff, "On Practicing Religiously: Music as Sacred in India," p. 157.

29.

What can I say of the Lord
who lifted me up for all time,
and made me himself, everyday?
My radiant one, the first one,
my Lord, sings of himself,
through me, in sweet Tamil.
TVM 7.9.1

30. See Norman Cutler, *Songs of Experience,* pp. 45–47.

31. A *paṭi* is a unit of thirty-two syllables, and the commentaries are known by the length of *paṭi*s.

32. Dr. S. Venkataraman does not give a date for the commentary but reports that the *araiyar*s consider it to date back to Nāthamuni's time. He also says that the present manuscript (which has been copied through the centuries) is about 150 years old. He notes that this is close to the commentary of Piḷḷāṉ and that the author claims to have been "a servant" of Nāthamuni. S. Venkataraman, *Araiyar Cēvai,* pp. 74–76.

33. Venkataraman, *Araiyar Cēvai,* p. 2.

34. The *Tiruvāymoḻi* has inspired a long line of commentaries in which the community relives and reexperiences the emotions of the *āḻvār*s. Sanskrit literature, on the

other hand, is perceived as embodying one truth for all time—after Rāmānuja's commentary on the *Bhagavadgīta* and the *Brahmasūtras*, no Śrīvaiṣṇava wrote another commentary on them. Usually, commentaries preserved the correct interpretations and the right opinions on a text; interestingly enough, the commentaries on the *Tiruvāymoḻi* preserve a diversity of opinions. However, it is important to note that this diversity did not at any time involve important theological issues pertaining to the supremacy of Viṣṇu, his auspicious nature, and other doctrines cardinal to the community, but usually reflected the flavor of the teachers' enjoyment of the poem.

35. Venkataraman, *Aṛaiyar Cēvai,* p. 9.

36. These are 1.1.1, 2.10.1, 3.3.1, 4.10.1, 5.5.1, 6.10.1, 7.2.1, 8.10.1, 9.10.1, and 10.10.1. Two of these verses (5.5.1 and 7.2.1) are spoken by Nammāḻvār from the viewpoint of a girl.

37. See Venkataraman, *Aṛaiyar Cēvai,* p. 85.

38. In his *Orality and Literacy* (p.7), Ong says:

> Some non-oral communication is exceedingly rich—gesture, for example. Yet in a deep sense language, articulated sound, is paramount. Not only communication, but thought itself relates in an altogether special way to sound. We have all heard it said that one picture is worth a thousand words. Yet, if this statement is true, why does it have to be a saying? Because a picture is worth a thousand words only under special conditions—which commonly include a context of words in which the picture is set.

Thus, while the performative interpretation is extremely important for the *Tiruvāymoḻi,* it is important only in the context of the poem itself. In some ritual contexts, like the one just discussed in the text, the verbal comment is considered more sacred than gestures. Yet there have been other examples in the Śrīvaiṣṇava tradition where a person has said that he has been more moved by the emotion expressed by his teacher than by the teacher's verbal commentary.

39. During an *adhyayana utsava* an *aṛaiyar* was elaborating a line from Kulacēkara Āḻvār's poem. In this line the poet, identifying himself as an angry *gopī,* said, "I shall give vent to my anger." The *aṛaiyar* depicted emotions of rage, showing how "she" would hit Kṛṣṇa and claw at him. Empār (Rāmānuja's cousin), who was sitting in the audience, thought that his was not a fitting interpretation. The anger would be lost on Kṛṣṇa, who would actually *enjoy* the *gopī* kicking, hitting, and scratching him. Empār's suggestion, therefore, was that the *aṛaiyar* (impersonating the gopī) should show "her" anger *not* by hitting and screaming but by feigning indifference and hiding "her" face from Kṛṣṇa. By not showing her face to him, her anger would be justly—and effectively—communicated to Kṛṣṇa, who could not survive without her. This incident is reported by Uttamur Viraraghavacariyar, commentary on *Perumāḷ Tirumoḻi* 6.8.

40. Venkataraman, *Aṛaiyar Cēvai,* p. 85.

41. Ibid., pp. 66, 85.

42. The *cāṟṟumuṟai* ritual is the concluding ceremony in recitation.

43. I have heard this explanation from several Śrīvaiṣṇava teachers. Venkataraman

says, "On the eleventh day, Nammāḻvār ascends in his [earthly] body to heaven, is one with the Lord, but tells him 'I do not want heaven, I only want to live on earth' and comes back to the world. This is done in the *cāṟṟumuṟai* [concluding] rituals." *Aṛaiyar Cēvai,* p. 84.

44. This drama is enacted on the ninth night of the recitation of the *Tiruvāymoḻi* only in Alvar Tirunagari. It is conducted during the month of *citra* in Srirangam (but without the *aṛaiyar* participation) and not at all in Srivilliputur. The drama is read out in Tirumōkkūr and used to be acted out in Tirumāliruñcōlai. Venkataraman, *Aṛaiyar Cēvai,* p. 84. A partial analysis of this festival as celebrated in Srirangam is given by Paul Younger in "Ten Days of Wandering and Romance with Lord Raṅkanātaṉ."

45. Venkataraman, *Aṛaiyar Cēvai,* p. 91.

46. A third interpretation is possible: this would involve role reversals: Śrī portrays the Lord, and the Lord assumes the role of a wayward human being. This interpretation would not be consistent with other elements of the ritual where the Lord places his feet on Śrī's head. It may be recalled that according to Narasimmayyankar's suggestion, the Lord portrays the *mumukṣu* (human being who aspires for liberation) in other rituals on the first day of the Festival of Recitation.

47. Normally the "festival image," or *utsava mūrti,* is beside the primary image in the *garbha gṛha,* but when these *utsava mūrti*s are being taken in a procession, some items of *prasāda* are not given in the *garbha gṛha.* At these times when the *utsava mūrti* is away and is the focus of the liturgy, it is fully considered to be the Lord. During the time that the "festival image" is in the thousand-pillared hall, the *śaṭhāri* (a name of Nammāḻvār), which is a little silver crown representing the feet of the Lord, and which is placed on the devotee's head, is used only in the vicinity of the *utsava mūrti.* Its use in the *garbha gṛha* is temporarily suspended while the *utsava mūrti* is away. On the distinctive identity of the *utsava mūrti* see my article "Arcāvatāra: On Earth, as He Is in Heaven," pp. 56–58.

48. *Vedārtha Saṁgraha,* par. 214, trans. S. S. Raghavachar, pp. 168–169.

49. *Śrī Raṅgarāja Stava,* pt. 1, 20, 26.

50.

> Nañjīyar said: I have listened to the *Tiruvāymoḻi* three times from Piḷḷai Tirunaṛaiyūr Aṛaiyar. No word from that will leave me; but all that I think of is his being overcome by emotion while explaining a verse, losing control of himself and [seeing] his eyes filled with tears.

Vaṭakku Tiruvīti Piḷḷai, *Īṭu* (*Thirty-Six Thousand Paṭi*) commentary on *Tiruvāymoḻi* 6.9.1. *Bhagavad Viṣayam,* ed. Annangaracariyar, vol. 3, p. 311.

51. On this theme see David Haberman, *Acting as a Way of Salvation.*

52. Consider the following *Tiruvāymoḻi* verses, which say that singing of the Lord is one way to invoking the golden age on earth:

> Rejoice! Rejoice! Rejoice!
> The persisting curse of life is gone,
> the agony of hell is destroyed,

death has no place here.
The [force of] Kali is destroyed.
Look for yourself!
The followers of the sea-colored Lord
swell over this earth; singing with melody,
dancing and whirling [with joy].
We see them.

Tiruvāymoḻi 5.2.1

Those beloved
of the discus-wielding Lord
uproot disease, hatred, poverty
and suffering
which kill and conquer this earth.

Singing melodiously, they jump,
dance and fly all over this earth.
O servants [of the Lord!]
come; worship, and live.
Fix your minds [on him.]

Tiruvāymoḻi 5.2.6

53. *Śrī Raṅgarāja Stava,* pt. 1, 78.
54. Wulff, "On Practicing Religiously," p. 155.
55. *Śrī Raṅgarāja Stava,* pt. 1, 72.

REFERENCES

Annangaracariyar, P. B., ed. *Nālāyira tivviyap Pirapantam.* Kānci: V. N. Tevanātan, 1971.

———. *Pakavat Viṣayam. (Bhagavad Viṣayam).* 4 vols. (with Nañjīyar's *Nine Thousand,* Periyavāccāṉ Piḷḷai's *Twenty-four Thousand,* and Vaṭakku Tiruvīti Piḷḷai's *"Īṭu" Thirty-Six Thousand* commentaries). Kānci, 1975–76.

———. *Stotramala.* Kānci, 1974.

———. Kūrattāḻvāṉ, *Varadarājastavamum Śrīstavamum.* Madras: Freedom Press, 1970.

———. Kūrattāḻvāṉ. *Atimānuṣa Stava.* Kānci, 1971.

Arunachalam, M. *Nammāḻvār, Varalāṟum Nūlāraycciyum.* Srirangam: Srirangam Srinivasa Tatacariyar Svami Tirust Veliyitu, 1984.

Blackburn, Stuart. "Oral Performance: Narrative and Ritual in a Tamil Tradition." *Journal of American Folklore* 94 (1981): 372.

Blackburn, Stuart, and A. K. Ramanujan, eds., *Another Harmony: New Essays on the Folklore of India.* Berkeley: University of California Press, 1989.

Brown, C. Mackenzie. "Purana as Scripture: From Sound to Image of the Holy Word in the Hindu Tradition." *History of Religions* 26, no. 1 (August 1986): 68–86.

Carman, John, and Vasudha Narayanan. *The Tamil Veda: Pillāṉ's Interpretation of the Tiruvāymoḻi.* Chicago: University of Chicago Press, 1989.

Cutler, Norman. *Songs of Experience.* Bloomington: Indiana University Press, 1987.

Graham, William A. *Beyond the Written Word: Oral Aspects of Scripture in the History of Religion.* New York: Cambridge University Press, 1987.

Haberman, David. *Acting as a Way of Salvation.* New York: Oxford University Press, 1988.

Hardy, Friedhelm. 'Ideology and Cultural Contexts of the Śrīvaiṣṇava Temple." *Indian Economic and Social History Review* 14 (1977): 119–51.

Hari Rao, V. N., ed. and trans. *Kōil Oḷugu: The Chronicle of the Srirangam Temple with Historical Notes.* Madras: Rochouse and Sons, 1961.

———. *The Srirangam Temple.* Tirupati: Sri Venkateswara University, 1967.

Hein, Norvin. *The Miracle Plays of Mathura.* New Haven, Conn.: Yale University Press, 1972.

———. "Līlā." In *The Encyclopedia of Religion,* ed. Mircea Eliade et al. New York: Macmillan, 1986.

Kinsley, David. *The Sword and the Flute: Kāḷi and Krishna, Dark Visions of the Terrible and the Sublime in Hindu Mythology.* Berkeley: University of California Press, 1977.

Krishnasvami Ayyangar, S., ed. *Bhagavad Viṣayam.* 10 vols. (with Tirukkurukai Pirāṉ Piḷḷāṉ's *Six Thousand,* Naññīyar's *Twelve Thousand,* Periyavāccāṉ Piḷḷai's *Twenty-four Thousand,* and Vaṭakku Tiruvīti Piḷḷai's *"Īṭu" Thirty-Six Thousand* commentaries). Madras: Nobel Press, 1924–30.

Kūrattāḻvāṉ. "Vaikuṇṭha Stava," "Varadarāja Stava," "Atimānuṣa Stava," "Śrī Stava," and "Sundarabāhu Stava." In *Stotramāla,* ed. P. B. Annangaracariyar, 15–42. Kānci, 1974. See also Annangaracariyar.

Lutgendorf, Philip. *The Life of a Text: Performing the Ramcaritmanas of Tulsidas.* Berkeley: University of California Press, 1991.

Monier-Williams, Monier. *A Sanskrit English Dictionary.* Oxford: Clarendon Press, 1974.

Narasimmayyanker, Uttamanampi S. *Vaikuṇṭa Ēkātaci Utsava Vaipavam.* Srirangam: Komatam Catakopacari, n.d.

Narayanan, Vasudha. "Arcāvatāra: On Earth, as He Is in Heaven." In *Gods of Flesh, Gods of Stone,* ed. Joanne P. Waghorne and Norman Cutler in association with Vasudha Narayanan, 53–66. Chambersburg, Pa.: Anima Publications, 1985.

———. "Hindu Devotional Literature, the Tamil Connection." *Religious Studies Review* 12 (1985): 12–20.

———. *The Way and the Goal.* Washington: Institute for Vaishnava Studies; and Cambridge, Mass.: Center for the Study of World Religions, Harvard University, 1987.

———. *The Vernacular Veda: Revelation, Recitation, and Ritual.* Columbia: University of South Carolina Press, 1994.

———. "Oral and Written Comment on the Tiruvāymoḻi." In *Texts in Context: Traditional Hermeneutics in South Asia,* ed. Jeffrey Timm. Albany: State University of New York Press, forthcoming.

Ong, Walter. *Orality and Literacy: The Technologizing of the Word.* London: Methuen, 1982.

Parāśara Bhaṭṭar. "Śrīraṅgarājastavam" and "Śrīguṇaratnakośa." In *Stotramāla,* ed. P. B. Annangaracariyar, 43–62. Kānci, 1974.

———. *Śrīraṅgarājastavam,* pt. 1, ed. P. B. Annangaracariyar. Kumbakonam: Forward Press, 1954.

———. *Śrīraṅgarājastavam,* pt. 2, ed. P. B. Annangaracariyar.Kānci: Krantamala Office, 1974.

Parthasarathi, Vanamala. *Evolution of Rituals in Viṣṇu Temple Utsavas, with Special Reference to Srirangam, Tirumalai and Kānci.* Ph.D. diss., University of Bombay, 1983.

Piṉpaḻakiya Perumāḷ. Jīyar. *Āṛayirappaṭi Guruparamparāprabhāvam,* ed. S. Krishnasvami Ayyankar. Tirucci: Puttur Agraharam, 1975.

Raman, K. V. "Divyaprabandha Recital in Vaishnava Temples." In *Professor T. K. Venkatasraman's 81st Birthday Commemoration Volume,* ed. S. Nagarajan. Madurai: Madurai Tamilology Publishers, 1981.

Rāmānuja, *Śrībhāṣya, Vedārtha Saṁgraha, Gītābhāṣya, Gadya Traya.* In *Rāmānujagranthamāla,* ed. P. B. Annangaracariyar. Kānci, 1974.

———. *Vedārtha-Saṅgraha,* trans. S. S. Raghavachar. Mysore: Sri Ramakrishna Ashrama, 1968.

The Splendor. See Piṉpaḻakiya Perumāḷ Jīyar.

Tiruvallikkēṇi Śrī Pārthasārathi Svāmi Tēvastāna Vēta Atyāpaka Kōṣṭi Ciṛappu Malar [Sri Parthasarathi Temple Veda-Reciters' Felicitation Volume]. Madras: 1985.

Tivyap Pirapanta Ilakkiya Viḻā Viḻakkam. Cuddalore: T. K. Narayanacami Nayutu, 1973.

Uttamur Viraraghavacariyar. *Kulacēkara, Perumāḻ Tirumoḻi* [*with*] *Prabandha Rakṣai* [*commentary*]. Kānci: Sri Venkatesvara Press, 1955.

Vedānta Deśika. *Srīmad Rahasya Traya Sāram,* 2 vols., ed. Śrī Rāmatēcikācāriyar. Kumbakonam: Opilliyappan Sanniti, 1961.

Venkataraman, S. *Aṛaiyar Cēvai.* Madras: Tamilputtakālayam, 1985.

Wulff, Donna Marie. "On Practicing Religiously: Music as Sacred in India." In *Sacred Sound,* ed. Joyce Irwin, pp. 149–72. JAAR Thematic Studies 50, no. 1. Chico: Calif.: Scholars Press, 1983.

Younger, Paul. "Singing the Tamil Hymnbook in the Tradition of Rāmānuja: The Adhyaynotsava Festival in Śrīraṅkam." *History of Religions* 20, no. 3 (February 1982): 272–93.

———. "Ten Days of Wandering and Romance with Lord Raṅkanātan: The Paṅkuni Festival in Śrīraṅkam Temple, South India." *Modern Asian Studies* 16, no. 4 (October 1982): 623–56.

12

Draupadī Cult *Līlās*

ALF HILTEBEITEL

This essay will discuss some of the reciprocal issues raised by the "*līlā*" traditions of the Tamil Draupadī cult for the study of *līlā* traditions more widely: in particular, in the north Indian dramas of the *rām, rās,* and *pāṅḍav līlās*. The accent will thus be on *līlās* as dramas, looked at primarily in their theological and ritual contexts. Draupadī cult dramas are normally designated by two terms evoking dance–drama: one Sanskritic (*nāṭakam,* used in Tamil, but from the Sanskrit word for "drama"), the other Tamil (*kūttu,* with dictionary glosses of "dance" and "drama").[1]

There is, however, also one more term for the dramas that are performed at Draupadī festivals. The authors who composed chapbook editions of some of the most important plays, from the early nineteenth to the early twentieth centuries, called them *vilācam.* The term includes much the same semantic range as *līlā:* "dalliance of men and women," "a kind of dramatic rhyme" (Fabricius 1972, s.v.); "sport, play, pastime, pleasure, diversion," "dramatic composition" (*Tamil Lexicon,* 1982 s.v.). One of the dramas to be called a *vilācam* is *Śrī Kaṇṇaṉ Jalakkimīṭai yeṉṉum Kiruṣṇa Vilācam* (Śrī Kṛṣṇa's Water Sports, called Kṛṣṇa Vilācam). This play is about Kṛṣṇa's youthful sports: from his birth to his "water sports" or "water play" (*jalakkirīṭai*)[2] with the Gopīs, referring to the episode when he steals their saris while they are bathing. The cycle of *Mahābhārata* dramas thus begins with Kṛṣṇa's youthful *vilācam–līlā–krīḍa*—his "play–play–play"—and extends to other *vilācams* in which he is at play with the Pāṇḍavas. The implication is that his play extends from his youth to his epic adulthood, in which, among other things, he restores the saris of Draupadī just as he stole those of the Gopīs (Hiltebeitel 1988a:183–90).[3] Finally, at Draupadī temples across the Tamilnadu–Andhra border, in Chittoor District, Andhra Pradesh, the preliminary drama on the youth of Kṛṣṇa is just called "Sri Krishna Leela" (Chandra Shekar 1961:108).

It is my sense, however, that for all the "*līlā*"-drama traditions we are discussing, *līlā* is more than drama. For *rās līlā*s it is a whole atmosphere of imaginative evocation of religious moods and sentiments (Hawley 1981:16, 40, 239). For *rām līlā* and *pāṇḍav līlā* it would seem that *līlā* means a whole festival, with mutually reinforcing recitative, dramatic, and "spectacular" components, or as Richard Schechner has put it, "texts" (Schechner 1983:239, 278). Nor, of course, are these categories—atmosphere versus festival—mutually exclusive in the instances cited. The threefold composition of the *rām-* and *pāṇḍav līlā*s is basically congruent with the three components of a typical Draupadī festival, which involves (1) recitation of the Tamil *Makāpāratam* by Villiputtūr Āḻvār (called *pārata piracaṅkam,* (2) *terukkūttu* dramas, and (3) ritual (Hiltebeitel 1988a:139; 1988b, Part 1). The ritual high points involve comparable spectacles to those at *rām līlā*s, as we shall see.

A Draupadī festival is not called a *līlā*. The usual Tamil word for festival is used: *viḻā* or *tiruviḻā*. But there are special reasons to single out Draupadī festivals as being more directly comparable to our three examples of north Indian *līlā*s than most other south Indian, or at least Tamil, festivals. First, as just mentioned, Draupadī festival drama cycles often begin with a play about Kṛṣṇa's childhood, fusing his youthful *līlā*s with his adulthood among the Pāṇḍavas. One might thus see the Draupadī festival dramas as a fusing of *rās līlā* elements (though minus that particular scene: Kṛṣṇa's circle dance with the Gopīs) and *pāṇḍav līlā* elements. I would not, however, suggest that the similarities result from any direct influence either way. Second, as I will discuss further, the Draupadī festival, *pāṇḍav līlā*s, and *rām līlā*s share affinities through common connections with Dasarā. Before taking up that issue, however, I would like to present an overview of some of the more instructive points of connection, comparison, and contrast between Draupadī cult "*līlā*s" and these northern counterparts, and then focus on the chief point in a Draupadī festival where recitation, drama, and spectacle converge in a "*līlā*"-like atmosphere: the death of Duryodhana.

Avatars and Icons

It can hardly be accidental that *līlā*s of the type we are discussing concern themselves primarily with three textual themes: *Mahābhārata, Rāmāyaṇa,* and the youth of Kṛṣṇa (textually, that is, first *Harivaṃśa,* then *Bhāgavata*

Purāṇa). The first thing this should tell us is rather obvious: that *līlā* traditions are rooted in *bhakti,* as are these texts: no less in their Sanskrit versions[4] than in their vernacularizations, which our *līlā*s enrich and build upon most directly: the *Rāmacaritmānas* of Tulsidas and the great Hindi poets (Hein 1972:156–57) for the *rām* and *rās līlā*s, the Tamil *Makāpāratam* of Villiputtūr Āḻvār for the Draupadī cult.

It may be that one can find partially or even wholly comparable phenomena elsewhere, particularly in connection with folk epic–based hero cults (Beck 1982; Roghair 1982) and goddess cults, as, for instance, especially in the Pattini cult described by Obeyesekere (1984). But whatever the affinities, these traditions do not rely ultimately on what I have suggested elsewhere (1988a:185) are the three great founding mythological texts of the Sanskrit *bhakti* tradition. As far as I know, there is no *līlā* tradition based on any of the Śaiva *purāṇa*s, or on the *Devī-Māhātmyam,* the founding Sanskrit *bhakti* text for the goddess (though Hein mentions something comparable, the *nirtakali* in Bihar, where, as reported by Francis Buchanan, "the impersonation of Śiva and Parvati was done entirely by boys" [Hein 1972:266]—and, of course, Durgāpūjā in Bengal and Orissa is in some ways a *līlā*-like Dasarā variant of *rām līlā*).[5] The obvious point here, however, is that our main *līlā* traditions have not only to do with *bhakti* but with *avataraṇa* and, more specifically, the human "descents" of Rāma and Kṛṣṇa (young and middle-aged).

This is nothing new; all I am attempting to do is alter the depth of field. As Hawley has nicely said, "It is consistent . . . that the theology of the avatar is usually conceived in dramatic terms. . . . In Vaiṣṇavite thought . . . the whole world process is conceived as a drama. All the world is literally a stage and God (Viṣṇu/Krishna), in many forms, is the actor. He creates, if it can be called that, in play only (the word is *līlā*) and the form of what emerges is dramatic. Then, in a special role, he enters the drama himself: that is what happens when Krishna is born" (1981:60). "In descending to earth from time to time he plays various roles: these are his avatars" (16). But *avataraṇa,* as we know from Madeleine Biardeau (1976, 1978), involves not just Viṣṇu but Śiva, the goddess, and indeed the whole Hindu cosmology, including its social order (see note 4). Thus when Kṛṣṇa is born, his indispensable dark "foster" sister is the goddess Yoganidrā.

Looking at *līlā* dramatic traditions comparatively, *rās* and *rām līlā*s are certainly the most prestigious and widely known. *Mahābhārata* drama cycles are less common, or at least less publicized. *Rās* and *rām līlā*s seem to be largely the expressions of high-caste traditions of Brahmans and merchants, and of panregional values. The central actors, the *svarūp*s, who impersonate the principal figures of devotion (Rādhā and Kṛṣṇa; Rāma, his brothers, and Sītā), are Brahman boys: chosen in both *līlā* traditions for their "good looks," good family, and so forth (Schechner 1983:265; Hein 1972:135–36, 158, 227; Swann 1990b:228, 234 [noting exceptions]): a selection process that appears to go back to the very founding of these *līlā*s in the sixteenth to seventeenth centuries (Hein 1972:108–9, 224–27, 274). *Rās* līlās at Brindavan are patronized by the town's Brahman temples (159), while seeming to attract the occasional royal patron such as Jai Singh of Jaipur "during his tenure as governor of the Moghul province of Agra (1721–1728)" (Hawley 1981:277; cf. Swann 1990a:210). The maharaja of Banaras, meanwhile, is a Brahman himself, like the *svarūp*s (Schechner 1983, 266).[6] Elsewhere, *rām līlā*s seem to be patronized above all by merchant classes (Sax 1991: Swann 1990b:218–19), also by Brahmans, and sometimes by municipal governments (Hein 1972:95–96). No doubt numerous castes and even Muslims (95–96) are among those who patronize the *rām līlā* in various cities and towns, but the Ramnagar *rām līlā* certainly realizes an ideal, if it does not necessarily set a norm.

Mahābhārata dramas, at least in the two cases under discussion, seem to be more regionally intensive and cult-specific, and—though a full spectrum of castes, including Brahmans, may have festival roles—they are tied in primarily with the values of the dominant landed castes who sponsor most of the festivals in which the plays are performed. Rather than focusing on relatively pure male deities who should be impersonated by Brahmans, they focus on female deities whose violent and impure side is registered by their associations with Kālī.

As Sax informs us, the *pāṇḍav līlā*s involve ritual dramas sponsored by dominant-caste Rājputs, who are regarded by themselves as well as other castes as *Kṣatriya*s. They claim descent from the Pāṇḍavas and regard their region as one in which certain epic events—the Pāṇḍavas' births, their Himalayan ascent to heaven—took place. The Pāṇḍavas are regarded as "personal deities" (*iṣṭadevatā*s). The *līlā*s are ways of worshiping Kālī, and Draupadī is regarded as Kālī's *avatāra* (Sax 1986, 1987). In one case where a predominantly Brahman village sponsored a *pāṇḍav līlā,* it was regarded by Rājput informants as "a matter of 'false impersonation' " and was considered as something of a botched job (Sax 1987:15).

Most of these features are paralleled, with instructive south Indian variations, in the Draupadī cult. Dramas are sponsored mainly by regionally dominant Vaṉṉiyars (in South Arcot) or Vēḷāḷars (in North Arcot), who claim either descent from Kṣatriyas (Vaṉṉiyars) or certain Kṣatriya prerogatives (Vēḷāḷars) (Hiltebeitel 1988a:32–39). Brahmans and other castes do not, however, regard either community as having legitimate Kṣatriya status, such as is attributed to Rājputs in Garhwal. With the prevailing sentiment being that there are no legitimate Kṣatriyas or Vaiśyas in Tamilnadu, the general perception is that the chief sponsoring and participating castes at Draupadī festivals are Śudras. Accordingly, prominent registries of "high" and "low" run through various aspects of the cult and its festivals, bearing not only on participants but on the different forms taken by the deities.

Kṛṣṇa is repeatedly said to be higher than Draupadī (Hiltebeitel 1988:275–77). Draupadī is worshiped as a manifestation of the supreme goddess Parāśakti (6, 79, 81; 1991:46), as an incarnation of Śrī (Hiltebeitel 1988b, Part 2), and as a multiform of Durgā (Hiltebeitel 1988a:368–82; 1991a:227, 242, 288, 327, 360, 458). But her rituals and myths center most often and most directly on her affinities with Kālī, whose "form" (*kālīrūpa*) she takes on in her most violent and impure aspects (Hiltebeitel 1988a:289–95, 434; 1991a:397–416, 430, 437, 473). Draupadī is also said to have taken on a special regional aspect in her Gingee *avatāra:* that is, her second birth in Gingee, the Vijayanagar Nayakate capital, to rescue an ancient Gingee king who descended from the Pāṇḍavas (Hiltebeitel 1988a:3–4, 8–9, 65–92; 1991:483–89).

Actors are mainly Vaṉṉiyars, or in some areas Tampiraṉs (a subgroup of Paṇṭārams, non-Brahman temple priests) or Vaṇṇārs (washermen) (Hiltebeitel 1988a:138; Frasca 1990:190–98). I cannot imagine a Tamil Brahman village wanting to perform a Draupadī festival. But some Draupadī temples and festivals outside the Gingee–Tondaimandalam core area have been variously Brahmanized or Sanskritized, as, for instance, in Thanjavur District just to the south of the core area (Hiltebeitel 1991:112–16, 314, 388, 408–29), and at Dindigul, farther south, in Madurai District (Hiltebeitel 1988a:43–51). Within the Gingee core area, Brahmans often play significant roles at Draupadī festivals' opening ceremonies of flag hoisting, fire offering, and wristlet tying (Hiltebeitel 1988b, Part 1; 1991, 79–86), and also, more rarely, serve as *Mahābhārata* reciters called *pāratiyār*s or *pārata-piracaṅki*s (Hiltebeitel 1988a:78 n. 11). Meanwhile, though most drama troupes will have one or two youths, who often achieve great audience appeal, there is no special group of youths like the *svarūp*s, and the youngest actors rarely play the chief devotional roles of Draupadī, Arjuna, and Kṛṣṇa. These are usually reserved for seasoned and accomplished actors who, in any case, are never Brahmans.

The roles of the *svarūp*s in the *rās* and *rām līlā*s also serve to point up some other instructive comparisons. It is clear that in both of these northern traditions the *svarūp*s are comparable to icons. In the *rās līlā*s, "people know perfectly well that these [the *svarūp*s] are normal children. . . . The mystery is quite the other way around. These are plays in which children enact the naturalness of childhood in order to stir the imagination of adults: the best Krishna is the one who acts most like himself, a child unbridled" (Hawley 1981:18). In well-known companies especially, the boys playing Kṛṣṇa and Rādhā are apt to receive special deference and affection (18). At Ramnagar, across the Ganges from Varanasi, the five *rām līlā svarūp*s are *mūrti*s, carried to keep their feet from touching the ground while they are in costume after a performance. Like temple icons, they are put away for the night (Schechner 1983: 261, 263). In *rām līlā*s other roles may be performed by members of any of the four castes (Hein 1972:72). Indeed, one would like more information on whether there are differentiations among those who play forest Ṛṣis (in the *Rāmāyaṇa* mostly, but significantly not all, Brahmans), kings queens, monkeys, bears, and *rākṣasa*s. But the *svarūp*s must be Brahman boys—indeed, local boys, carefully selected, as we have seen, and surely pure as well as charming.

Certainly Hein is right that the use in these *līlā*s of prepubescent boys (who may in the *rām līlā*s grow a little beyond this) is a transformation of earlier folk drama traditions in which the actors were adults (1972:72, 230–31). Hein probably goes too far in suggesting that the *kumāri-pūjā* (virgin girl worship) of Śāktism lies behind this transformation (265–71), but the two are no doubt parallel developments. The intention was surely from the beginning to create a devotionally inspired theater in which actors, playwrights, and producers would ''suffer none of the contempt that ancient India heaped upon the stage profession'' (274). More suggestive is Hein's remark that the five *svarūp*s of the *rām līlā* must be Brahman ''because when they appear in costume and crown as the very embodiments (svarūps) of the divinities, even brahmans will bow down to them and worship them'' (72). To explain this phenomenon historically, it would be better to look at the regional sociology that fed into such transformations locally—against the background of Muslim rule—than to seek an explanation from outside influences.

In the Draupadī cult things are rather different. The drama troupes are itinerant, and they contract for each festival at which they perform. Their status is not high, being lower than that of the *Mahābhārata* reciters. *Pārata-piracaṅki*s sometimes disdain the dramatists for vulgarizing the *Mahābhārata*, and there is certainly no closely cued correlated alternation between epic textual recitation, which takes place in the afternoon, and the dramas, performed at night, as there is between the simultaneously performed recitation of the *rāmāyaṇi*s who sing from Tulsidas and the *svarūp*s who speak most of the dialogues (*saṃvād*s) at Ramnagar (Schechner 1983:239, 272–73, 278; cf. Hein 1972:79). Similarly, trustees often treat the *terukkūttu* actors poorly in forging contracts and in making local arrangements for their stay in a particular village. Normlly they have only the thatched green room behind the stage to sleep in during the hot days after their nightlong performances, and no one puts them to bed like icons.

Yet at one level that is what they still are, though in ways whose differences require us to begin thinking about the nature of ''village goddess'' cults and of the *Mahābhārata*. All of these *līlā* traditions give pause and movement to what can be called iconic bhakti tableaus, moments of living *darśana,* often with surprising ironies and inversions (see, e.g., Schechner 1983: "Rāma's playful, even ironic omnipotence is shown by the way he not only breaks Śiva's bow but exposes it as a stage prop"). They also actualize the mythological settings (Brindavan, Ayodhya, Lanka, etc.); at Draupadī cult dramas the audience is continually addressed as "members of the court" (Sanskrit *sabhā;* Tamil *capaiyōrkaḷē*), which is especially powerful at the disrobing of Draupadī. Then there are those beautiful liminal moments of transition when dramas begin, and especially when they are over, when the actors receive worship and the audience (in Hawley's closing words) "walks into the play" (1981:274; cf. 226).

Here, however, we can note some distinctions. At Brindavan the *svarūp*s are offered *ārati* (waving of light), and spectators come to touch their feet (Hawley 1981:226; cf. Hein 1972:90, 138). At Ramnagar, after the last drama, even the maharaja's family worships them, washing their feet (Schechner 1983:261). When Draupadī cult plays conclude at dawn, the status of the actors is, as we would now expect, lower. They do not receive *ārati* from the audience (though the Draupadī actor may have earlier received the tray onstage to offer *ārati* to the Kṛṣṇa actor), and no one touches or washes their feet. Rather, upon the conclusion of the drama, the one or two actors who have played the leading devotionally significant roles (Kṛṣṇa, Draupadī, Arjuna, Śiva, Pārvatī, etc.) circumambulate the processional icons that have come on a "chariot" (*tēr, ratha*) to watch the play after touring the village in the late hours of the previous night. The actors perform *dīpārādhanā* (offering of light) to the processional icons and then dispense *prasāda* in the form of turmeric powder to those who have come forth from the audience (Hiltebeitel 1988b, Part 2).

The actors, still in costume and makeup, are an iconic presence but one that is decidedly low, and can actually be ranked in relation to others. Highest are the icons in the temple sanctum, the *mūlavar*s. Next are the processional icons (those of five metals [*pañcaloha*] being higher than those in wood, if a temple has both), which are themselves like *avatāra*s in that they represent the forms in which the deities descend from the temple onto the village stage and ritual grounds where the *Mahābhārata*'s conflicts are reenacted (Hiltebeitel 1991:39–52, 142–65). Then one comes to the actors, or rather the roles they embody. Before certain killing scenes, the slayer and victim will go together to worship the *mūlavar* in the sanctum (Hiltebeitel 1988a:418). Or if the stage is not near the temple, the Duḥśāsana actor, when he is about to attempt the disrobing of Draupadī, may beg forgiveness of the portable icon of Draupadī on the chariot that faces the stage (facing east, like the temple icon), after which the processional icon may be screened by a yellow cloth so that "she" (the higher wooden or five-metal processional form of Draupadī) does not have to see "her own" (the lower Draupadī actor's) disrobing (Hiltebeitel, 1988b, Part 1). Lower still than the actors are those in the audience who become possessed during such scenes of sacrificial violence and sexual violation, and who thus embody Draupadī and perhaps other Draupadī cult deities in this additional way (Hiltebeitel 1988a:276).

One could also go on to various pots used in procession that embody the goddess, though these do not fit into this chain of descent in any readily recognizable way and are most important in connection with the cult's fire-walking rituals (Hiltebeitel 1991:451–58). Clearly, though, taken as a whole, "descents" into the "mixed" and multicaste world of the *Mahābhārata* are rather different from those into the worlds of the cowherds and Rāma. If one wanted to represent and preserve the ideals of pure Brahmanic Hinduism, there would be no point in dressing up little boys as Draupadī, Arjuna, and Kṛṣṇa–Pārthasārathi at Kurukṣetra. But then, of course, the Draupadī cult does not represent pure Brahmanic Hinduism but a popular Hinduism sponsored primarily by communities that Tamil society at large regards generally as Śūdras—though for present purposes it must be stressed again that the cult is not without its Brahmanic components.

The Death of Duryodhana

Against this background let us now take up the scene at Draupadī festivals that, as I described it earlier, has the most to tell us about continuities between the Draupadī cult and the *rām* and *pāṇḍav līlā*s. The scene is the death of Duryodhana, which I will introduce by way of some comments about improvisation before turning to the Dasarā-rooted themes that relate the three traditions just mentioned.

One of the most attractive things about *līlā*s is their improvisational character, which Hawley has caught most vividly in his description of the *rās līlā,* with its emphasis on imagination (1981:17–18). Let us note in particular the spontaneity achieved through temporal anachronisms: the irrelevance of the order of the *rās līlā*s as a cycle (104, 106–7) and the supposedly "later" *Mahābhārata* events that are sometimes referred to as if they had already happened (219–20). In the *rām līlā, pāṇḍav līlā,* and Draupadī cult traditions, there is generally a fidelity to the familiar epic temporal sequences[7] but no lack of "novel" episodes, whose generation is fascinating in all cases (see especially Hein 1972:74–75, 156, 274; Hiltebeitel 1988a:153–448). According to my two main *terukkūttu* actor informants, their true guru is their "imagination'' (*karpaṉai*) (Hiltebeitel 1988b, Part 1; 1992). As to *rām līlā,* standardization has apparently resulted in improvisation being more restricted at Ramnagar (Schechner 1983:278) than elsewhere.

In any case, it was in making my film of a Draupadī festival at Mēlaccēri village, Gingee Taluk, South Arcot, in 1986 (Hiltebeitel 1988b) that I was most deeply struck, after writing most of a book on the subject (Hiltebeitel 1988a), by the improvisational vitality of Draupadī cult dramas. I take as an example the play that closed the Mēlaccēri festival cycle, with its enactment of events building up to the death of Duryodhana and the rebraiding of Draupadī's hair. To set the stage, one must know that on the previous afternoon the *pārata-piracaṅki* had brought his recitation of Villiputtūr Āḻvār's Tamil classical version of the epic to its close, with a narrative version of Duryodhana's death. All that night the drama called ''Eighteenth-Day War'' carried the same basic narrative through the deaths of Śakuni and Śalya to the same culminating point. At last, at dawn, the final scenes, to be captured on video, were to be played out. I had seen four versions, all different, of this finale, two by this same troupe. None, however, included the two following ''novelties.''[8]

First, when Kṛṣṇa learns that Duryodhana has made Aśvatthāman his fifth marshal and commissioned him to kill the Pāṇḍavas in their sleep, he concocts a new scheme to trick Aśvatthāman into killing the Pāṇḍavas' children instead. Rather than having the Pāṇḍavas move camp on some pretext, he calls forth one of the *terukkūttu* chorus, introduces him as the Sage Who Never Lies (*poy-colāta-muṉivar*), and tells him that when Aśvatthāman comes looking for the Pāṇḍavas, the truthful *ṛṣi* should tell him they are under his asshole. This, Kṛṣṇa explains, will not be a lie because he (Kṛṣṇa) will indeed dig a pit for the Pāṇḍavas to hide in. Kṛṣṇa then leaves the *ṛṣi* to squat over the alleged pit until Aśvatthāman arrives. When Aśvatthāman hears the *ṛṣi* tell his outrageous and unbelievable truth, he of course goes on looking elsewhere, and soon finds and kills the Pāṇḍavas' children by mistake (Hiltebeitel 1988b, Part 2). On this bawdy and irreverent material, quite typical of the *terukkūttu,* I would just note that it is rather different from the tastes of the *rām līlā,* in which, according to Hein, ''nothing indecent is even hinted at'' (1972:98).[9] I know of nothing to suggest that it is not similarly different from the *rās,* with its emphasis on ''solemnity and piety'' (Swann 1990a:199). Sax, however, indicates that bawdy humor is also typical of the *pāṇḍav līlā*s (1991).

Now the five Pāṇḍava children whom Aśvatthāman kills are, of course, Draupadī's children. Tamil *Mahābhārata* traditions, which the *terukkūttu* follows, actually have Duryodhana lament their deaths, since the five are his nephews, whose killing portends, as far as he knows, the end of his family and its dynastic line (Hiltebeitel 1988a:423–24; 1988b, Part 2; Shulman 1985:144–45). He thus curses Aśvatthāman for his mistake. In some of the versions I have seen of the end of this play, Draupadī starts to put up her hair in anticipation of fulfilling hers vow—uttered after her violation at the dice match—of oiling it with Duryodhana's blood. But when she sees her slain children, she laments bitterly, again unfurls her hair, and makes a second vow that she will now not put up her hair until she is brought Aśvatthāman's head. Eventually, thanks as usual to an intercession by Kṛṣṇa, who knows Aśvatthāman's connections with Śiva prevent any possibility of killing him, Draupadī finally accepts Aśvatthāman's tiara (with which Duryodhana had installed him as his last marshal) in lieu of his head. Only then does she finally put up her hair (Hiltebeitel 1988a:413–44).

Now, however, something unexpected occurs. In the version captured on video, Draupadī never laments her children or demands the death of Aśvatthāman. Rather, she and Kṛṣṇa engage in a repartee that handles the themes of birth, death, the motherhood of the goddess, and even the final message of the *Mahābhārata,* in other but no less striking ways.

As Duryodhana lies dead on the musicians' bench, Kṛṣṇa calls for Draupadī—his "sister" Yākatēvi, "the Goddess of the Sacrifice"—to come forth to fulfill her vow. He leads her, circling the battlefield–stage, pointing out the dead warriors, and finally shows her Duryodhana and invites her to tie up her hair with his blood. At this point Duryodhana's corpse makes a surprising move, raising its right arm from the elbow with the hand closed in a fist. Draupadī draws back, startled:

DRAUPADĪ: But I cannot do it. Why is his fist closed?

KṚṢṆA: Yes. A man is born. He had his hand closed. When a person dies, the fist is stretched open. How beautifully my younger sister asks this question.

DRAUPADĪ: But this man has one fist closed. There is a reason for it. What is the reason?

Kṛṣṇa then tells how Duryodhana died counting five things on his fingers, any one of which, had he availed himself of it properly, would (he thought) have won him the war. We need only note here the dialogue over the fourth finger:

KṚṢṆA: *Parimukaṉar cēnāpati,* the horsefaced marshal. *Pari* means horse. Aśvatthāman was born out of a horse's womb.

DRAUPADĪ: True.

KṚṢṆA: [Duryodhana thought] "If only I had given the marshalship to Aśvatthāman earlier, he would have killed the Pāṇḍavas. I gave it to him at dusk, the time the light is gone. Without realizing it, he killed the young Pañcapāṇḍavas."

DRAUPADĪ: True. [In this version this is Draupadī's only response to the death of her sons, which she seems to know about already.]

KṚṢṆA: "If only I had thought about it, Aśvatthāman would have killed the Pāṇḍavas for sure." Like this, Duryodhana thought about it in his mind. Thus the fourth finger.

Finally, having gone through all of Duryodhana's five closed fingers and having reassured Draupadī, with the inevitable smile, that he had five countermeasures in store anyway, Kṛṣṇa convinces her that Duryodhana is dead, and that she can go stand on his chest unafraid and finish her vow, which she does. What is striking here is that Draupadī feels she cannot fulfill her vow—which involves not only dressing her hair with Duryodhana's blood but using his ribs as a comb and his intestines as a garland—because Duryodhana reminds her of a baby that has just been born. Indeed, in this version Duryodhana, who appears like a baby, is the only one to have lamented Draupadī's own slain children. As she prepares to dress her hair with his blood, she is on the verge of appearing like Kālī as the mother who delights in the blood of her own children. For not only have her five sons now died in the war their mother required; as the supreme goddess appearing in Kālīrūpa, the form of Kālī, Draupadī is the mother of all, including Duryodhana. One is reminded of well-known myths in which Kālī ceases her wild dance when she sees Śiva in the form of a baby (Hiltebeitel 1991:364). Here, Kṛṣṇa's reassurances have the similar purpose of dispelling this image of Draupadi as Kālī, so that her *kālīrūpa* can in effect be deactivated when she ties up her hair (Hiltebeitel 1991:364, 392, 405, 475; 1992).[10]

Once this play is over, the shift is completed from recitation to drama to ritual spectacle. The latter takes place at a ritual battlefield site called the *paṭukaḷam,* separate but often not far from the *terukkūttu* stage. It involves the construction of a huge prone clay effigy of Duryodhana (facing up, from forty to over a hundred feet in length) surrounded by pits lined with margosa leaves for the reenactment of the deaths of Draupadī's children. The spectacle, however, is all-inclusive, involving roles for the *pārata-piracaṅki,* who recites at key points and may serve as a sort of master of ceremonies, and actors from the drama troupe. A vast crowd, equaled only by the one that will return for the afternoon's fire walk, gathers by the time the effigy is finished. For our purposes the main order of events can be outlined as follows:

1. Two actors replay the final duel between Bhīma and Duryodhana. The Duryodhana actor finally lies on the thigh of the effigy at a point that has been filled with reddened water (= blood), and the Bhīma actor cuts the effigy's thigh.

2. As Duryodhana (the effigy) lies dying, five men carry out traditional

roles, often passed down through their families, of representing the five Pāṇḍava children slain in their sleep.

3. After the five have risen up, with various connotations of their revival, Draupadī's processional icon (*pañcaloha* if possible, otherwise of wood) is brought on her portable palanquin–"chariot," and as it is carried over Duryodhana's prostrate form, "blood" is taken up from the effigy's thigh and smoothed into the Drupadī icon's hair while the hair itself is tied, with red or orange flowers, into a knot.

4. An actor impersonating Draupadī now mounts the effigy's chest and replays the rebraiding scene. Sometimes the Draupadī actor gets possessed and laments her sons, who may be ritually revived but are still narratively dead. In such cases there is a contrast: the icon represents the goddess in her victorious aspect, atop her fallen foe; the actor represents the suffering goddess, the heated goddess, the goddess as victim who suffers for her children.

5. Finally, in a scene that has no precedent in the earlier *pārata-piracaṅkam* or drama, Duryodhana's wife comes forth with her hair disheveled, beating her breasts in a mock lament, and then holding a winnow. Her entrance fulfills another dimension of Draupadī's vow: that upon the rebraiding of her hair, the Kaurava women would suffer this reversal of fortunes.

Clearly it is at this point that the three "scripts" of recitation, drama, and ritual converge with the greatest intensity and symbolic multivalence. Indeed, they are rebraided like Draupadī's hair. At the fire walk that follows, the actors are normally absent, or at least have no scripted role.[11]

All this activity around Duryodhana's effigy invites, and indeed requires, as I see it, some discussion of parallels with *rām līlā* rites and the relation of both configurations to Dasarā. Before we can turn to such parallels, however, we must note a feature of Dasarā that has left traces in both *rām līlā*s and Draupadī festivals that has so far gone largely unnoticed.

The chief matter to concern us at Dasarā is the *śamī pūjā,* the worship of the *śamī* tree.[12] At royal celebrations of Dasarā or Vijayādaśamī, *śamī pūjā* is part of a complex with two other rites: *sīmollaṅghana,* or "crossing of the boundary" of the capital, and *aparājitā pūjā,* worshiping the goddess under the name Aparājitā, "the Invincible." The three rites form part of one procession to the *śamī* tree, which is itself invoked as Aparājitā. And the "crossing of the boundary" occurs either before or after the *śamī pūjā,* depending on whether the *śamī* tree is inside or outside the capital limit.

In addition, the *āyudha pūjā,* or "worship of the royal weapons," which usually occurs on the previous ninth day before Dasarā's "tenth," may also be done conjointly with the *śamī pūjā:* the weapons being taken to the *śamī,* worshiped with it, and then carried back from the *śamī* to the palace. The worship of weapons and crossing of the boundary under the protection of the invincible goddess opens the season of military campaigns at the end of the rainy season, and may further involve a rite calling for the king to shoot arrows in each of the four directions, or at a symbolic enemy, or set off a fusillade of guns (see, among others, Biardeau 1984:8–13; 1989, 299–317; Ramakrishna Rao 1921:305–8; Fuller and Logan 1985:85, 89; Masilamani-Meyer, in press; Kane 1975. Vol. 5, Part 1: 177–95; Tod 1972, vol. 1:467; Kinsley 1986:106–11).

Now *rām līlā* is a Dasarā without a king. Or, more precisely, it is a Dasarā that is usually performed without a king or, more exactly, with Rāma as the substitute king. The main popularity of the *rām līlā* is in villages and towns, and within wards of cities, much as is the case with Draupadī festivals. Ramnagar is a rare exception, the festival there apparently having been royally appropriated and reformed in the first third of the nineteenth century (Schechner 1983:256, 258; Hess 1988:4).

On Dasarā day the maharaja performs the *āyudha pūjā* in the courtyard of his fort, which is also the staged environment for Rāma's fort–capital of Ayodhya, and then "in an extraordinary and magnificently theatrical procession of elephants," he sets off on the more than five kilometers to Laṅkā, to the southeast, where Rāvaṇa is represented in his fort by his huge standing effigy. Before he reaches Rāvaṇa's fort, at what would appear to be a boundary point between the two forts, the king comes to a *śamī* tree, which he circumambulates and worships.[13] Now the origin of the *śamī pūjā* is often credited to Rāma, though it does not appear in the *Rāmāyaṇa* (Biardeau 1984:6; 1989b:302–3), just as it is often given a source in popular versions of the *Mahābhārata* (Biardeau 1984:7; Hiltebeitel 1991:152–56, 316). The king then rides up, over, and past the battleground outside Rāvaṇa's fort, whereupon, after a brief ten minutes, he turns around to make his way back to his own fort.

Schechner senses the mystery—"it is the only time in the Ramlila that the Maharaja literally invades the performing space"—and rightly calls attention to the combination of *āyudha-pūjā* and *sīmollaṅghana,* though not mentioning the related *śamī pūjā:* the royal practice of kings "to march their armies to the borders of their domain, proclaim the territory as theirs, confront their opposing number across the border, and go home" (1983:249–50, 270–71). Significantly, the maharaja also explains the brevity of his stay in Laṅkā by his reluctance to see "the killing of a king" (269; cf. Hess 1988:40). The maharaja claims to differ in this aversion from his great-grandfather, who stayed to watch the enactment of Rāvaṇa's death. Hein describes what is surely a more typical enactment (one that is reminiscent of the well-choreographed dance–duels between Bhīma and Duryodhana around Duryodhana's effigy): "Two carriages bearing impersonators of Rāma and Rāvaṇa circled round and round in lively imitation of the tactical gyration of the chariots of the two champions in combat. A great shout went up as Rāvaṇa was struck down,'' after which Laṅkā is stormed and the effigies burned (Hein 1972:76–77). At Varanasi the Rāma actor shoots thirty-one arrows at the effigy: one to dry up Rāvaṇa's navel (his vital point), the rest for his twenty arms and ten heads. The Rāvaṇa actor then shows these effects by removing his twenty arms and ten heads and bowing before Rāma, ''symbolizing his union with the lord in death.'' After nightfall the effigy is then burned to represent Rāvaṇa's cremation (Hess 1988:41).

The maharaja is thus not the only king to enter Lankā. The other is, of course, Rāma himself. As far as I can see (though the information is sketchy), virtually all *rām līlā*s include a nine- or ten-day period that culminates with the death of Rāvaṇa on Dasarā or Vijayādaśamī (Hein 1972:96–97). But whether others include a *śamī pūjā* on Dasarā day is uncertain. Considering the textual footing of the *rām līlā,* the absence of information should not be surprising. Rāma performs no *śamī pūjā* either in the Vālmīki *Rāmāyaṇa* or in Tulsidas's *Rāmacaritmānas.* Tulsidas, however, does include an episode unknown to Vālmīki—one that seems to have pan-Indian recognition due to its association with the famous pilgrimage site of Rameshwaram. It is an apparent equivalent of, and possibly even a substitute for, the *śamī pūjā:* Rāma's *liṅga pūjā* at Rameshwaram. There are traditions that Rāma offers a *liṅga pūjā* both before he crosses the Palk Strait to Laṅkā from Rameshwaram and after he returns.[14] But most interesting for our purposes is the former tradition, given pride of place by Tulsidas (Hill 1952:367–68), in which Rāma initiates this ritual, while his monkey allies build their bridge, before crossing the ultimate boundary of India to invade the kingdom of Laṅkā and confront his enemy Rāvaṇa. Leaving aside for now the question of how a *liṅgam* could be a substitute for a *śamī* tree, let it suffice to say that what is interesting about the Rameshwaram *liṅgam* is its boundary position.[15] In oleograph print depictions of this scene, which represent the most popular aspects of this popular tradition, Rāma and Lakṣmaṇa perform the *liṅga pūjā* before a stone votive *liṅgam* with *yoni* pedestal while the monkeys construct the *setu* toward Laṅkā in the background (see Vitsakis 1977:31, plate 11).

In any case, when one looks to popular *Rāmāyaṇa* traditions beyond the *Rāmacaritmānas* and the *rām līlā,* the *śamī pūjā* reappears in structurally much the same position as Rāma's *śivaliṅga pūjā.* Indeed, the *śamī pūjā* is itself often explained with reference to the Rāmāyaṇa. Rāma does not, however, do his founding *śamī pūjā* in sandy Rameshwaram but in Laṅkā itself, and not before he has killed Rāvaṇa but after. Thus in one such account, ''Rāma, unable to get the better of the ten heads of Rāvana which grow back as soon as he cuts them off, addresses a prayer to Durgā. Durgā grants him the prayer of killing Rāvaṇa precisely on the day of Durgāṣṭami, the day of the buffalo sacrifice [of Navarātra]. On the day of Dasarā, Rāma offers a *pūjā* to the *śamī* and sets off back to Ayodhyā on his celestial chariot'' (Biardeau 1984:6). The boundary of Rāma's realm has, as it were, been extended into Laṅkā itself, especially now that Rāvaṇa has been defeated. There are also numerous *purāṇic* and popular traditions linking Navarātra and Durgā Pūjā more generally with founding prayers and offerings by Rāma to Durgā: again, both just before and just after the killing of Rāvaṇa (Kinsley 1986:108–9). Here, however, one often finds no reference to the *śamī pūjā,* which seems to be typical of Durgā Pūjā celebrations. Like *rām līlā,* the Durgā Pūjā seems to be another substitute for Dasarā without a king. Or, more exactly, Durgā Pūjā is a celebration in which Durgā (rather than Rāma) substitutes for, or at least takes priority over, the king (see, e.g., Östör 1980:33–97).[16]

It seems, finally, to be a reasonable supposition that both *rām līlā* and Durgā Pūjā are what can profitably be called popular substitutions *at the Brahmanic* level for Dasarā celebrations without a king, or at least—as with Durgā Pūjā, at which the role of regional kings is more in evidence (Eschmann 1978:279 and passim; Biaradeau 1989:67–79, 270, 281, 300)—with Hindu kings very much in eclipse. They are found in the great central belt of north India, from Orissa and Bengal, in the case of Durgā Pūjā, through Bihar, Madhya Pradesh, Uttar Pradesh, and Panjab, in the case of *rām līlā* (Hein 1972:101). And I think that what Hein (100), Schechner (1983:256–57), and Hess suggest about *rām līlā* would also apply to Durgā Pūjā as well: that these rites developed against the background of Muslim, and then British, rule as symbolic expressions of the ideal of an alternate mythical and ritual Hindu *rāj.* Indeed, one could regard the recent Rāmjanmabhūmi agitation as an attempt to sponsor a multimedia pan-Indian *rām līlā* against the background of a secularism that devolves precisely from Islamic and colonialist antecedents. In all such *rām līlā*s, the energy comes mainly from wards of cities and towns, where their popular character becomes increasingly evident. But they retain their Brahmanic structure.

As to Draupadī cult ''*līlā*s'' and *pāṇḍav līlā*s, they are popular, as we have seen, at a largely non-Brahmanic level: that is, among regional landed dominant castes. These castes, however, are the ones that take on symbolic royal functions at the regional and village level. And though they transform them, and often change their calendrical timing (Draupadī festivals seem to be variants of a spring Navarātra; *pāṇḍav līlā*s take place in the winter), they seem to have at one of their forts the ritual inscription of Navarātra-Dasarā. In the Draupadī cult, when Draupadī's ''chariot'' is led over the effigy of Duryodhana, the chariot itself may be led by the portable icon of Draupadī's guardian Pōttu Rāja, or ''the Buffalo King,'' who, as has been shown elsewhere, is not only mythically the ''reformed'' transfiguration of the Buffalo

Demon but ritually a multiform of the *śamī,* the *lingam,* and the sacrificial stake (Biardeau 1989; Hiltebeitel 1988a:76–88, 333–93; 1989; 1991:103–56). The fact that in the *pāṇḍav līlā*s centrality is given to the *līlā* in which the Pāṇḍavas hide their weapons in the *śamī* tree (Sax 1986:8–11) encourages us to look in the same direction: for one thing, the *śamī*—or more exactly its pine tree substitute—is in evidence at the epic's postwar *aśvamedha* (see Hiltebeitel 1988:133). Indeed, as Biardeau has shown (1984:7), the story of the Pāṇḍavas and the *śamī*—not the hiding of the weapons alone but the retrieval of the weapons before the war—is another piece of Dasarā folklore, and, as with the explanation through Rāma, another popular explanation for the origin of the *śamī pūjā.*

Finally, it is also clear that the *rām līlā* and the Draupadī cult *paṭukaḷam* have similar elements beyond the *śamī pūja.* The impersonation by local men of the death and revival of the Pāṇḍavas' five young (and unmarried) children bears a *ritual* analogy with the function of the five *rām līlā svarūp*s. The five men who impersonate the dying and rising "Young Pañcapāṇḍavas" at Draupadī festivals are usually senior temple officials, typically Vaṉṉiyar, and in any case never Brahman. But their impersonation of these "sixteen-year-old" children requires preliminary purification rituals that include sexual abstinence and vegetarian food, or just milk (Hiltebeitel 1991a:345–46). While some temples perform this "Young Pañcapāṇḍava" ritual, others perform an alternate ceremony involving sword pressing (*katti cēvai*) by real "youths" (*kumāra*s) (351). Ceremonies similar to the "Young Pañcapāṇḍava" rite, but involving or recalling five young or immature children, are also found in popular Dasarā traditions in Maharashtra and Karnataka and in a buffalo sacrifice in Andhra (369–70).

Further parallels are evident in the construction and demolition of effigies of the chief epic demons (Duryodhana and others in the Draupadī cult; Rāvaṇa and usually Kumbhakarṇa and Indrajit in the *rām līlā*s), and in the rituals and myths found in both traditions about the confrontation between the kings of two forts, and the construction of a battlefield fort as the main ritual terrain (Hiltebeitel 1991:294–96, 332–38, 399–432).

The founding of the *rām* and *rās līlā*s seems to go back to the sixteenth to seventeenth centuries (Hein 1972:108–9; 224–27, 274): a time that could well also be that of the consolidation of Draupadī cult *paṭukaḷam* rites in the Gingee core area. Not only are both epics thus tied into the popular mythology of Dasarā; they have supplied the myths for similar battlefield rituals that in the *rām līlā* and the Draupadī cult, and apparently in the *pāṇḍav līlā* as well, involve popular transpositions of Dasarā rites into idioms of ritualized epic conflict.

NOTES

1. There is also, however, a folk etymology bringing *kūttu* close to the meanings "play, sport." According to the icon sculptor and repairer N. Dandapani, an informant on the two partially overlapping *Mahābhārata* folk cults of Draupadī and Aravāṉ-Kūttāṇṭavar (Arjuna's son [Sanskrit Irāvat] with the serpent-woman Ulūpī-Nākakkaṉṉi), the name Kūttāṇṭavar, "Lord of Kūttu," derives from a demon he defeated named Kūttācuraṉ, who was born after his two spirits (*āvi*) were "joined" (*kūṭṭu*). Playing on the similarity between *Kūttu* and *Kūṭṭu,* and hypercorrecting the latter to *Kuṟṟu* (which can mean "death, Yama," as well as "utterance, declaration, proclamation"), Dandapani continues: "If you join two things into one, that is called *kūṟṟu*. And when people say, 'I am a *kūṟṟu,*' it means they are just part of the play (*kūṟṟu*). What we dance is *kūttu*. We are all dancing from the order of God (*kaṭavul amaippu*). Whatever he wishes, we do. That is *kūṟṟu*."

2. Sanskrit *jalakrīḍa: krīḍa,* Sanskrit "play, sport."

3. Other than the drama about Kṛṣṇa's youth, whose author is unknown, the only other Draupadī festival dramas I know of that are called *vilācam* are all by Irāmaccantira Kavirāyar: "Dice Match and Disrobing," "Arjuna's Tapas," "Bending of the Bow for Draupadī's Marriage," and "The Poison Pond" (*Naccupoykai,* in which the four younger Pāṇḍavas drink water from a pond and fall dead, until Yudhiṣṭhira saves them by answering a Yakṣa's questions) (Hiltebeitel 1988a:456–57). It is Irāmaccantira Kavirāyar who seems, in the early nineteenth century, to have played the seminal role in reworking traditional oral and palm-leaf versions of the plays into authored chapbook publications (157–67). It may be that he called the plays *vilācam*s to link them with the Kṛṣṇa cycle and/or give them a Sanskritic tone.

4. It is gratifying to see Pollock come to the formulation that the divinity of Rāma as "divine king" has been integral to the *Rāmāyaṇa* since it took on its "monumental" form under the hand of the poet or poets we call Vālmīki. Pollock interprets this as a current of "political theology" that runs through the text (1991:15–54, 64–65, 68). It remains to explore the relation between this "political theology" and what Madeleine Biardeau calls the "universe of bhakti," which she sees pervading both epics and the *Harivaṃśa* (Biardeau 1976, 1978).

5. Coburn (1991:168) shows how a modern-day devotee of the *Devī-Māhātmyam* can interpret the main action of the text as "the Mother's cavorting in, and as, the universe (*līlā*)." But this involves no dramas.

6. Sax (1991), however, indicates that "the fact that Vibhuti Narayan Singh is a Brahman is an anomaly (he was adopted—is he technically a Brahman anymore?)."

7. Epic chronology is generally kept more faithfully in the drama cycles than in the rituals. See Hiltebeitel (1988a:165–66; 1991:229–30, 287–88, 328–29, 404).

8. For a fuller discussion of these innovative episodes, see Hiltebeitel (1992).

9. Kumar (1988:180–97), however, describes an exception in the "crude actions" and "verbal obscenities" (190) that formed part of one episode of the *rām līlā* of the Chaitganj section of Varanasi from about 1890 until reform forces achieved its "sanitation" in the 1930s. The *līlā* in question, the *nākkaṭayyā,* or "cutting off of the nose" by

Lakṣmaṇa of Rāvaṇa's sister Śūrpanakhā, results in the gathering together of Rāvaṇa's "demon army" for an all-night procession of costumed grotesqueries involving mainly lower castes. This can be instructively compared to some of the nighttime "demon army" processions that form part of larger festivals, in Kerala (cf. Hiltebeitel 1991:176–77). There may be other examples where both the *rām līlā* and *rās līlā* include raw humor, but probably not, I suspect, with the same *normalcy* as the *terukkūttu* or, I suspect, the *pāṇḍav līlā*.

10. The theme of the five closed fingers has a famous counterpart in the story of the great Śrī Vaiṣṇava theologican Rāmānuja's arrival before the corpse of his precursor, Yāmunācārya. Seeing three fingers closed on Yāmuna's hand, Rāmānuja asked whether Yāmuna had died with any unfulfilled wishes and was told by the latter's disciples that there had indeed been three: to write a Vaiṣṇava commentary on the *Brahmasūtra,* to express his gratitude toward Vyāsa and Parāśara, and to show his great affection for the Tamil saint Nammāḻvār. When Rāmānuja said he would try to fulfill these wishes, the dead Yāmuna's three fingers straightened out, and Rāmānuja was acclaimed his successor (Carman 1974:30).

11. Portions of the preceding summary are incorporated from Hiltebeitel (1991:324–31).

12. Portions of the following summary are incorporated from Hiltebeitel (1991:142–54).

13. I thank Philip Lutgendorf and Linda Hess for their information on this point. There is no mention of a *śamī* tree at Ramnagar, or other *rām līlā*s, in any of the sources I have consulted.

14. The tradition at Rameshwaram is that Rāma could not touch food without *darśan* of Śiva. Because at the seacoast such a *darśan* was difficult, "he had to make an earthen image of Śiva for darsan before taking food." Śiva then "blessed him with the promise of his success." Then, after killing Rāvaṇa, upon return to Rameshwaram, Sītā performed her fire ordeal there(!) and Rāma relieved his sin of *brahmahatyā* (brahmanicide) for killing Rāvaṇa, which required a *śivaliṅga.* Hanumān set off to bring one from Mount Kailāsa, but when the auspicious time for the worship was in danger of passing, Sītā made one out of sand that miraculously turned solid and immovable when Hanumān, annoyed at returning too late and at the neglect of the *liṅgam* he had taken such troubles over, tried to lift the sand *liṅgam* with his tail. Rāma then ordered that Hanumān's *liṅgam* be set up to the left of the main one, to receive the first worship. It is also at Rameshwaram, before building the bridge, that Rāma challenges the ocean king Sagara, threatening to kill him with his arrows if he does not dry up the ocean (Das 1964:70–74): a reminder of the challenge to enemies, real or substitutional, that is also part of Dasarā. See Jagadisa Ayyar (1982:492): there are actually eleven *liṅga*s there, one established by Nala, the monkey architect of the *setu* (bridge); cf. also Shulman (1980:50–51).

15. One should better say *liṅgam*s in light of the complexities and variants of the Rameshwaram myth, which differs at key points from the traditions found in Tulsidas; see note 13.

16. Coburn (1991:153) refers to *rām līlā* and Dasarā as "royal festivals" with which

Durgā Pūjā "overlaps." I assume he is contrasting a nonroyal Durgā Pūjā with the royal character of the other two. Durgā, however, is as royal as Rāma. The real contrast is between a festival requiring real human kings, and festivals for which a deity may substitute for a human king.

REFERENCES

Beck, Brenda E. F. 1982. *The Three Twins: The Telling of a South Indian Folk Epic.* Bloomington: Indiana University Press.

Biardeau, Madeleine. 1976 and 1978. "Études de mythologie hindoue," 4 and 5, "*Bhakti* et *avatara. Bulletin de l'Ecole Française d'Extrême-Orient* 63:87–231, 65:111–263.

———. 1984. "The Śamī Tree and the Sacrificial Buffalo." *Contributions to Indian Sociology,* n.s., 18, no. 1: 1–23.

———. 1989. *Histoire de poteaux: Variations védiques autour de la déesse hindoue.* Paris: École Française d'Extrême-Orient.

Carman, John Braisted. 1974. *The Theology of Rāmānuja: An Essay in Interreligious Understanding.* New Haven, Conn.: Yale University Press.

Chandra Shekar, A. 1961. *Fairs and Festivals:* 8. *Chittoor District.* Part 7B of *Census of India* 1961, vol. 2: *Andhra Pradesh.* Delhi: Manager of Publications.

Coburn, Thomas B. 1991. *Encountering the Goddess: A Translation of the Devī-Māhātmya and a Study of Its Interpretation.* Albany: State University of New York Press.

Das, R. K. 1964. *Temples of Tamilnad.* Bombay: Bharatiya Vidya Bhavan.

Eschmann, Annecharlotte. 1978. "Prototypes of the Navakalevara Ritual and Their Relation to the Jagannatha Cult." In *The Cult of Jagannath and the Regional Tradition of Orissa,* ed. Hermann Kulke Eschmann and Gaya Charan Tripathi, pp. 265–84. New Delhi: Manohar.

Fabricius, Johann Philip. 1972. *Tamil and English Dictionary.* 4th ed., revised and enlarged. Tranquebar: Evangelical Lutheran Mission Publishing House.

Frasca, Richard Armando. 1990. *The Theatre of the* Mahābhārata: Terukkūttu *Performances in South India.* Honolulu: University of Hawaii Press.

Fuller, C. J., and Penny Logan. 1985. "The Navarātri Festival at Madurai." *Bulletin of the School of Oriental and African Studies* 48: 79–105.

Hawley, John Stratton. 1981. *At Play with Krishna: Pilgrimage Dramas from Brindaban.* Princeton, N.J.: Princeton University Press.

Hein, Norvin. 1972. *The Miracle Plays of Mathura.* New Haven, Conn.: Yale University Press.

Hess, Linda. 1988. *The Ramlila of Ramnagar: An Introduction and Day-by-day Description.* Berkeley and Varanasi: Anjaneya Publications.

Hill, W. D. P., trans. 1952. *The Holy Lake of the Acts of Rāma.* London: Oxford University Press.

Hiltebeitel, Alf. 1988a. *The Cult of Draupadī*. Vol. 1, *Mythologies, From Gingee to Kurukṣetra*. Chicago: University of Chicago Press.

———. 1988b. "Lady of Gingee: South Indian Draupadi Festivals." Parts 1 and 2. Video film. George Washington University. Distributed by South Asia films, University of Wisconsin, Madison.

———. 1989. "Draupadī's Two Guardians: The Buffalo King and the Muslim Devotee." In *Criminal Gods and Demon Devotees: Essays on the Guardians of Popular Hinduism*, ed. Alf Hiltebeitel, pp. 339–71. Albany: State University of New York Press.

———. 1991. *The Cult of Draupadī*. Vol. 2, *On Hindu Ritual and the Goddess*. Chicago: University of Chicago Press.

———. 1992. "Transmitting *Mahabharatas*: Another Look at Peter Brook." *The Drama Review* 36: 131–59.

Jagadisa Ayyar, P. V. 1982. *South Indian Shrines*. Revised and enlarged ed. New Delhi: Asian Educational Services.

Kane, P. V. [1930–62] 1975. *History of Dharmaśāstra*. 5 vols. Poona: Bhandarkar Oriental Research Institute.

Kinsley, David. 1986. *Hindu Goddesses: Visions of the Divine Feminine in the Hindu Religious Tradition*. Berkeley: University of California Press.

Kumar, Nita. 1988. *The Artisans of Banaras: Popular Culture and Identity, 1880–1896*. Princeton, N.J.: Princeton University Press.

Masilamani-Meyer, Eveline. "Durgā in Tamilnadu." In *Durgā and the Buffalo*, ed. Gunther D. Sontheimer and M. L. K. Murth. Heidelberg: South Asia Institute, forthcoming.

Obeyesekere, Gananath. 1984. *The Cult of Pattini*. Chicago: University of Chicago Press.

Östör, Ákos. 1980. *The Play of the Gods: Locality, Ideology, Structure, Structure and Time in the Festivals of a Bengali Town*. Chicago: University of Chicago Press.

Pollock, Sheldon I., trans. 1991. *The Rāmāyaṇa of Vālmīki: An Epic of Ancient India*. Vol. 2, *Araṇyakāṇḍa*. Edited by Robert P. Goldman. Introduction and annotation by Sheldon Pollock. Princeton, N.J.: Princeton University Press.

Ramakrishna Rao, Rajakaryaprasakta B. 1921. "The Dasara Celebrations in Mysore." *Quarterly Journal of the Mythic Society* 11: 200–211.

Roghair, Gene H. 1982. *The Epic of Palnāḍu: A Study and Translation of Palnāṭi Vīrula Katha, a Telugu Oral Tradition from Andhra Pradesh, India*. Oxford: Clarendon Press.

Sax, William S. 1986. "The Pāṇḍav-Lila: Self-Representation in a Central Himalayan Folk Drama." Unpublished manuscript presented to the Graduate Seminar on South Asia, University of Chicago.

———. 1987. "Ritual and Performance in the Pāṇḍavlīlā." Draft of paper presented at the American Academy of Religion Meeting, Boston.

———. 1991. Personal correspondence concerning this article.

Schechner, Richard. 1983. *Performative Circumstances from the Avant Garde to Ramlila*. Calcutta: Seagull Books.

Schechner, Richard, and Linda Hess. 1977. "The Ramlila of Ramnagar [India]." *Drama Review* 21: 51–82.

Shulman, David Dean. 1980. *Tamil Temple Myths: Sacrifice and Divine Marriage in South Indian Saiva Tradition*. Princeton, N.J.: Princeton University Press.

———. 1985. *The King and the Clown in South Indian Myth and Poetry*. Princeton, N.J.: Princeton University Press.

Swann, Darius L. 1990a and 1990b. "Rās Līlā" and "Rām Līlā." In *Indian Theatre: Traditions of Performance*, eds. Farley P. Richmond, Darius L. Swann, and Phillip B. Zarrilli, pp. 177–214, 215–36. Honolulu: University of Hawaii Press.

Tamil Lexicon. [1926–39] 1982. 6 vols. Madras: University of Madras.

Tod, James. [1829–32] 1972. *Annals and Antiquities of Rajasthan*. London: Smith and Elder.

Vitsakis, Vassilis G. 1977. *Hindu Epics, Myths and Legends in Popular Illustrations*. London: Oxford University Press.

13

Some Concluding Reflections

JOHN B. CARMAN

Indian languages, like English and many European languages, have many words that can mean both sport (playing at games) and drama (putting on plays). What is striking in Hindu usage is the prominence of the religious meanings of both sport and drama, as well as a third concept related to both: dance. These meanings, moreover, can refer to human religious activity, divine activity, or both human and divine activity. The essays gathered together in this volume discuss various instances in which the term *līlā* and a number of partial synonyms convey one or more of these meanings.

The first theological meaning discussed has its textual basis in the *Vedānta-sūtra* 2.1.33. Divine activity in periodically creating, maintaining, and dissolving the universe is said to be "like sport" (*līlāvat*). For Rāmānuja this means the activity of a great king at leisure, when he is free to do anything he wishes, neither compelled by any past action nor propelled toward any unrealized goal. It is also possible, in the second place, to interpret the metaphor as the spontaneous and joyful play of a child, or even as a child's playful mischief, so contrary to the rule-bound character of the workaday world. Third, *līlā* can have the sense of love play, of amorous sport between lover and beloved.

In earlier Vaiṣṇava usage *līlā* is a metaphor for Viṣṇu's cosmic activity and does not apply to Viṣṇu's descent as an *avatāra* to restore the rightful social order (*dharma*). Divine activity in righting wrong or rescuing the good is purposeful and therefore not "like sport." In the versions of the Kṛṣṇa story told in the *Viṣṇu Purāṇa* and the *Bhāgavata Purāṇa*, however, it is precisely the *avatāra* Kṛṣṇa whose activity is playful, "like sport," in all the senses just mentioned.

The activity of Śiva is also "like sport," and it is exemplified in Śiva's sports (Tamil *vilayātu*), his appearances in this world to his devotees, appearances that often express mischief, disregard of moral convention, and apparent cruelty, as befits the all-powerful Lord of cosmic destruction. The figure of the dancing Śiva, king of the dance (*naṭarāja*), also expresses divine *līlā,* with the emphasis on spontaneity and graceful movement. There are other conceptions of Śiva in which he sits or lies motionless while all activities are carried out by his consorts or where Śiva's destructive power is expressed in a special emanation. The power of the goddess Kālī is also "like sport," expressed in a cosmic dance motivated by what Malcolm McLean calls "willfulness" (*icchāmoy*), which may perhaps be understood as the exercise of an arbitrary and untrammeled will by an unlimited power.

Kṛṣṇa, too, can be represented in dances of destructive power, as when defeating the serpent Kāliya, but in the later versions of the Kṛṣṇa story the preeminent dance is Kṛṣṇa's circle dance with the milkmaids of Braj, a dance in which Kṛṣṇa multiplies himself to dance individually with each of the young women in the cowherd village.

For the human women (if they are regarded as human), relation with Kṛṣṇa involves teasing sport (more being teased than teasing), dance, and erotic play. This relation is also expressed in a series of plays or dramatic scenes in which the *gopīs* reenact Kṛṣṇa's mischievous deeds and heroic feats to console themselves with remembrance and re-presentation during his absence. Here we encounter *līlā*'s second major meaning as drama, and here, too, one significant dimension of *līlā* is dance.

Līlā is drama portraying or imitating divine action or divine–human interaction. It is human action distinct from the normal human activity of work, it is "playacting." Such drama sometimes includes antinomian "games" or roughhouse, which suggest a temporary dissolution of the moral order. In these plays there are different degrees and types of identifications of the action with their role models. Sometimes the deity possesses the human actor for the duration of the performance, and in other sacred dramas the audience treats the actors as temporary avatars, indeed as embodying the divine essence (*svarūp*).

Such ritual drama is close to what Śrīvaiṣṇavas include in their worship but call, not *līlā,* but *utsava,* which, as Vasudha Narayanan explains, means festive celebration. The image incarnation of Viṣṇu at the most important temple is called the "Lord of the Sacred Stage" (*Śrīranganāthan*): the Lord enjoys the songs and dances performed on this "stage," depicting his glorious deeds and his loving care of his devotees. Unlike north Indian Vaiṣṇavas, Śrīvaiṣṇavas largely restrict *līlā* to designating the Lord's cosmic character;

neither the Lord's descents nor his devotees' celebrations are called *līlā*, yet music, dance, and drama all play a vital role in Śrīvaiṣṇava worship.

In the worship of Śiva there is *līlā* both in the divine action and in the devotee's response, yet there are some significant differences from *kṛṣṇa līlā* that the contributors to this volume make clear. In some ways the concept of *līlā* is even more systematically connected with Śiva's character than with Viṣṇu's, and this is a mysterious and paradoxical playfulness that constantly suggests that the "make-believe" of *līlā* is more real than the "real world." Bettina Bäumer notes that divine playfulness is pervasive in the Trika philosophy of Kashmir Śaivism: all five activities of Śiva are related to *līlā*. She adds Abhinava Gupta's view that the root of the word for deity (*div*) means "to sport." The understanding of play in these traditions explicitly connects with "the yogi shaking or reeling under the impact of inner bliss." It also seems to fit with the image of Śiva as the master dancer exhibiting both rigid form and amazing spontaneity. The connection of Śiva's activity with drama is explicit, both a king's pleasure in playing at being a simple soldier or taking on some other role and the playwright's or stage director's delight in creating the interplay of characters in their various roles. In the monistic philosophy of Kashmir Śaivism, the individual finite self is the stage upon which the true Self plays, assuming his various roles.

Two kinds of issues recur in the various essays and were prominent in the discussion at the conference. The first concerns the way in which a general Hindu concept of *līlā* should be defined. The second deals with the appropriate ways, if any, for *līlā* to be discussed outside the traditional terminology of *līlā* as a Hindu concept and/or Hindu institution. Both issues involve Western scholarship as well as Indian subject matter.

The first issue can be expressed as a question: is there a particular defining instance or paradigmatic instance of *līlā*? It is Norvin Hein's contention that there is, that in the *kṛṣṇa līlā* of Brindavan and the surrounding Braj region the theology of Kṛṣṇa's playful activity and the liturgical dramas about Kṛṣṇa and his companions are fully integrated, far more so than in any other belief or practice concerning *līlā*. Many of the other participants, however, do not agree that *kṛṣṇa līlā* is the only full exemplification of the complex Hindu concept of *līlā*. Hein's view raises at least two different questions. First, is the primary Hindu significance of *līlā* its *combination* of two major meanings: the playfulness of divine action and the importance of human plays to remember God's actions through dramatic reenactment? Second, even if this combination is crucial, is it unique to *kṛṣṇa līlā*?

The essays discussing Śaiva interpretations of *līlā* suggest that both divine playfulness and human plays are important for Śaivas, and that both meanings sometimes occur together. Śaivas, however, are generally less interested in combining these meanings than are the participants in the *kṛṣṇa līlā*. When we turn our attention to dance, which I suggest is a third and intermediate meaning of *līlā,* it is evident how important divine dance is for worshipers of Śiva and Kāli, as well as for worshipers of Kṛṣṇa. It is also readily apparent how for all three types of worshipers there is some form of human imitation or replication of the divine dance.

This first issue reflects the tension common to Indian and Western scholarship between the general and the specific. It is the latter that supplies the richness for this book's content, but without some general definition the subject expands indefinitely in all directions. The various attempts at general definitions, not surprisingly, show the strong influence of the usage of *līlā* studied by each essayist, but they also illustrate a common effort to bring together the two major semantic fields of *līlā*. My own suggestion here is simply that the intermediate meaning of dance may help us to understand the link Hindus see between divine playfulness and human play.

The second issue reflects not so much different regional or sectarian fields of study as the diversity of modern Western methodological approaches. Both historical and ethnographic studies are sufficiently diverse that the methodological differences are much more complicated than any single bifurcation of scholarly views. Many of the essays restrict themselves to translating Indian terms relating to *līlā* as closely as possible into English, and some focus entirely on the meaning of these terms to a particular community of Hindu interpreters.

There are also a number of essays, however, that seek to illuminate the subject by bringing the more narrowly defined religious concept and/or practice of *līlā* into relation with some other type of discourse. Perhaps the shortest step beyond the usual religious circles of meaning is made in the essay by Robert Goodwin. His analysis of classical Sanskrit drama shows the connection between the conception of *līlā* as divine activity and the "play world" of the human characters in the drama. He comes close to suggesting that the divine role-playing of the one true person (Śiva) proves a heavy burden for the human hero emulating Lord Śiva: the notion of one ultimate reality assuming various roles and reflecting back to himself from his temporary manifestation can easily drift, Goodwin believes, "toward the solipsistic consciousness of aesthetic hedonism." There is a counterbalance: "The Radiant Female . . . is an irreducible Other," which "is a force undermining the autonomy of the subject's play fantasy." The hero in the *Śakuntala* must somehow in the latter part of the play "translate the elation of the first three acts into the actual world of the court."

This heroic human imitation of the timeless drama between Śiva and the Goddess is quite different from *kṛṣṇa līlā,* in which Kṛṣṇa and Rādhā are both divine and (apparently) human, but in relating to Kṛṣṇa the limitations of our human world are, if anything, even more forcefully present. If even the divine Rādhā must face permanent separation from Kṛṣṇa, how much more poignant is the plight of Kṛṣṇa's human devotees? Yet the drama itself provides a means of coming to terms with and in some fashion overcoming that separation: through remembrance and reenactment. In this sacred drama the divine prince is not a model for human princes aspiring to superhuman powers, as in classical Sanskrit dramas. Kṛṣṇa is the central figure but not a role model; Rādhā comes closer to being a role model, though only in the symbolic sense of representing all devotees of Kṛṣṇa, both women and men. Except for the Sahajiya Vaiṣṇavas of Bengal who sometimes adopt Tantric sexual ritual, there would seem to be no connection between Kṛṣṇa's love play and acceptable sexual behavior in daily life. Is there indeed no connection, even with the love play of married couples? This question should perhaps be asked first about the most elaborate drama in which ordinary Hindus who are not actors participate: the ritual surrounding the wedding. How seriously do bride and groom take their roles as God and Goddess?

A number of essays take a step beyond comparing human and divine *līlā* by speculating on the various social contexts of *līlā* and its synonyms. One suggestion is that *līlā* is an attempt to escape from the restrictions of social *dharma* in a way that changes, levels out, or reverses the usual social status of the participants and/or provides them with some psychological relief from social structures that are felt to be confining or oppressive. It is important to recognize that this kind of interpretation moves outside the traditional modes of Hindu self-understanding and is implicitly or explicitly comparative. I am hesitant to seek such a social or psychological explanation for an important Hindu concept. In any case, some comparison with non-Hindu societies seems implicit. This kind of comparison is at the opposite extreme from the type of comparison that suggests there could be a Hindu contribution to a Western theology of play. That proposal argues that Hindus have a genuine insight into divine playfulness that Western theologians need in order to correct their overly serious notion of God.

If the discussion of *līlā* is to pursue and critically examine such interpretations, then more explicit comparison with other societies and other theologies is needed, far more than is possible within the scope of this volume. What of the suggestion that *kṛṣṇa līlā* conjured up an ideal world of Hindu rule against the political realities of Mughal or British dominance? It seems important both to examine the specific evidence and to consider the general implications of this kind of explanation. This is also the case with Nita Kumar's analysis that men in Banaras have made "imitation" of Śiva's playfulness the characteristic mark of the Banaras male lifestyle, a style from which women are excluded. *Līlā* in the sense of "drama" clearly involves imitation and identification. Kumar's analysis reminds me of a caution well known in the Vaiṣṇava treatment of Kṛṣṇa's playfulness: that this is something to be admired, indeed adored, but not to be imitated in daily life!

A more limited comparison is one that does not deal with either the social utility or the metaphysical truth in the Hindu concept of *līlā* but instead draws on Western religious concepts in an effort for greater understanding. The theological concept of *līlā* stands in clear contrast to most human activity, which Hindus believe is determined by *karma,* the consequences of previous actions. *Līlā* stands in a somewhat less clear contrast to purposeful activity. In Rāmānuja's interpretation of the Vedanta, God's cosmic activity is like *līlā;* God's governance of individual souls is determined by *their* "beginningless *karma";* but God's descents are not "like sport" nor determined by *karma.* They serve the double purpose of sustaining *dharma* and providing to finite beings a saving vision of their compassionate and forgiving Lord. In later north Indian Vaiṣṇavism the divine descent of Kṛṣṇa is also part of the Lord's *līlā.* Like the Tamil Śaiva "sports," the Lord's descent is an appearance in which the Lord transcends human purposes and therefore appears both mischievous and baffling, not least when he disappears. This, too, is *līlā.*

As a theological concept, *līlā* suggests some extraordinary activity, even if there is some partial human analogy in the action of young children or royal princes. When such divine *līlā* includes dance, *līlā* can suggest either an activity in which human beings can share (*kṛṣṇa līlā*) or a unique activity of the Lord of the Universe (Śiva's dance). Like the concept of *bhakti* with which it is often connected, *līlā* suggests both transcending uniqueness and shared experience. If the latter invites human analogies and explanations, the former represents inexplicable transcendence.

Contributors

BETTINA BÄUMER's doctoral dissertation (Munich, 1969) is entitled *The Concept of Līlā in Hinduism: Its Philosophical and Theological Significance*. She is presently research director of the Alice Boner Foundation for Research in Fundamental Principles of Indian Art at Varanasi, India. Her main interest is in Kashmir Śaivism and in the *śilpaśāstra*s (texts on temple architecture and sculpture) of Orissa. She has coedited *Kalātattvakośa: A Lexicon of Fundamental Concepts of the Indian Arts*. Her latest publication is *Śilparatnakośa: A Glossary of Orissan Temple Architecture*.

JOHN B. CARMAN is Parkman Professor of Divinity and professor of comparative religion at Harvard Divinity School. His most recent book is *Majesty and Meekness: A Comparative Study of Contrast and Harmony in the Concept of God*. His previous publications include: *The Tamil Veda: Pillan's Interpretation of the Tiruvāymoḻī* (with Vasudha Narayanan), *The Theology of Rāmānuja: An Essay in Interreligious Understanding*, and *Village Christians and Hindu Culture: Study of a Rural Church in Andhra Pradesh, South India* (with P. Y. Luke).

ROBERT E. GOODWIN taught Sanskrit and Sanskrit literature at Brown University for over ten years until his retirement in 1993. He now devotes himself to the study of music and has opened a music store in Saratoga Springs, New York. He has published numerous essays on Indian aesthetic theory. His book *The Playworld of Sanskrit Drama* is forthcoming.

JOHN STRATTON HAWLEY is director of the Southern Asia Institute at Columbia University and is professor and chair in the Department of Religion at Barnard College. His published works include several books on the devotional literature of Kṛṣṇa, a coedited study of Indian goddesses entitled *The Divine Consort*, and an introductory survey of the major poet-saints of North India entitled *Songs of the Saints of India* (with Mark Juergensmeyer). Two edited volumes, *Fundamentalism and Gender* and *Sati, the Blessing and the Curse,* appeared in 1994.

NORVIN HEIN was, prior to his retirement, professor of comparative religion at Yale University, where he taught Asian religions from 1950 until 1985. His interest has focused mainly on the Kṛṣṇa cult, the subject of his major study *The Miracle Plays of Mathura* and of many essays in edited volumes. He has written the section on Hinduism in a much-used university-level text entitled *The Religions of the World.*

ALF HILTEBEITEL is professor of religion at George Washington University. He is the author of *The Cult of Draupadi* (vol. 1: *Mythologies: From Gingee to Kurukṣetra;* vol. 2: *On Hindu Ritual and the Goddess*). He has also written *The Ritual of Battle: Kṛṣṇa in the Mahābhārata,* as well as numerous essays on Kṛṣṇa, the Mahābhārata, and other topics in Hinduism.

CLIFFORD HOSPITAL is professor at Queen's Theological College and in the Department of Religious Studies of Queen's University at Kingston, Canada. He is the author of *The Righteous Demon: A Study of Bali* and *Breakthrough: Insights of the Great Religious Discoverers,* and has written numerous articles, mainly on the *Purāṇa*s, religion in Kerala, and theological approaches to religious diversity.

NITA KUMAR is a fellow (associate professor) at the Centre for Studies in Social Sciences, Calcutta. She is the author of *The Artisans of Banaras: Popular Culture and Identity, 1880–1984* and *Friends, Brothers, and Informants: Fieldwork Memoirs of Banaras,* and the editor of *Women as Subjects: South Asian Histories.* She has recently completed a book on *Schooling in 19th-20th-Century Banaras: The Social Construction of Meaning* and will be writing a volume for the New Cambridge History of India on *Education and the Rise of a New Intelligentsia.* She is also an activist who works in her husband's innovative school, Southpoint Vidyashram, and is involved in other projects.

MALCOLM MCLEAN is a senior lecturer in religious studies at Otago University, Dunedin, New Zealand. His main research interest is Saktism in Bengal, and he has published papers on Ramakrishna, and Ramprasad Sen. He is presently working on a book on Ramprasad.

VASUDHA NARAYANAN is associate professor of religion at the University of Florida. Her other books include *The Way and the Goal, The Vernacular Veda: Revelation, Recitation, and Ritual,* and *The Tamil Veda: Piḷḷāṉ's Interpretation of the Tiruvāymoḻi* (with John Carman).

WILLIAM S. SAX is senior lecturer in the Department of Philosophy and Religious Studies at the University of Canterbury, Christchurch, New Zealand. His has written *Mountain Goddess: Gender and Politics in a Himalayan Pilgrimage,* as well as several articles on pilgrimage, gender, and performance in north India.

DONNA M. WULFF is associate professor of religious studies at Brown University. Her publications include *Drama as a Mode of Religious Realization: The Vidagdhamādhava of Rūpa Gosvāmī,* as well as articles on Sanskrit aesthetic theory, the sacredness of sound and music, and a contemporary Bengali form of dramatic, devotional musical performance.

Index

Abhinavagupta, 37–38, 42–45, 59–61, 227. *See also* Aesthetics; Kashmir Śaivism
Advaita Vedanta, 14–15, 37
antipathy to *līlā*, 7, 51–56, 69–70, 79 n. 17
Aesthetics, 36, 50–86, 76 n. 2, 78 n. 14, 130 n. 18. *See also* Abhinavagupta; Kashmir Śaivism: aesthetic theory of
of *araiyar*'s performance, 191–92
in Kashmir Śaivism, 38–47
theory of Rūpa Gosvāmī, 102–3
Āgni Purāṇa, 26
Anandavardhana, 50, 57–58, 61, 69
Araiyar, 8. See also *Utsava*
cēvai of, 185–90, 197–98 n. 25
definition of, 185, 198 n. 26
embodiment of Nammālvār in, 191
performances of, 183–90, 195 n. 17
Aśvaghoṣa, 56
Aurobindo, Shri, 18–19
Avatāra, 8. *See also* Embodiment
concept of, in Srīvaiṣṇava literature, 179–80
in *līlā* traditions, 205–6, 209–11
in early Vaiṣṇava literature, 21–31, 225–26

Bābājī, Rāmdās, 107
Bādarayana. See *Vedāntasūtras*
Balarāma, 25, 27–29
Banaras and *banārasīpan*, 160–74
Bäumer, Bettina, 5, 6, 76 n. 6, 231
Berger, Peter, 22–23
Bhagavadgītā, 15, 24, 180
Bhāgavata Purāṇa, 21–27, 129 n. 5
in Bengali Vaiṣṇavism, 101–3
as devotional text, 29, 205–6
as source of Kṛṣṇa mythology, 16, 112 n. 8, 116, 225–26
on not imitating Kṛṣṇa, 19
Rāmānuja's use of, 18
Bhakti
and *līlā*, 230
as democratizing movement, 99–100, 110–11
dualism of, 51
in Kashmir Śaivism, 41
in *līlā* traditions, 205–6, 209–10
as romantic "devotion," 63
Bhaṭṭa Nāyaka, 57, 77 n. 12, 78 n. 14, 78–79 n. 16
Bhaṭṭa Tauta, 59, 79 n. 21, 80 n. 26
Bhaṭṭar, Parāśara, 193
Bhoja, 79 n. 22
Biardeau, Madeleine, 206
Bodhapañcadaśikā, 45
Brahmā, 22, 25–26
Brahmāṇḍa Purāṇa, 27
Brahmasūtras, 21, 36. See also *Vedāntasūtras*
Brahmavaivarta Purāṇa, 18
Braj, 16, 17, 29, 115
Brown, Cheever M., 196 n. 20
Byrski, Maria Christopher, 83 n. 36

Caitanya, 14, 15, 18, 100–102, 105–6, 110
Caṇḍī. See *Devī Māhātmya*
Carman, John, 8, 231
Chāndogya Upaniṣad, 24